ULTIMATE JOURNEY

ULTIMATE JOURNEY

Death and Dying in the World's Major Religions

EDITED BY STEVEN J. ROSEN

Westport, Connecticut
London

Library of Congress Cataloging-in-Publication Data

Ultimate journey : death and dying in the world's major religions / edited by Steven J. Rosen.

    p. cm.

Includes bibliographical references and index.

ISBN 978-0-313-35608-7 (alk. paper)

1. Death—Religious aspects. I. Rosen, Steven, 1955–

BL504.U48 2008

202′.3—dc22   2008023719

British Library Cataloguing in Publication Data is available.

Library of Congress Catalog Card Number: 2008023719

ISBN: 978-0-313-35608-7

First published in 2008

Praeger Publishers, 88 Post Road West, Westport, CT 06881

An imprint of Greenwood Publishing Group, Inc.

www.praeger.com

Printed in the United States of America

The paper used in this book complies with the Permanent Paper Standard issued by the National Information Standards Organization (Z39.48-1984).

10 9 8 7 6 5 4 3 2 1

12/08
Pfst

Contents

Introduction

Steven J. Rosen

> What can we know of death,
> We, who cannot understand life?
>
> —*Gates of Prayer*, Jewish prayer book

We all know that death awaits us. Yet we tend to avoid the subject as if our lives depend on it.

We don't live as if we know we're going to die. Instead, we try to camouflage the oncoming train of death with material possessions, reputation, popularity, and the pleasures of the senses. We sometimes conceal this truth consciously, though most of the time it is quite unconscious.

Perhaps we avoid the subject because we think it somewhat morbid. True, there are people who contemplate death to an excessive degree, making it an obsession and letting it get in the way of life.

But it doesn't have to go there. Rather, a natural curiosity about the nature of life and its inevitable demise can be healthy. After all, death is one of the few certainties we have. And knowing what to expect, what various deep thinkers have had to say about it, and what the great religions of the world tell us is in store for us—all of this can be edifying, preparing us for the unavoidable journey that each of us must take.

It's not that we have to believe every proclamation that well-meaning thinkers, scriptures, or theologians have made on this subject. But it behooves us to listen with an open mind, for these are resources that claim the secrets of life and death as their main concern; they have deeply contemplated life's ultimate journey, and we can benefit from their insights.

WHAT IS DEATH?

Until relatively recently, people were declared dead when their heartbeat and breathing came to an end. But with emerging techniques, such as CPR and prompt defibrillation, we have entered a new era, for now a person's breathing and heartbeat can often be restarted. Similarly, life can sometimes be sustained with a series of life support devices, organ transplants, and artificial pacemakers. Thus, when heartbeat and breathing stop, we refer to it as "clinical death." It is not considered the ultimate end of life.

Today, experts usually use the terms "brain death" or "biological death" when indicating the absolute end of life processes: People are considered dead when the electrical activity in the brain comes to an end. This cessation of brain activity, says modern science, indicates the end of consciousness as we know it. For this to be true, however, suspension of consciousness must be permanent and not temporary, as when one is asleep or in a coma. If it is permanent, it is called death.

But isn't there more to death than this? Or, to state it more directly: Isn't there more to life? Clearly, we're not just machines that begin to malfunction and ultimately succumb to planned obsolescence. Life is more than that, isn't it? And while we're on the subject, what *is* life? In fact, wouldn't knowledge of what life really is be prerequisite for a true understanding of death? Indeed, the body is just a machine, but life is not. We all sense it. Life goes beyond the technical apparatus of our external shell (bodily existence). It is known by the presence of consciousness.

Science often talks about the electrical processes of the brain and attempts to equate these processes with consciousness. The usual claim is that consciousness is an emergent property of complex bioelectrical activity in the brain, but solid evidence for this is not to be found. No scientists can tell us exactly what electrical process results in consciousness. And yet consciousness exists. We love, hate, desire, feel and want, quite unlike other substances that are products of electrons or electromagnetic fields. The point is this: Mere objects, such as electrons, do not feel anything at all; objects are not self-aware, and yet such awareness is the hallmark sign of a conscious entity. Thus, electrical impulses, in the brain or anywhere else, do not cause consciousness.

Rather, an alternate model must be put forward regarding the nature of the self. Religions throughout the world refer to this as the soul, a nonmaterial entity the likes of which cannot be explained by common materialistic definitions. And this would fit: Consciousness is the symptom of that which is referred to as the actual self. Call it what you will—*atman, ruach, nephesh, anima*, spirit. What's being referred to is the same life force, that indefinable something that separates a living being from inanimate objects.

The obvious existence of this "spiritual element" is the only premise of this book. With that as a given, this work will offer much perennial wisdom and food for thought.

THE ULTIMATE JOURNEY

The essays in this book were written by experts in their respective fields, people who have studied the subject of death from a particular vantage point and who want to share their wisdom and knowledge for the benefit of those who want to know. They offer traditional points of view as well as the insights of mystics. Consider their words deeply, for their research offers detail, clarity, and, in many ways, solace. Accept what makes sense to you, and discard the rest. In the end—whatever you accept or don't accept—you'll become privy to age-old wisdom, the cumulative knowledge of generations of seekers and prophets.

Interestingly, the world's many religious traditions, as outlined here, share certain key points in common—one notices an overarching unity in the midst of superficial differences. Along these lines, it is important to remember that Judaism, Christianity, Islam, Buddhism, and Hinduism, the religions addressed in this book, came of age in different regions, with their own languages, customs, rituals, and so on. In other words, they were born and developed in culturally specific circumstances, giving rise to variations in nomenclature, methods of communication, conceptions of time, biological detail, environmental landscape, and so on. Thus, the exact terminology of where one goes after death, how one journeys to the next destination, how long it takes to get there, and the names and appearances of supernatural beings associated with the dying process—all of these will vary. And yet the essential information is the same: The soul journeys to various lands—metaphysical lands, perhaps—after death, with the help of supernatural entities; ultimately, the soul is on its way to a supreme destination, which may take many lives, and it goes through numerous tests and trials, which enhance its character, rendering it ready to meet its Maker.

But the book you now hold in your hands is not just about the dissemination of information and age-old wisdom. Chaplain David Carter offers us concluding words of a practical nature. He ministers to the dying on a daily basis, and he brings to this book a sort of "hands on" dimension. He shows how a spiritual approach to death, whatever one's particular orientation—religious or not—has incalculable value, making the transition smoother, easier, even blissful. Thus, the ultimate journey need not be disorienting, painful, confusing, or sad. Rather, through time-tested procedures and a certain adjustment in one's consciousness, death and dying can be filled with dignity, grace, and a sense of happiness.

Judaism: The Journey of the Soul

Rabbi Arthur Seltzer

THE MAINSTREAM: AN OVERVIEW

In the Jewish tradition, death is considered an integral part of the experience of life, leading from the antechamber of this life into the next. The time of transition of the soul from its incarnation in the physical body to the beginning of its journey in the next is considered to be a time of great sacredness, for if man is created in the image of God, then the form that once contained that soul is now relieved of its task, and the godly soul begins its return to its divine source.

Judaism has developed a large body of quite specific rituals and traditions with which to mark this time of transition, and these are intended to assist in the process of the separation of the soul from the body. Inherent in these traditions is the understanding that those remaining in life, the mourners, by their actions, contribute significantly to the separation, elevation, and transformation of the soul.

Before death comes, it is considered to be of great merit to recite the "Viddui," the confessional, with the dying. If it is possible for the dying person to recite the "Viddui" on his own, he should do so. If it is not possible, then one close to him should recite the confessional on his behalf, seeking forgiveness for his sins, asking for healing, even at this extreme time, but accepting the divine decree whatever it is to be.

It is considered immensely significant to be with the dying in their final moments and to witness and to assist the soul's passing into the next realm. The eyes of the deceased are to be closed by those present and a sheet or covering drawn over their face.

The body should be placed with feet facing the door and with a candle placed at the head of the deceased. This time is also one for family and friends to offer prayers, asking forgiveness of the deceased for any wrongs they may have caused him during his life.

If death occurs at home, all mirrors are covered, both to avoid instances of personal vanity in the face of death, and, it is said, to acknowledge the now diminished image of God in the once animated human form.

While it is traditional to recite Psalms in the presence of the deceased, Psalms 23 and 91 are particularly included in this recital. Since the deceased may not be left alone at any time from death to interment, a *shomer*, or watchman, is appointed, preferably from the family, to remain with the body and recite Psalms throughout this period.

In the presence of the deceased, only the highest degree of respect may be exhibited. It is forbidden to eat, drink, or smoke in their presence, and only positive thoughts and recollections may be shared concerning them.

The Chevra Kaddisha, the burial society, is to be called to care for the remains. It is the responsibility of the Chevra Kaddisha to deal with all medical/legal issues, and to make arrangements for the interment. Among the most important tasks of the Chevra Kaddisha, and one considered to be of the greatest merit, is the Taharah, the ritual purification of the body before burial. Not only does Taharah require the physical cleansing and preparation of the body, but also those performing Taharah are required to recite specific prayers asking God to forgive the sins of the departed and to grant his soul eternal peace. Those who perform Taharah must be fully trained, themselves highly qualified, on a personal and spiritual level, to render such a holy act.

The Jewish tradition requires that all Jews must be buried in a plain, white shroud made of muslin, cotton, or linen, for at death all stand equal before God. It is also taught that at a time when a person stands before his Maker, he should do so in simplicity and dignity. For males, the *tallit* or prayer shawl is then wrapped around him.

According to Jewish law, the deceased is to be interred in a plain wooden coffin, with no extraneous decoration whatsoever. In fact, since nothing is to hinder the decomposition of the body, holes are sometimes made in the bottom of the coffin to assist this process. Therefore, the use of lined caskets meant to prevent decomposition of the body is a clear violation of Jewish law.

It is also a custom to place a small amount of soil from the land of Israel inside the coffin with the deceased as an aid to the final resurrection of the dead at the time of the coming of the Messiah.

According to Jewish tradition, burial is to be performed as soon after death as possible, preferably on the same day, but certainly within twenty-four hours after death. It is understood in the tradition that for a body to linger once its soul has moved on to the next world is shameful, for the body is now only a vestige of what it once was. Only under specific circumstances (which may add to the honor of the dead) may burial be delayed, such as the need to wait for relatives to arrive for the funeral service from long distances away.

Prior to the funeral service, *kriyah* is performed, the ritual rending of a garment of the mourners, with the accompanying statement that "the Lord has given and now taken.... He is the judge of truth." In Jewish law, a mourner, with specific ritual responsibilities to the deceased, is defined as father, mother, brother, sister, son, daughter, or spouse.

The funeral service itself is brief, simple, and intense. It is focused on the honor and dignity of the deceased and the reality of death. It is not intended to be a time of consolation for mourners, which it nonetheless is by virtue of those who join to share in the mourner's loss. More to the point, however, the funeral service is intended to focus on the life, now ended, of the deceased, and to join together in sending the soul off to its journey in the next world. It is understood that it is from all the mourners and their prayer, as well as the *Mitzvot*, the good deeds, they perform in memory of the deceased, that its soul receives the energy to elevate its level in the World to Come.

Burial in the earth is considered the only appropriate way to bring the body to its resting place, so that it may return to the dust from which it came. Thus, cremation is forbidden by Jewish law, as are vaults and mausoleums. Furthermore, it is considered an act of great merit for those attending the burial to assist in the filling of the grave with earth. It is a profound statement of the finality of death and of the concern of all in attendance that the body of the dead is properly returned to its source.

Within the body of burial service, the burial Kaddish, a doxology in praise of God, is recited by the mourners, and in somewhat shorter form, it is recited by the mourners three times a day at each of the required daily prayer services (for the next eleven months). The main responsibility for the Kaddish recitation falls on a child to be enacted for the parent. In the Orthodox Jewish tradition, this typically manifests as the son saying Kaddish for his parents throughout the approximately year-long period of mourning. The tradition teaches that this forms a binding link between the generations, and it is through the energy of the recitation of the Kaddish that the soul of the deceased may elevate.

With the conclusion of the burial service begins Shivah, the seven-day period of mourning during which the mourners remain at home, comforted by visitations from family and friends. Shivah is most assuredly not a social occasion. Indeed, the tradition teaches that we may not speak until the mourner speaks to us first and that the conversation should focus on the qualities of the deceased or the well-being of the mourners.

The Shivah period is itself divided into two, with the first three days encompassing the period of deepest mourning and the last four days beginning our slow readjustment to the world around us. Only at the end of Shivah may one return to work and begin normal day-to-day activities.

About a year after the burial, a Matzevah, a monument, is erected and consecrated over the grave as a permanent memorial for the deceased. Also, a year after burial is the observance of the Yarzeit, the anniversary of the death of the deceased. It is a special time for the recitation of the Kaddish and the performance of good deeds in memory of the departed loved one. Also, four times a year—on Yom Kippur, Pesach, Shemini Atzeret, and Shavuot—Yizkor, memorial prayers on behalf of the departed, is recited.

It is apparent from this description that in the Jewish tradition, the departed are intimately interwoven into family and community life, remembered, and prayed for and are the object of meritorious and special deeds throughout the year. From the perspective of the Jewish mystical tradition, the Kabbalah, this is understood to be the result of the intimate connection between soul, even after death, and its energetic relationship with those in the world left behind, as it moves onward on its journey of transformation and elevation. While offering interpretations often unique and originally different from the mainstream Jewish tradition, the Kabbalah teaches a rich, insightful, and detailed understanding of the soul as it moves along its journey both within its life in the physical world, as well as along its journey in the postmortem world of the Afterlife. It is to the mystical texts that we now turn.

THE MYSTICAL UNDERPINNINGS OF DEATH: AN INTRODUCTION

In the Jewish tradition, death is understood as the separation of the eternal, spiritual soul from the material body, the two of which were joined together at the time of conception. While the physical body returns to the ground of matter from which it originated, the eternal soul begins its journey of transition from this world to the next, as it tends to its task of elevation, refinement, and transformation.

According to the Jewish tradition, the soul retains memory of its lifetime on earth, and in its individuality, it is held accountable for its actions and thoughts while incarnate in a physical body. Therefore, death marks a radical transition from physical life in this world, but it does not end consciousness and awareness of personal identity, nor does it end the spiritual demand for continuous internal refinement.

In fact, all of the Jewish customs regarding death and dying, as outlined above, serve to assist the soul in its metaphysical adventure in the World to Come. For example, at the time of the Yarzeit, the anniversary of the death, Jews not only remember the departed, but also seek to elevate the soul to a higher level through the performance of good deeds, such as the giving of charity and the learning of Torah. The specific statement is made to the family, "May the soul of the departed experience an elevation."

Indeed, there are some traditions at which family members visit the graves of the departed at this time of Yarzeit, not only to remember the departed and be reminded of the brevity and fragility of life, but, more importantly, to seek advice and counsel from them. This clearly implies the notion that the dead know of the activities of the living in the physical world, are concerned with their welfare, and, in the appropriate manner, can be of assistance and insight.

At the time of Yizkor, the memorial prayers recited for the departed at major Jewish festivals, a similar wish is expressed for the elevation and refinement of the departed soul, with the hope that the soul now resides in the Garden of Eden, one of the levels of Paradise.

Most important is the requirement for a mourner, as defined by Jewish law, to recite the Kaddish doxology three times a day for the departed for a period of eleven months. As with Shivah, the common perception is that Kaddish is recited for the healing of the grief of the mourner. In truth, Kaddish is an obligation upon the mourner in order to assist in the elevation of the soul of the departed. This teaching is a very pointed one: first, that souls require human energy and intent to succeed in their process of elevation and second, that humans have the ability to affect the welfare of the departed just as the departed are capable of being of assistance to us in this physical world.

The Jewish mystical tradition, the Kabbalah, teaches that souls not only seek to transform and elevate themselves in the afterlife, but also do so as well while incarnated in physical bodies, for the transformational work of souls is never-ending. The Alter Rebbe, the first Chabad Rebbe, speaks of souls as literally being part of God Himself, and as such, their seeking to elevate back to their divine source is a constant expression of their very nature. Thus, within the Kabbalah, a fully developed typology exists describing the journey of souls both within life in this world and in the next.

JOURNEY OF THE SOUL

The mystical tradition teaches that the embodied soul is understood to be constantly on a journey of refinement and elevation. We are taught that the soul consists of five levels. From lowest to highest they are *nefesh*, the vital soul; *ruach*, the level of emotional interaction with the world; *neshamah*, the intellectual soul; *chayah*, the level of soul that is part of all that lives; and *yechidah*, the unitary oneness with all that is.

Further, the Kabbalistic tradition teaches that each level of soul contains within itself all other levels of soul as well. It is these levels of soul, and their sublevels, which themselves define the parameters of the soul's work of elevation while incarnated into physicality. Therefore, a soul may begin its journey within physical incarnation on the lowest of levels, that "of *nefesh* of *nefesh*," and spend an entire lifetime in this world completing and rectifying that level. Conversely, although quite unusual, it may happen that a soul rectifies the *nefesh* levels of *both nefesh* of *nefesh* and *ruach* of *nefesh* in one embodied incarnation, moving on in the next reincarnation to rectify the level of *neshamah* of *nefesh*. The sixteenth-century mystic, the Ari'zal, taught that we rectify and elevate a soul level through the study of the Torah and the keeping of its *Mitzvot*, its commandments, on the appropriate soul level.

Implicit in this Kabbalistic structure and process of embodied soul refinement is the necessary reincarnation of the soul over numerous incarnations. Therefore, from the Kabbalistic perspective, the soul's journey of elevation and rectification is not limited to the embodied state only, but includes as well postmortem soul refinement and transformation following each reincarnation into the embodied state, with postmortem soul rectification itself influencing the level and *tikkun*, type and quality of life task, of the following embodied incarnation. Thus, the journey of the soul encompasses both realms, this world and the next, with each aspect of the journey influencing the soul work of the other.

It is the purpose of this chapter to describe the postmortem journey of the soul as described in selections from the Jewish mystical literature, specifically, the *Zohar*, the Book of Splendor, and related texts. Within the *Zohar*, which will be our main source in this chapter, are contained numerous and extensive descriptions of the various stages through which the postmortem soul travels—from impending death and the separation of the soul from the body; interment; transition from this world; cleansing; self-evaluation; Gehinnom (hellish existence); Lower Paradise; further soul evaluation; Upper Paradise; the Bond of Life and the Divine Throne; and finally, the soul's return to the physical world through reincarnation informed by its *tikkun*, life task.

THE PREDEATH PROCESS ACCORDING TO THE KABBALAH

The *Zohar* describes how, at the time of death, the four elements that combine to constitute the human body as container of the soul—earth, water, fire, and air—begin to quarrel among themselves. This same text tells us that when the day comes for a person to depart from the world, four quarters of the world indict him, as it were, with punishments rising up from all four directions. At this time, a voice goes forth and makes a proclamation, the *Zohar* explains, that is heard throughout the cosmos.

If it is deemed at that time that a man is worthy, all dimensions of existence welcome him with intense happiness, but if not, that person will suffer greatly.[1]

This separation of the soul from the body is not a process of a moment's duration, for the *Zohar* teaches that this separation occurs over a period of thirty days, during which profound changes begin to occur in the body and soul relationship. Specifically, the text tells us that, when death approaches, a bold announcement about the dying person is made for thirty days, with even the birds of heaven proclaiming his fate; if such a person is particularly virtuous, the *Zohar* further reports, his fruitful journey is announced for thirty days among the righteous in the Garden of Eden.[2] It is also mentioned that during these thirty days a person's soul departs from his body every night, ascending to the other world; here, he looks carefully at his place to be.[3]

The *Zohar* further teaches that this progressive separation of the soul from the body can be a most difficult experience:

For love is strong as death: It is strong like the parting of the spirit from the body, as we have learnt that when man is about to depart from the world and sees strange things, his spirit courses through all his limbs and goes up and down like a boatman without oars who is tossed up and down on the seas and makes no progress. It then asks leave of each limb; and its separation is only effected with great violence.[4]

The *Zohar* elaborates on this theme of difficulty in regard to the soul and body's separation, adding as well the notion that this also represents a time of great judgment and the beginning of a long journey of soul rectification. The text tells us that there is no solution for such a man unless he repents in due course. Otherwise, until his very last moment, he knows great fear, hopelessly endeavoring to hide himself in terrible shame. The *Zohar* further informs us that such a person is forced to gaze upon "the Angel of Death," ultimately surrendering himself to his inevitable fate.[5] This is considered the moment of "the Great Judgment"—an experience all will be subjected to in this world.

The spirit actually undergoes a journey through its own body, struggling with each separate member, or limb, as it parts from it; as the soul does this, each limb withers away. The *Zohar* offers graphic detail in this regard: When the spirit is about to make its final exit from the body, having thus dealt with each limb, the Shekinah stands over the empty shell, and the spirit continues its journey, leaving the body behind.[6] The rabbis of the *Zohar* tell us: "Happy is the portion of whoever cleaves to Her! Woe to the sinners who keep afar from Her!"[7]

"Indeed," reflect the writers of the *Zohar*, "what a number of ordeals man has to undergo in passing out of this world!"[8] The text then makes a list of seven such ordeals: (1) The first is when the spirit leaves the body, as just described. (2) The second is when his actions and statements precede him and proclamations are made concerning each of them. (3) Another ordeal manifests when entering the tomb, or one's burial place. (4) And then there is the tomb itself, which is ghastly for the spirit, as (5) its body soon undergoes an ordeal being eaten by worms. After this, (6) one approaches Gehinnom, a sort of hell for the soul. Finally, (7) there is the constant roaming in the world, yet again, in which the spirit finds no resting place, at least until its necessary tasks are accomplished and it is able to move on. According to the *Zohar*, these are the seven ordeals through which all must pass.[9] Hence, the text proclaims, "it behooves man while in this world to acknowledge his Master. One should also carefully examine his daily works, sincerely repenting any misdeeds he may have committed before his Maker."[10]

Jewish mystical texts further inform us that when man's judgment hour is near, a new spirit enters into him from above, and he is able to see things that he could not see before; this occurs just before he departs from the world. So it is written: "For man shall not see me and live; in their lifetime they may not see, but at the hour of death they may."[11]

The question remains, however: What indeed is the vision that the dying person sees at this time of soul transition? The *Zohar* suggests a number of possibilities. First is that the dying man sees Adam, the first man.[12] A second *Zohar* tradition states that a person on his deathbed will see the Shekhinah:

R. Eleazar said: "When a man is on the point of leaving this world, his soul suffers many chastisements along with his body before they separate. Nor does the soul actually leave him until the Shekhinah shows herself to him, and then the soul goes out in joy and love for the Shekhinah. If he is righteous, he cleaves and attaches himself to Her. But if not, then the Shekhinah departs, and the soul is left behind, mourning for its separation from the body, like a cat which is driven away from the fire."[13]

The above *Zohar* text would seem to indicate that depending on the righteousness of the dying person, different qualities of visions and their implications occur, leading to different pathways to be traversed by the departing soul. This point is further emphasized in *Zohar* I, which tells us that by one's acts, by one's words, and by one's intensity of devotion, one draws to himself that spirit from on high.[14] The same section of the *Zohar* relates that if a man attaches himself in this world, he will find himself similarly attached in the next one: If he is holy in this life, he will be holy in the next, and if he is defiled, that's what he will know in the world to come. But he is still a soul, moving ever closer to his source.

It would seem, then, that all souls departing this world merit seeing the Shekhinah. However, whether a soul is allowed to then cleave to the

Shekhinah, or is deserted by Her, depends on the worthiness of the soul's life on earth. Further, being deserted by the Shekhinah implies that one will be drawn to the side of uncleanness, making the challenges of the Afterlife far more foreboding.

To be thorough: A third tradition concerning deathbed visions is that of seeing deceased relatives and friends who come to assist the soul on its journey, its destination depending on the person's merit acquired in this life.[15]

The principle of judgment is central to the *Zohar*'s understanding of the postdeath process. As a result, it also speaks at some length of deathbed visions as pertaining to the judgment that awaits all souls in the world to come. Therefore, a fourth tradition of vision is that of the "Life Review," both on the part of God and on that of the individual. As the *Zohar* says, three appointed messengers descend upon the dying man—one of them will make a record of all that person's meritorious deeds, as well as his misdeeds; a second messenger tallies up and concludes with a reckoning of his days; and the third is a special entity who has accompanied the dying man from the time when he was in his mother's womb.[16]

It's described that when God desires to take back a man's spirit to His own kingdom, all that person's days pass in review before Him. The only people who can properly rejoice, then, are those who have lived a righteous life—for the *Zohar* says that they draw ever nearer to God. But those who were consciously wicked throughout their days will not "draw near," and of them it is written: "The way of the wicked is like thick darkness, they know not on what they stumble." (Prov. IV, 19).[17]

The *Zohar* is clear: "On the day when man's time arrives to depart from the world, when the body is broken and the soul seeks to leave it, on that day man is privileged to see things that he was not permitted to see before, when the body was in full vigor." And again it says, "Every man seals his fate with his own hand": He will be judged in the next world for all his actions, former and later, old and new, not one of them is forgotten—every man must acknowledge his works, for all the deeds that he committed give an abiding account of his next destination.[18]

A fifth tradition of deathbed vision is that of the Angel of Death. Unlike some of the more benign visions previously discussed, this is a vision of intensity and fear, leading to the final separation of body and soul, and of a person's ultimate surrender to this particular angel. The *Zohar* describes a fearful scenario: The Angel of Death's officer advances toward the dying man, holding in his hand a sharp sword. At that moment, the man looks up and sees the wall of his house in a blaze of fire—with he himself as the culprit. After this, he sees before him a demon with eyes all over his body, clothed in fiery garments. The very sight of this being causes tremendous fear, as the dying person's body shivers uncontrollably.

The *Zohar* again informs us that there is no alleviation for such a man unless he repents in due course. Until his last moments, he subsists in fear.

Aware of his own helplessness, he opens his eyes and gazes at the Angel of Death with full consciousness, surrendering himself, body and soul. It is, again, the moment of the Great Judgment, to which man must be subjected as part of life in this world. But then, when the spirit is about to depart, having thus taken leave of the whole body, acknowledging each of his bodily limbs, the Shekinah stands over the body—and the spirit leaves for his next destination. The *Zohar* affirms: "Happy is the portion of whoever cleaves to Her! Woe to the sinner who keep afar from Her!"[19] The text further states, "Hence a man should constantly be in fear of that great day, the Day of Judgment, the day of reckoning, when there be none to defend him save his own good deeds that he performed in this world."[20]

The importance of Torah study is then underlined: "Now the soul of one who has labored in the study of the Torah, when it leaves this world, ascends by the way and paths of the Torah—ways and paths familiar to them. They who know the ways and paths of the Torah in this world follow them in the other world when they leave this life."[21]

Therefore, for the righteous, the moment of death is painless and effortless, "like drawing a hair out of milk," whereas for the wicked, it is a moment of agitation and pain, like "pulling a tangled rope through a narrow opening."[22] This is the sum and substance of Judaic teaching on death and dying.

POSTDEATH EXPERIENCE

Jewish texts speak of a complex process of postdeath interaction between the body and the soul. According to these sources, while death results from the separation of the soul from the body, the soul nonetheless remains in the vicinity of the body for a time even after the separation.

According to the *Zohar*, once the Angel of Death removes the soul from a person's body, death occurs instantaneously. At that point, the person's spirit comes out and sits on the tip of the nose until the body begins to decay. After this, the spirit is taken to the courtyard of the dead, to join other such spirits in an interim state.[23]

Not only does the soul remain in the vicinity of the body immediately after death, but it also travels back and forth between the grave and its former home, aware of all that takes place there:

For seven days the soul goes back and forth—from his house to his grave and from his grave to his house—mourning for the body. This corroborates that which has already been written: "His flesh shall suffer pain for him, and his soul shall mourn for it" (Job XIV, 22), and it grieves to behold the sadness in the house.[24]

Seven days constitute the period of Shivah, the period of sitting and mourning by the family for the deceased. The implication of this *Zohar* text is that during this period, the soul seeks to retain its ties to the people and places it knew so well in life. Further, the *Zohar* suggests that disembodied souls retain consciousness and memory and retain awareness of events occurring in the physical world. This closeness continues until the soul becomes aware of and saddened by the inevitable disintegration of the physical body in the grave. The *Zohar* states, "... and as for the *nefesh*, it wanders around the world, observing the body that was once its home, now devoured by worms and suffering the judgment of the grave. This leads to intense mourning."[25]

Another version of the soul remaining near the body after death is found in *Midrash Rabbah* (18:1): "For three days [after death] the soul hovers over the body, intending to re-enter it, but as soon as it sees its [the body's] appearance change, it departs...."

According to the *Zohar*, the viewing by the soul of the disintegration of the body in the grave is a most painful experience and is considered to be one of the trials it must endure in its postdeath journey. Not only is the experience a painful one, but it attests to the soul irrefutably that its place in physicality is now itself disintegrating and that it must move on. The process is known as *Chibut Hakever*, the "Purgatory of the Grave," and can only be averted by the good deeds acquired during one's lifetime.

KAF HAKELAH: THE HOLLOW OF THE SLING

After the separation of the soul from the body, a process begins of eliminating impurities from the soul, which remain from its physical existence with the body, preparing the soul for its future journey. If a soul is deemed worthy, it may be spared the experience; if not, it must submit. Like *Chibut Hakever*, *Kaf Hakelah* can only be avoided through good deeds, learning of the Torah, and the performance of the *Mitzvot* (following of the commandments) one has acquired and achieved during his lifetime.

The *Zohar* confirms this, adding that those who defile their body through sinful and degraded acts are "tossed about like a stone from a sling. Woe to them! Who shall plead for them?"[26] Conversely, the same text teaches that righteous people are happy and God is pleased to take them back to Himself. "But if a man is not deemed worthy," says the *Zohar*, "woe to his spirit, which has to be purified and to be prepared before it can bask in the Body of the King. And if it is not prepared, it, too, must roll about 'like a stone in a sling'" (cf. I Samuel).[27]

THE CELESTIAL GARMENT

Now that *Chibut Hakever* and *Kaf Hakelah* have cleansed the soul of much of the physicality in which it had previously been immersed, it is now given a new garment—a spiritual body—to sustain itself in the transcendent realm:

When souls ascend to the place of the "bundle of life" (v. I Sam. XXV, 29), they feast their eyes on the beams of the "refulgent mirror," which radiates from the most sublime region. And were the soul not clothed in the resplendency of another (i.e., non-flesh) garment, it would not be able to approach the effulgence. The esoteric doctrine is that in the same way as the soul has to be clothed in a bodily garment in order to exist in this world, so is she given an ethereal supernal garment wherewith to exist in the other world, and to be enabled to gaze at the effulgence of life radiating from that "land of the living."[28]

Yet another section of the *Zohar* tells us more along these same lines. First is that until the soul is divested of its physical garment and given new supernal clothing, it cannot proceed along its spiritual journey. Secondly, that this supernal garment is the same one that the soul had to remove before entering this physical world. In essence, the *Zohar* suggests that, after death, we again put on our own garment that was ours prior to our incarnation into physicality and in which we experience great joy.

The text further tells us that all the images and forms of this material world were fashioned after those in the Spiritual Kingdom. This Kingdom is the abode of all spirits, both of those that have appeared in this world and also of those who have not yet come here. Those who are about to come are given "garments," i.e., faces and bodies, like those from above, and they gaze upon the glory of their Lord until the time comes for them to appear in the material world.[29]

According to the *Zohar*, many souls make their abode in this world in the garments and bodies fashioned from the seed of suitable parents. So when the time comes for the spirit to leave this world again, it cannot do so until the Angel of Death has taken off the garment known as this body. Once this process is completed, the spirit again puts on that other garment in the spiritual realm, of which he had had to divest himself when he entered this world of matter. The text concludes by mentioning that the soul's real joy is in the celestial body, not in his material form. In that higher body, he rests and moves, all while contemplating the supernal mysteries of life—even though, when he was in his earthly body, he could neither grasp nor understand them.[30]

It should be noted that the celestial garment is not available to all souls, only to the worthy. As the *Zohar* informs us, "If the soul is worthy and wears its precious protecting garments, multitudes of holy hosts stand ready to join her and accompany her to Paradise. But if she is not deemed worthy of that garment, the 'strange' hosts compel her to take the path that leads to Gehenna. These are angels of destruction and confusion, and they gladly take their revenge on wayward souls."[31]

GEHENNA

The intent of Gehenna, Purgatory, is not for punishment alone. In the *Zohar*, it becomes clear that the purpose of Gehenna is for refinement and purification of the soul from the dross of sin and physicality, making it possible for the soul to progress to the next supernal level, that of the Lower Garden of Eden. Certainly there are specific areas of Gehenna for specific types of sinners, but for all, the period of confinement in Gehenna is at most twelve months, with only the few most incorrigible souls remaining in the level of Gehenna known as Abbadon.

This is confirmed in the *Zohar* as follows: "Sinners are subjected to Gehenna for twelve months, half with fire, half with snow. When they go into the fire they say: 'This is really Gehenna!' When they go into the snow they say the same. The supreme punishment is with snow."[32]

But the text goes further. It tells us that the Holy One eventually raises them out of Gehenna, after they have undergone sufficient purification. At this time, they remain sitting at its gate, and when they see sinners enter there to be punished, they ask for mercy on their behalf. In time, the Holy One shows pity and brings them to a certain place for their betterment.[33]

The soul soon rises from Gehenna, says the *Zohar*, purified of its guilt like iron purified in fire, and she is carried up to the Lower Garden of Eden. Here the soul is cleansed in the waters of Paradise and perfumed with its spices. The soul will remain here until the appropriate time, when she departs from the abode of the righteous. After this, she is carried up toward the Supreme Destination, step by step, like a sacrifice to the altar.[34]

The *Zohar* gives exacting detail: At first, the text relates, the soul is taken to an area called Ben-Hinnom, where souls are cleansed and purified before they enter the Lower Paradise. Two angel messengers stand at the gate of Paradise, calling out to the leaders who are in charge of that portion of Gehenna. They repeatedly ask the powers that be to receive the expected soul who is now approaching, and during the entire process of purification they continue to utter the word *hinnom*, which means, "Here they are." When the process is finally over, those in charge take the soul from Gehenna and lead it to the gate of Paradise. At that point, they again say to the angel messengers standing there: "Hinnom, behold, here is the soul that has come out pure and white." The soul is then brought into the realm of Paradise.[35]

Most interestingly, the *Zohar* teaches that in the midst of a soul's twelve-month period in Gehenna, its punishment ceases each Sabbath, the day of rest, for the peace of the Sabbath extends even to the depths of Gehenna itself:

Every Sabbath evening, when the day is sanctified, heralds are sent to proclaim throughout all of Gehenna: "Please stop punishing the sinful! The Holy King has arrived; the Sabbath is about to know sanctification. And so they are all under His protection." Because of this, all chastisements cease and the wicked find repose for a certain time.[36]

THE LOWER PARADISE

The *Zohar* describes how a soul, upon completing its time in Gehenna, is prepared, while still in the hellish region, for its elevation to the Lower Paradise, as described above.

Also as noted previously, change of spiritual status is reflected in a change of garments, which more appropriately reflects the newly elevated status of the soul.

As the *Zohar* says, a man's soul does not appear before the Supreme unless she is first deemed worthy in terms of her divine raiment. In the same way, the soul does not manifest in the material world unless she is clad in appropriate garments. The text further tells us that even heavenly angels—if they need to execute a message in this world for one purpose or another—do not appear here unless they clothe themselves in the proper garments of this world. In other words, the "attire" always has to be in harmony with the place visited.[37]

As described by the *Zohar*, the Lower Paradise is itself a place of further preparation for souls, who, when and if found worthy, then ascend to the Upper Paradise itself, the ultimate goal of all souls. Yet the difference between the Lower and Upper Paradise is considered to be enormous: "... those who have not merited to ascend so high are assigned a lower place according to their deserts. They are stationed in the lower Eden, which is called 'lower Wisdom,' and between which and the higher Eden there is a difference as between darkness and light."[38]

Nevertheless, the *Zohar* stresses the interrelated nature of the Upper and Lower Paradise, so that on the Sabbath, souls are permitted to rise from the Lower to the Upper Paradise to stand before the Throne of Glory. Eventually, the soul in the Lower Garden of Eden may be deemed worthy to rise to the celestial level of the Upper Garden, where it again receives new raiment.

The soul's garments are made out of the good deeds performed by her in this world—in obedience to the commands of the Torah. While in the Lower Paradise, the soul is sustained by these deeds—even clad in garments that are made out of them! So says the *Zohar*. But when the soul progresses through purification and the grace of the Almighty, other precious garments are provided of a more exalted order. This dress is fashioned from the enthusiasm and devotion that characterized the soul's study of the Torah and its most sincere prayers. On the highest level, in fact, garments of light are made for the soul in order to ascend on high. The former garments, as already noted, depend on the soul's actions in the world of three dimensions, but the higher garments depend on devotion and love, which qualify their owner to join the company of angels and divinely inspired spirits.[39]

UPPER PARADISE

In order to enter the Upper Garden of Eden, still one more trial of purification awaits the soul before it can stand before the "Sovereign of the Universe."

While in the Lower Paradise, the soul still has remnants of the mundane world in its consciousness, and this needs to be fully purged before it is fit to ascend on high. For this reason, the *Zohar* tells us, the soul passes through a "river of fire," after which it will emerge thoroughly purified. In this way, it comes into the presence of the Ultimate Sovereign, purified of all material conceptions and pollutants. According to these same Kabbalistic texts, there are also rays of celestial light, which further adds to the souls' healing. Since this is the ultimate stage of purification, the souls then stand garbed in their appropriate raiment before their Maker, and they know unending bliss.[40]

At this point in the *Zohar* we learn that the highest level of all is that of Tzror Hachayim, "the bundle of the living." It is literally the return of the soul to its preincarnation source. It is here that the soul encounters "that holy superior grade called the super-soul (*neshamah*), and it regales itself with supernal delights."[41] This is when the spirit ascends and basks in its association with the super-soul.

A NOTE ON REINCARNATION

According to the *Zohar*, Tzror Hachayim, as mentioned here, would seem to be the place or dimension in which souls finally complete their post-life journey, now purified, and worthy of dwelling in the highest reaches of the Upper Garden of Eden—figuratively, in the King's Palace itself. However, rather than a place of eternal rest, it seems clear that Tzror Hachayim is the final place of preparation for the soul's future incarnation.

This is clear from even a cursory reading of the *Zohar*, which tells us that all souls must undergo transmigration: they incarnate in bodily form repeatedly, until they learn their lessons and purify their consciousness. As the texts say, "Many are the worlds through which they [the souls] revolve, and each revolution is wondrous in many hidden ways. But men neither know nor are they able to perceive these things! Nor do they know how the souls roll about 'like a stone inside a sling' (I Sam. XXV, 29)."[42]

Based on this statement—and similar ones—from the *Zohar*, we learn that reincarnation occurs numerous times to all souls, for it is an integral part of the very process into which souls are brought forth and in which they do their "work" of rectification and purification. The *Zohar* teaches yet another reason for reincarnation, for it suggests that the purpose of incarnation is not only the perfection of the soul, but also the perfection as well of the physical body, so that it may become perfect in the image of God. Says the *Zohar*: "If but one part of a body is not perfected, then reincarnation [gilgul] must occur until perfection is achieved, for both the body and the soul."[43] The texts are quite explicit:

If there is even one limb in which the Blessed One does not dwell, then the soul will reincarnate again into the world because of that limb, until he becomes perfected in his parts—for all of them must be perfect in the image of the Holy Blessed One.[44]

We see then that according to the Kabbalistic tradition, the journey of the soul continues long after physical death, leading to its purification and rectification in the next world, preparing for yet further incarnations into physicality to continue to elevate itself and to elevate and transform the physical world around it:

Each and every new soul must fulfill all 613 commandments. There are many sources in which all the souls of the world are divided. Each source is a particular organ or limb from one of the organs or limbs of the soul of Adam. Each and every source is divided into many sparks, each spark a particular soul without end. Each and every spark must keep all 613 commandments because there is no limb or organ that does not include 248 organs and limbs and 365 sinews, equivalent to 613. An old soul that has been reincarnated and returned to this world does not have to complete all the precepts in order to correct its soul, but only has to keep those precepts that it did not fulfill in its first life. At the same time, it does have to be careful not to sin through neglecting a positive precept or transgressing on a negative precept....

When a person neglects to fulfill a commandment, then he will be compelled to reincarnate in order to fulfill it.... After having fulfilled this precept connected to a particular soul in this world, he then can return to the Garden of Eden, the place of souls.[45]

It is clear that according to this tradition, only in this world of physicality can souls do the "work" of their *tikkun*, which ultimately enables them to earn their place in the highest levels of the Garden of Eden. However, it is through the work of cleansing and elevation in the next world that a new and more productive *tikkun* can be realized in the subsequent incarnation.

In a sense, the *Zohar* suggests that the very purpose of the creation of souls is birth, death, and rebirth and that their elevation through this process results in their essential refinement:

Let Aaron be gathered unto his people, etc. R. Hiya adduced here the verse: "Wherefore I praised the dead which are already dead," etc. (Eccl. IV, 2). How could King Solomon praise the dead more than the living, seeing that he is called "living" who walks in the way of truth in this world, while the wicked man who does not walk in the way of truth is called "dead"? We must, however, look at the words that follow, "which are already dead." This refers to one who has already died but who has the opportunity to return to this world in order that he may rectify (his previous life); verily this one is more to be praised than the other dead, because he has received his punishment, and he is more to be praised than the living who have not yet received their punishment. Such a one is called "dead" because he has had a taste of death, and although he is in this world he is dead and has returned from the dead; whereas "the living who are still alive" have not yet had a taste of death, and have not received their punishment and do not know if they will be worthy of the other world or not.... These, then, are they whom Solomon called "the living who are still alive," but the others "who have already died" and who have received their punishment once and twice are in a higher grade than they, and are called refined silver that has been purified of its dross.[46]

Interestingly, the Kabbalah suggests that it is not only a question of appropriate punishment that inevitably determines the process of reincarnation, but that the interaction with repentance can determine whether a soul must return to this world for further rectification or not.

The concepts of *teshuva* [repentance] and reincarnation, says the Kabbalah, are diverse, stemming from two different sources. The source of repentance is in Imma, the Divine Mother, while the source of reincarnation is in Abba, or the Ultimate Father. Therefore, for one who commits sin and does *teshuva*, or repentance, the supernal mother (Imma) will correct his blemish and set him right. If the man is not inclined to repent, then he will need to reincarnate to correct his blemish, and this is done through the grace of the supernal father (Abba).[47]

Finally, *Shaar Hagilgulim* adds the notion that a soul may need to reincarnate not only for its own rectification, but to guide and assist another soul in its own work as well:

Regarding reincarnation of souls, why do souls reincarnate? There are various reasons why they do: (a) They have transgressed on a particular commandment of the Torah laws; (b) To correct a commandment that was neglected and is lacking by them; and (c) For the sake of others, to guide them and help to correct them.[48]

This last point is an interesting one, for if all souls come from the Bundle of Life, then there is a clear notion that all souls benefit by the rectification of one another and that a soul's *tikkun* in this world can be for the purpose of helping other souls as well as, and for the benefit of, one's own soul. The unity of all souls and of all life in a dynamic divine process leading to unity with the divine itself is clearly implied.

RESURRECTION

The Kabbalists understood that the doctrine of reincarnation raised a serious question concerning another central Jewish doctrine: resurrection. According to Maimonides, the doctrine of resurrection was one of the thirteen cardinal principles of the Jewish religious tradition, and according to some Talmudic sources, one who doubted the doctrine of resurrection would not be able to enter the World to Come.

Although combining within itself numerous nuances of interpretation, the doctrine of resurrection posits that all who are born will die, and one day, be born again as soul and body together at the time of the coming of the Messianic age. Some versions speak of resurrection only for Israel, others for all mankind. Some speak of resurrection only for the righteous, others for all. Some versions speak of resurrection only for those in the Land of Israel, others, for everyone, no matter where they may be. Nonetheless, all versions speak of a time when the dead will rise again, in their same bodies, filled with the knowledge of God in a world transformed into its full spiritual possibilities.

The question for the Kabbalists was a pointed one. If there is to be a resurrection of body and soul, and if, according to the doctrine of reincarnation, a given soul will have incarnated into numerous bodies—then which soul/body combination will become the resurrected one?

In response to this question, the *Zohar* states that those bodies that were unworthy and did not achieve their purpose will be regarded as though they had never existed—like a withered tree in this world, which serves little or no purpose. So will such bodies be regarded at the time of the resurrection. In fact, *only the last body*—the one that has been firmly planted and took root and prospered—will come to life. As the scripture says, "For he shall be as a tree planted by the waters ... but its foliage shall be luxuriant, etc." (Jer. XVII, 8).

The *Zohar* states it directly: "The Holy One will thus in the future raise the dead to life again, and the good principle will prevail in the world and the Evil One will vanish from the world, as already said, and the previous bodies will be as though they never had been."[49]

CONCLUSION

As the *Zohar* describes at great length, the journey of the soul in the next world is a long and arduous one. Yet also implied in the *Zohar* is that this is the very purpose and intent for the creation of souls—to elevate themselves and the bodies into which they incarnate, so that Godliness will become increasingly manifest in the material world. The ultimate goal of this most complex process is the preparing of the world and its spiritual level for the time of the coming of the Messiah, and the Resurrection of the Dead.

We see then that the doctrine of reincarnation is not in opposition to the doctrine of resurrection, but, rather, is the expression of the Kabbalists' understanding of how resurrection and the Messianic era are to be achieved, through the constant elevation of the spiritual and the material through soul reincarnation.

When combined with the Arizal's teachings concerning the journey of the soul while in life in this world, a complete scenario is developed concerning the purpose of spiritual life both in this world and the next and their intimate and necessary relationship with each other. From the Jewish mystical perspective, then, we were created for the work of the soul, both in this world and in the next. This is the most basic meaning and purpose of both life and death.

NOTES

1. See *Zohar* II, 218b. All references to the *Zohar* can be corroborated with reference to Harry Sperlin and Maurice Simon, trans., *The Zohar*, vol. 1–5. London-New York: Soncino Press, 1984.
2. *Zohar* II, 217b.
3. Ibid.
4. *Zohar* II, 245a.
5. *Zohar* V, 126b–127a.
6. Ibid.
7. Ibid.
8. Ibid.
9. Ibid.
10. Ibid.
11. *Zohar* II, 218b.
12. *Zohar* I, 57b.
13. *Zohar* V, 53a.
14. *Zohar* I, 100a.
15. *Zohar* II, 218a–218b.
16. *Zohar* IV, 199a.
17. *Zohar* I, 221b.
18. *Zohar* I, 78b–79a.
19. *Zohar* IV, 126b.
20. *Zohar* II, 202a.
21. *Zohar* II, 175b.
22. See *Midrash* on Psalms 11:6.
23. Ibid.
24. *Zohar* I, 218b-219a.
25. *Zohar* III, 142a.
26. *Zohar* I, 77a–77b.
27. *Zohar* II, 217b.
28. *Zohar* I, 65b–66a.
29. *Zohar* IV, 150a.
30. Ibid.

31. *Zohar* III, 97a.
32. *Zohar* II, 238b.
33. *Zohar* I, 107b–108a.
34. *Zohar* V, 53a.
35. *Zohar* IV, 211b.
36. *Zohar* IV, 150b–151a.
37. *Zohar* IV, 229b.
38. *Zohar* V, 182b.
39. *Zohar* IV, 210a–210b.
40. *Zohar* IV, 211b–212.
41. *Zohar* V, 71a.
42. *Zohar* III, 99b.
43. *Tikkunei Zohar*, 70, 132a.
44. Ibid.
45. See "The Jewish Concept of Reincarnation," *Shaar Hagilgulim*, 89–91.
46. *Zohar* V, 182a–182b.
47. See "The Jewish Concept of Reincarnation," *Shaar Hagilgulim*, 113–14.
48. Ibid., 45.
49. *Zohar* II, 131a.

SELECTED BIBLIOGRAPHY

Goldberg, Rabbi Chaim Binyamin. *Mourning in Halachah*. Brooklyn, NY: Mesorah Publications, 1991.

Lamm, Maurice. *The Jewish Way in Death and Mourning*. New York: Jonathan David Publishers, 1969.

Pinson, DovBer. *Reincarnation and Judaism: The Journey of the Soul*. Northvale, NJ: Jacob Aronson, 1999.

Raphael, Simcha Paull. *Jewish Views of the Afterlife*. Northvale, NJ: Jacob Aronson, 1994.

Solomon, Lewis D. *The Jewish Book of Living and Dying*. Northvale, NJ: Jacob Aronson, 1999.

Sperling, Harry, and Maurice Simon, trans. *The Zohar*, vol. 1–5. London-New York: Soncino Press, 1984.

Wexelman, David M. *The Jewish Concept of Reincarnation and Creation*. Northvale, NJ: Jacob Aronson, 1999.

2

Preparation for Eternal Life: Christian Teachings on Death and Dying

Francis V. Tiso

On my desk, I have a small, framed picture of one of the frescoes in the caves at Subiaco, in Central Italy, where according to tradition St. Benedict lived as a hermit in the early sixth century of the Common Era. Three young men in noble costume are out hunting with falcons in the woods; they come upon a lonely chapel cared for by an aged hermit. He shows them three coffins containing the bodies of three dead men in three distinct stages of decomposition. The message is clear: *As these are, so will you be; therefore, take up an approach to life that will prepare you for the time of death in a meaningful way, for after death comes judgment. Do not waste your time while here on earth!* This image resonates with the ancient call to the ascetic life in Buddhist texts and perhaps offers us a universal point of departure: The archetype of bodily death as a sign that has a powerful impact on the way we live our daily lives, consciously or not.

Over the past sixty years, human populations have become more and more attuned to mass phenomena, mediated by means of increased social communication, better known as "the media." With the usual human tendency to imitate, follow along, and identify with the experiences of others, it should not be a great surprise that the death process of diverse cultures is receiving a great deal of attention. In the United States, the World War II generation is dying off, bearing the noble title of "The Greatest Generation": the people who lived through the Depression of the 1930s and the war and came to preside over our institutions during the decades of great prosperity and deepening doubts from 1945 to 1990 or so.

The Greatest Generation became the parents of the "Baby Boomers," that numerous population that was shaped by the constructed social perspectives of the 1950s and 1960s. This author falls into the latter category statistically, but shares with (perhaps) a minority of that statistical grouping a viewpoint of skepticism with regard to the value of the way we were brought up and, even more so, the way we were taught by advertising and politics to think about ourselves. From that doubting perspective, I would like to take up the question of death, fully aware that what I am saying should not only fairly represent the faith of Christians, but should also be helpful to those whose Greatest Generation relatives are dying and who will themselves confront personal death over the next few decades.

Some of what I say may not match the experience of the middle of the sociological bell curve. I am a Catholic priest who spent a large portion of his ministry in rural Europe and who studies Indian and Tibetan cultures, so this should not come as a surprise. However, the view of life coming from the margins can sometimes provide the kind of perspective that allows the reader to come to his or her own conclusions without being clubbed over the head with statistical data.

As children of "the media," we are persuaded to believe or do things on the basis of what are purported to be trends that cannot be evaded. Instead, I would hope that the reader will think critically from a position of inner freedom from coercion. I therefore make no apologies for my Catholic Christian point of view, with its accompanying perspective of doubt with regard to stringently secular worldviews. I will discuss other Christian viewpoints, where their role in illuminating Christian diversity bears insistently upon the discussion.

THE PROBLEM OF DEATH IN THE MODERN WORLD

Cultural deficiencies that can turn up in any society can make it very difficult for people to benefit spiritually from the fact that we are all going to die. Our life is a "life unto death" we are told by more solemn philosophers, but we easily forget. It is not just that we forget: we let the lessons of life and death slip from our grasp. St. Benedict, in his *Rule for Monks*, taught the "Instruments of Good Works," one of which was to "Keep death daily before our eyes." This was meant as a meditative practice, not just a passing idea.

Preparation for death and for eternal life is a spiritual necessity. However, human beings seem to need reminders—pointing out simply and directly that they will come to an end, at least in their present form. In spite of the large number of deaths that are reported in the mass media, not to mention in popular entertainment circles, people have a habit of shunting aside consideration of one's own personal bodily death. The continued use of euphemisms to refer to death, the reported decline in the number of religious funerals, and the increase in the number of anonymous nonceremonial cremations—as if death were simply a problem of hygiene rather than of philosophy or religious faith—indicate the persistence of denial in popular culture.

People need to be reminded. In fact, when properly reminded, human beings can be changed and even improved by such reminders, particularly when the reminders are themselves life-threatening, such as accidents and diseases. Sometimes the death of a close friend or family member, or mass deaths such as those of 9/11, can impact people's lives so deeply as to motivate moral, life-altering change. What the perennial philosophy has called the "rich inner life" or "the examined life" makes sense for many people only when there has been a dramatic encounter with the reality of one's own mortality.

From the perspective of Christian faith, "Death is the end of man's earthly pilgrimage, of the time of grace and mercy which God offers him so as to work out his earthly life in keeping with the divine plan, and to decide his ultimate destiny."[1] The manner of a person's existence, at the center of which is a commitment to a life of faith in Christ, predisposes that person and those around him or her to death as the gateway to eternal life in God. Thus, everything connected with the bodily death of a person has the character of an affirmation of the faith of the person and of the community.

In the "Introduction" to the *Rite of Christian Funerals,* the point is clearly stated: "The Church's belief in the sacredness of the human body and the resurrection of the dead has traditionally found expression in the care taken to prepare the bodies of the deceased for burial. The prayers and gestures of Catholic funeral rites likewise affirm the Church's reverence for the bodies of its deceased members. That reverence is not always shared by the society in which the Church exists. An exaggerated sense of privacy and individualism often prevents family members from providing the custody and care of the body that is properly theirs. This same concern with privacy, combined with a denial of the reality of death and human mortality, has resulted in an increasing tendency to shorten the period for mourning the passing of the deceased person. These practices contradict the Church's emphasis on the indispensable role of the wider community in the dying and death of a Christian."[2]

General deficiencies of a religious nature have settled into the practices of many churches.[3] Nevertheless, I have noticed that people of faith protest unashamedly the trivialization of death in popular culture and in popular preaching. The clergy should know better, but often they feel pressured to give in to bad taste and bad theology. Many clergy fear a reputation of being overly serious. There is always the threat that telling the truth will not be popular. In short, there is the fear that parishioners will "drift away." In reality, however, there is a spiritual hunger in the general population that is not satisfied with pious euphemisms and humorous anecdotes. What could be less spiritually illuminating than a trivial homily on the occasion of someone's death? What could be more offensive than a funeral celebrated with haste and lacking any sense of aesthetics, moral balance, and respectful dignity? How can we expect people to value their own lives, and the lives of others around them, when the deepest hopes of persons are reduced to ham-handed humor?

Funerals celebrated with dignity and intelligence can be a valuable teaching moment in the life of a Christian community. I think that the key insight here is that there is continuity between life and death. As one lives, one dies. As one lives, so does one approach the prospect of life after death. The perplexity of the clergy is perhaps understandable when one realizes that even families that consider themselves "believers" are reluctant to participate fully in the *dying process* in a truly Christian manner. To the extent that old age, sickness, death, and eternal life are unspoken features of a human life, so too has pastoral care of the dying become an "unmentionable" topic.

Thus we have the anomalous situation of a public ritual of the church, a funeral, in which neither the participants nor the clergy truly know one another in terms of pastoral care and shared faith. The experience of making the passage into eternal life is missing and an opportunity is lost. In a community of vibrant faith, the time of illness, dying, and burial becomes a time in which to deepen faith and widen the embrace of Christian love. At such times, believers are reassured about their connectedness to God and to one another; skeptics are invited to reconsider their views; all are asked to open their imaginations to the message of resurrection and eternal life.

In practice, these deficiencies reflect a lack of proper preparation for death. Again, from a faith perspective: "The Church encourages us to prepare ourselves for the hour of our death.... Every action of yours, every thought, should be those of one who expects to die before the day is out. Death would have no great terrors for you if you had a quiet conscience.... Then why not keep clear of sin instead of running away from death? If you aren't fit to face death today, it's very unlikely you will be tomorrow...." (*The Imitation of Christ* 1, 23, 1).[4]

Deficiencies in the Attitude toward Sickness, Suffering, and Death

If our whole life can be seen as a preparation for death, or more precisely, as a preparation for eternal life, it would be logical to set up a courageous program of life, a "rule of life," by which to regulate one's conduct such that virtue is cultivated and faults are cured. This would be our *remote preparation* for death. When there is a serious illness, however, we enter into the time of *proximate preparation*. All the merits, virtues, and wisdom of the remote preparation come to fruition at this time; unfortunately, a very flawed remote preparation shows itself in the anguish and confusion of the time in which death approaches quickly. I have seen patients so traumatized by a fatal diagnosis that no sedatives could calm them down. We have the bad habit of interpreting sickness and suffering as signs of God's disfavor, of some kind of punishment, of the "universe being against us." As a result, we waste a great amount of time that could be more fruitfully spent on working with the phenomena associated with bodily deterioration. We can turn those phenomena into forceful opportunities to offer ourselves completely to God, gaining in detachment and inner freedom at every painful cycle of breath. It would be very helpful for the dying to have as much spiritual companionship as possible; having friends and family who value the dying process is a great benefit at this time.[5]

CLASSIC CATHOLIC CHRISTIAN TEACHINGS ON PREPARATION FOR DEATH

> God becomes Man in order to divinize Man.... *theoria esti telos tou biou*: contemplation is the purpose of life.
>
> —Clement of Alexandria

One of the classics of European early modern spirituality is *The Preparation for Death* (*Apparecchio alla Morte*) of Saint Alfonso Maria de' Liguori, published in 1758. This book is a mirror of the kind of popular preaching that Saint Alfonso was promoting with dramatic effect in the Kingdom of Naples at the time. The preaching of "missions" to the largely unlettered and pastorally neglected masses bore fruit in a great spiritual revival. A key feature of these missions was the sermon on the Four Last Things: Death, Judgment, Heaven, and Hell.

However, at the heart of the preaching is an intense awareness of Christ as the Loving Redeemer. Therefore, the overarching theme of this book is to obtain and remain in the love of God and to persevere to the end of one's life. The approach is to reflect on the brevity of life and the inevitability of death and to consider the risks of prolonging repentance. The great peril of this method, which is after all not a theological treatise but a work of popular piety, is that it risks stirring up objections in the form of parodies of its own excesses. In other words, it lacks irony and so brings out the human inclination to cynicism and irony as a form of psychological self-defense.

In the context of eighteenth-century Naples, in which a certain amount
of secularism had begun to take hold, this was a very real risk. As at the
royal courts of Europe, society easily became divided into the "devout,"
who were willing to take on the rigors of living a fully Catholic Christian
life, and the "libertines," who either chose to delay repentance or who
openly mocked the way of life of their believing contemporaries. The
social dualism that ensued entered into the idiomatic speech of the people, and the spiritual power of a certain kind of pious rhetoric thus found
itself reduced to the level of cynical popular proverbs. As also in the case
of Jean Baptiste de la Salle's *Introduction to a Devout Life*, the emphasis
on avoiding and resisting temptations that come one's way depending on
one's "state in life" seems to overpower the joy of the Christian life and
even to obscure the nature of sanctity.

At times, reading these works one can only wonder at the kind of personality that might measure up to the standards of holiness therein
described. The purgative and illuminative ways, given to penance and
acquiring the virtues, are given due emphasis, but the unitive way (when
mentioned at all) is depicted in such lofty terms that it seems reserved
for elect souls confined to the cloister. This is in spite of the fact that
these writers were considered at the time to be "progressives," seeking to
engage the laity in a deeper and more authentic form of Christian piety.
Fortunately, there were a number of great souls of those times in whose
lives we have a glimpse of deeply committed Christians who were faithful to the moral norms, but who also found ways to express their faith
in remarkably subversive, unconventional ways. St. Vincent De Paul,
St. Gerard Maiella, and St. Louis de Montfort are three examples that
could be cited.

In the best parts of St. Alfonso's *Preparation*, the affirmation of the
fullness of life in God overpowers the grim words of warning that take
their power from reflection on physical death. St. Alfonso was a mystic
of love expressed as total self-surrender; his popular preaching clearly situates these values at the heart of Christian life, in spite of the fact that
there is for our taste too much of a cult of death and a psychology of
guilt. In the comments that follow, my intention is to derive an image of
the mentality that we find in the *Preparation for Death* so that we can
sort out the enduring wisdom of the Catholic Christian approach from
the psychologically problematic aspects of the saint's rhetoric.

One of the functions of guilt in society is to gain control over others.
Making a person feel guilty is a way of controlling that person. If our
image of God is that of a grim old man whose day consists entirely of
counting up people's faults and seeking ways in which to chastise them,
we can easily imagine that such a God might not be very believable.
However, for some people such a God is a handy weapon against those
who disturb the peace. A parent, for example, can use guilt to control a

child well into adulthood so that the child feels perennially guilty for any thought, word, or deed conceived in the freedom of one's own spirit, whether for good or ill. In some parts of St. Alfonso's text, it seems that God is a rather ineffectual and complaining old grandfather, unable to rescue his grandchildren from the schemes of the ever-fascinating demon, who moves much more quickly, seems always to be on hand, and is eager to offer his own version of the good life.

Meanwhile, the more one reads, the more one senses that God is rather a neurotic old fellow, very demanding of his grandchildren, lonely without them and critical of them when they are present, easily offended by the least mistake, and strangely eager to turn his back on the people whom, we are told, he has created and redeemed. It is as if, in God's eyes, the human race is so repellant that he wants nothing to do with it.

Even the Son of God, who should be known as love incarnate, has to be endlessly implored to come back into our arms. The soul is depicted almost as an unappealing young woman, entirely lacking in self-confidence, who has to beg for suitors to pay attention to her. She becomes quite neurotic trying to attract her eventual spouse, who seems always on the verge of running away, perhaps precisely because she is so boring, repetitive, and codependent. He is never around when temptation comes along, never around when she needs him; he has to be implored for the very favors that he is said to have already won for her at so great a price: his own death on the cross.

Even those graces that we need in order to take the first steps in spiritual life, without which we cannot be pleasing to God, seem to be bestowed with great reluctance and are all too easily lost by a single act of transgression. Many years of virtuous living can be reduced to nullity by one single serious sin. It is as if the great biblical drama of the rescue of humanity is replaced with another narrative, one in which neither God nor humankind comes off well. What ever happened to the great cosmic drama that God is willing to endure in Christ for our redemption? In many passages, a not very helpful worldview distorts the rhetoric of conversion of life. How many different ways of reading the following passage can be imagined? "My redeemer, you poured out all your blood, you gave your life to save my soul, and I lost it many times by the hope of obtaining your mercy—thus I made use of your goodness and why? To offend you even more? Just for this I merited that you should have killed me and sent me to hell."[6]

To the pious soul, perhaps this will give a moment of spiritual affection. But to the skeptic, it is nothing but a parody of a God who is called "love," for He seems to not know how to love those whom He has created. And to the exploitative person, it is the perfect excuse to impose a regimen of guilt on those over whom one has charge. Thus, the exercise of human freedom, without distinguishing transgression from creativity, is seen as hard to redeem, meriting homicide and eternal damnation. The imagery suggesting reluctance on God's part is troubling, something one would not expect from the One who preached about the Prodigal Son whose father *rushes* to embrace him *even before he asks for forgiveness*.

To be fair, St. Alfonso does reassure us: "The Lord does not wish to see us lost, and for this reason, he does not fail to urge us to change our way of life"—but, he adds: "with the menace of chastisement."[7] This is one of those ideas that might even be true in the way of analogy, but it carries a tremendous risk: That when I am being "chastised," it means I have been "bad" (and by way of a corollary, when I am feeling fine, I am being favored with divine grace). It is hard for the ordinary person to recognize in adversity a sign of purifying grace; even harder to be alert in prosperity for signs that things are not all as they should be. Experience teaches us to be wary of subjective feelings and emotions, which are after all mutable impressions that tell us more about the fickle mind of human beings than about the will of God for our salvation.

It is not that the saint did not know this—I am sure he did. The problem is in trying to create rhetoric that will get people's attention. Afterwards, however, this rhetoric takes on an unhealthy life of its own that requires considerable theological clarity and psychological realism to cure. The pessimistic and remote images of God lend themselves to very distorted and dysfunctional relationships in families and in society as a whole, wherever and whenever religion is used as a system of social control. Naturally, it is religion as an institution that ends up paying a terrible price when society rebels and sets up a new system, based on the "death" of such images of God.

Even St. Pio of Pietrelcina, a great Capuchin spiritual guide of the twentieth century, had to work hard to help himself and others break out of this trap of the misleading subjective feelings, impressions, and opinions that completely ruin our encounter with the living God. This is particularly evident in his brilliant letters to the Cerase sisters in Foggia, Italy, and to Maria Gargani, a young teacher who later founded a religious order of women. St. Pio wrote forcefully to these young women, whose timidity and health problems had burdened them with psychological anguish. His counsels led them from scrupulosity to greatness of spirit.

St. Alfonso's rhetoric on the state of the soul of a sinner at the time of death has tremendous force and fully reflects the rich Augustinian heritage of theology, psychology, and preaching. And yet there is a feeling that God has been all along powerless to move this soul to repentance. The sins that are mentioned include harming others, calumny, and oppression. St. Alfonso gives us a portrait of a despicable person who all along has not been trying to seek the good and has not only been weak many times, but even malicious; this is a person who did everything to avoid goodness and to justify evil acts. It is the habitual sinner, therefore, who is depicted and not the frail soul, perhaps aware of the gifts of grace and eager for good, but unable to carry out all his or her responsibilities perfectly. The distinction between the "untouched" sinner hard of heart and the contemplative who occasionally falls is essential to an accurate interpretation of this passage.

For my argument—that how we live is how we die—the deathbed scene is particularly poignant. St. Alfonso's description of the dying person's encounter both with memory and friends may be imagined to have contributed to the reluctance a family sometimes shows in inviting a priest to come to help the dying person because he says that everything will seem like a "thorn" to him at that time, even the crucifix.[8] So, to diminish his presumed pain, the family even hides the fatal diagnosis from the poor dying person, who is left feeling even more abandoned and terrified of what he may already have learned by intuition.

St. Alfonso says in *Consideration VIII* that the anguish the sinner experiences is not felt by the just (though many saints experienced other kinds of anguish in the time before death).[9] The valid point here is that the just souls longed for eternal life and practiced detachment in this life so they had an uncluttered mind when they died. However, detachment also means being interiorly free from the merely good and from various notions and opinions that may be useful remedies from time to time in the spiritual life, but which must be jettisoned as the soul matures toward perfect freedom, detachment, and openness to the will of God. This is where the real joy comes in, something that no misfortune can take away.

Frequently, St. Alfonso corrects his own rhetorical exaggerations with clarifications that come from the best of the theological tradition. For example: "Death is not to be feared, only sin that makes for a bad death." However, the risk inherent to exaggerated rhetoric is that the reader will focus on the unhealthy material rather than on the rational material; we know that there are times when preachers have been inclined to use hyperbole to get people's attention. The problem is that hyperbole has a way of becoming the normative voice of the Church.

One of the problems that St. Alfonso had to address in his time was Jansenism, an extremely pessimistic form of Catholicism that emphasized the need to avoid sin at all costs and, even more emphatically, sought to find the cause of guilty behavior even in the normal joys of life. St. Alfonso was himself accused of being too lax by followers of Jansenism active in the Kingdom of Naples. Incredible as it may seem, the fact that a men's prayer group that he started served veal cutlets on one occasion became something of a cause célèbre in which St. Alfonso was mocked as being "morally lax" for tolerating this "feasting." Those were the times.

St. Alfonso goes on in *Consideration X* to expound the value of preparing oneself spiritually for death, which is of course the very heart of the book. In spite of the psychological flaws of some of his rhetoric, he has not lost touch with the essential thread of a life-long preparation for death, understood as the "gateway to life," i.e., eternal life with God. Such preparation will include the following:

- Examination of conscience covering one's entire life (on retreat)
- General confession of one's sins (the general confession was an occasion, often during the course of a retreat, to establish a penitent in a firm state of conversion of heart)
- Daily Mass
- Meditation on the eternal truths of the Catholic faith
- Confession and reception of Holy Communion once every eight days
- Daily visits to the Blessed Sacrament and to the Blessed Mother, involving a short meditation and affective prayer
- Belonging to a spiritual association such as a Third Order or study group
- Spiritual reading
- Examination of conscience every evening
- Daily Marian devotions
- Use of short "ejaculatory" prayers during times of temptation
- Keep in mind that Jesus Christ wants one's salvation and provides the means for the realization of that end
- Detachment from worldly things: daily dying to selfishness
- Abandon temporal attachments
- Imagine yourself to be actually dead, done as a meditation once a month

These methods have much to recommend them. It is interesting that some of them turn up in other world religions in various ways. I would add two practices that should also be of great help in preparing one for the hour of death: (1) Frequent attention to one's state of mind in the course of the day, trying to cultivate recollection or mindfulness and cutting down distractions; (2) Works of charity especially to the poor and disabled, since this helps us fulfill a command of the Lord and also liberates us from self-centered preoccupations.

One feature of such preparation would certainly be to cultivate a sense that one is giving of oneself for the betterment of others so as to grow in the virtue of generosity. Having performed the works of mercy is a precondition for entering joyfully into eternal life because the works of charity allow God's love to flow to others through us. Thus we become habitually detached and we also gain a sense of compassion and solidarity with others. By giving of oneself, one symbolically "gives away" the body, which will have to be given away at the time of death. Over time, one will be conscious of the analogy between being habitually generous with time, talent, and treasure, and, at the end of life, accepting the time of death as itself a gift and as a time to "give away" everything. The integrity of a virtuous life can help one develop a great deal of inner strength. As a result, one's natural fear of death is overcome gradually and spontaneously in the course of the years that one dedicates to the loving care of other people.

What is needed today would be a new way to orient Christians to prepare themselves for death without the sense that a Christian way of life is grim, joyless, and uninspiring. This is why I would prefer to speak of a "preparation for eternal life," since that is what Jesus promised those who believe. Death is then the gateway to that gift of life in God.

Proper preparation for death requires a systematic, decisive, pondered, and frequently renewed spiritual battle against worldliness, superficiality, moral laziness, and spiritual obtuseness. The practices outlined by St. Alfonso are very effective weapons in this battle. People in our times are frequently surrounded by a limitless array of truly bad examples, promoted as admirable and imitable, especially the way celebrities are set up as role models. Beauty, wealth, and sexuality are touted as ideal, indeed indispensable, qualities that make one happy. Virtue, intelligence, courtesy, and refined tastes are mocked. It is therefore morally necessary for the average Christian to develop and cultivate a deep revulsion for these media and advertising-driven promotions. A skillful parent, for example, will impart to his or her children the ability to recognize fraud for what it is, making use of humor, banter, and debate. We have to become skilled at mockery, rejection, and suppression of the sources of misinformation and decadence that are forced on us.

When a person commits serious sins as a result of growing up in a decayed moral environment, we can be compassionate toward that person because we know that God is merciful and knows why people have become susceptible to dehumanizing influences. Of course, one of the reasons why people seem to behave so badly is precisely because they have had the virtues kicked out of them by the negative impact of bad role models; as a result, their conduct does not measure up to the requirements of positive social interaction. The notion of "culture wars" is perhaps too subtle for this phenomenon. It is not enough to say we have a violent, decayed culture; we have to look at the causes and conditions that have been constructed to bring this state of affairs into being. As in the time of the earliest Christians, candidates for adult baptism were expected to develop revulsion not only for personal sin but also for social constructions of injustice, violence, exploitation, abuse, and all forms of nonvirtuous living. We may have to leave behind certain occupations and activities that place us in a position to do harm or give a bad example.

In the later part of our lives, it will be hard to give up our bad habits and attachments in preparation for death, so it is a good idea to practice some form of asceticism and spiritual discipline when young and healthy.

It is pathetic to see elderly people needlessly making use of Viagra, seeking sex partners, engaging in gambling, and wasting precious time playing games and other fruitless leisure activities when they could be focusing on practices that will open up their spirits to the serenity and joy of eternal life. A materialistic, purposeless philosophy of life does not bring us happiness and it makes it very difficult to confront the real challenges of old age and the dying process.

What is sadder and more terrifying to watch than the old age and death of a person whose life has been a meaningless series of moral evasions? I have counseled young people working in healthcare who were devastated by what they saw happening when an old person dies in despair because that person never sought to live a virtuous human life. It is not a pretty sight, and it is shocking to think that this goes on more and more in our kind of society. One can only imagine the spiritual anguish of a person who has already contracted to have his or her life terminated in the case of a debilitating illness; here we are sunk in the worst excesses of the "hygienic" view of death, which is nothing but complete despair.

To die without the fear of death requires a deep inner conviction that we are guided by God, that our lives receive meaning and purpose from our relationship with God, that there is life after death, that good is rewarded and evil is punished, and that suffering is part of life and helps us become disentangled from attachments, opinions, and blind spots that impoverish our spiritual vision. Offering prayers and Masses for the dead also has a way of nurturing our sense of solidarity with others. Consciously praying for the dead helps us understand the communion of the saints that binds all believers together in one mystical reality. We are all sharing in the same Trinitarian life of love, a fellowship of divine life that we will all share forever, in community with all who are saved and sanctified by faith in Jesus. This is why I consider burial *ad sanctos* to be such an important sign and why I think the Church should encourage the use of collective columbaria and should where possible revive churchyard burial. This has recently been done in a beautiful way in the crypt of the Cathedral of Los Angeles. Being buried near a community that celebrates the Eucharist is an affirmation of solidarity with the whole church— militant, suffering, and triumphant, awaiting the return of the Lord in glory to judge the living and the dead, bestowing on the faithful "the life of the world to come" (*vitam venturi saeculi*. Amen).

WHAT IS DEATH?

The simplest definition of death is the cessation of bodily activity and the separation of the soul from the material remains. The traditional *Prayer of Commendation* states it with great clarity in a way that echoes the threefold formula of Christian Baptism: "Go forth, Christian soul, from this world in the name of God the almighty Father, who created you, in the name of Jesus Christ, Son of the living God, who suffered for you, in the name of the Holy Spirit, who was poured out upon you; go forth, faithful Christian." The rites contain prayers and readings that illuminate the dogmatic foundations of Christian belief about death, dying, and the life after death.

We readily notice that that which distinguishes a corpse from a living person is the absence of an energetic "presence" in the corpse. A corpse lacks both the psychological and transcendent features that accompany the material body of a living person, even when we have an emotional attachment to the deceased. A corpse appears to us as a body, recognizable for its physical features, but lacking the psychologically active and spiritually persuasive presence of a living person. The very "thing" that we recognize in photographs of ourselves or of our friends taken decades ago is absent in a corpse.

For a Christian, this absence does not diminish the fact that that corpse, as a once living body, participated in the process of sanctification and is therefore itself sacred. It is not reducible to a problem of hygienic disposal! The continuity from a life full of grace and the fulfillment of our desire for eternal life in God is mediated by the body that receives the sacraments in the course of a lifetime.

A person is a given reality, evident from moment to moment, in and through the changes that occur in its way of presenting itself to others. When a person becomes a corpse by dying, we might have an emotional reaction when we see the corpse because it looks strikingly like the deceased and, unlike an effigy, it was in reality the material basis by which we recognized the person with our senses when he or she was alive. However, it does not take long for us to awaken to the fact that the person is no longer "there," even though the "corpse" is there. Absence, not presence, is what we perceive with our ability to unite physical observation with intuitive cognition. We know that persons are dead because their current physical condition does not allow them to act so as to present themselves interactively with other living persons.

We know that even a corpse is unique from a biological point of view. But what strikes us particularly hard is that the uniqueness of a person comes across to us much more from the psychology of the person as he or she interacts with us, than from the material body per se. You can sometimes tell who your friend is even if she is wearing a mask and a well-designed costume. As for a person with whom one has shared a deep and long-term spiritual relationship, the process of intuitive mutual recognition is even more persuasive. Spirit knows spirit, taking into account even very subtle interactions between persons, not all of which can be attributed to body posture, scent, mannerisms, and so forth. By spirit, I mean the following features observable especially to the "contemplative person": (a) evident awareness; (b) openness to change and development; (c) willfulness, decisiveness, and freedom; (d) uniqueness and distinctiveness; (e) the will to create meaning; (f) enhancement of all features through relationships; (g) a continuity of cognitive abilities from sense data to subtle mystical phenomena; (h) actions that have a tendency toward "absoluteness" or finality even in particular circumstances; these actions are motivated by the classic qualities: beauty, goodness, truth, even when present as abstractions; and (i) an orientation toward God or the absolute as its overarching trajectory.

Human persons have these physical, psychological, and spiritual features of uniqueness. It does not take a great deal of reflection to recognize that once the body is dead, the uniqueness of a person in the perception of others is compromised. Unless someone has the preternatural ability to perceive spirit separated from embodiment, in the death of the body there is no basis for discussing the presence of a person, because our uniqueness is dependent on our ability to form a relationship. As a result, even if a hypothetical immaterial aspect of the person were to gather together and reassemble the material particles of a body, as if the "soul" were to function as a sort of magnetic field pulling together the elements of another body, there is no reason that would compel us to say that that person is the "same" as the person whom the soul had previously pulled together.

This is very evident in the case of those persons who are claimed to be the "rebirth" of a previous person, as in the case of reincarnate lamas from Tibet. These persons are formally recognized as reincarnations and spiritual heirs of their predecessors, who are usually abbots or other high officials in the monastic system. However, the historical record testifies very clearly that one incarnation can be very different from the previous one. The Great Fifth Dalai Lama, for example, was quite different from the controversial Sixth Dalai Lama. The Thirteenth Dalai Lama, who was a beleaguered but nonetheless admirable figure, was quite different in appearance and personality from the widely admired current Fourteenth Dalai Lama. Thus, even these reincarnate lamas present themselves with the uniqueness that we usually identify with a presumably "Western" notion of the person.

Even where we notice some physical similarities, as in the case of the Seventeenth Karmapa who has some features (bone structure of the forehead) in common with the remarkable Sixteenth Karmapa, the new rebirth is in many ways dramatically different from the previous Karmapa. So it would seem, from the point of view of a person as someone who presents a distinct manner of being alive in a unique embodiment, a reincarnate lama is a distinct person who is trained in each manifestation to take on the role of his or her predecessor, but whose distinctive personality shines through. Speaking hypothetically, should the same immaterial "magnetic field" of a particular entity leave one embodiment to take upon itself the material elements of a new embodiment, such an entity would not be the same "person" who was manifest in the previous rebirth. Thus, even from the perspective of interreligious dialogue, it is important to clarify what we mean by a person when we are talking about death and dying.

As We Live, so We Die, and Are Born to Eternal Life

Continuing our reflection on theological foundations, we turn to the New Testament and Church history.[10] The redeeming death of Jesus and transforming power of His resurrection are called the "Paschal Mystery" and are affirmed in the New Testament and in the liturgy, shaping our theological convictions about death and life after death.[11] Some theologians, reflecting on the question of the afterlife over the past century or so, have interpreted the text of the New Testament as exclusively a proclamation of the resurrection of the body. As a result of this attempt at recovering the presumed "original" Christian belief, any discussion of the immortality of the soul appears to have been jettisoned as a merely philosophical, Hellenistic intrusion into the presumably pure, uncontaminated world of Judaic "wholeness of body and soul."

My own research over the past thirty years suggests that this is an oversimplification. It ignores the three centuries–long process of Hellenization that Judaism underwent before the coming of Jesus. It cannot be said that the Hellenization of Judaism was irrelevant to early Christian experience. Indeed, it clearly was not.

As a result, the early Christian communities quickly recognized a connection between how one lives and how one approaches the threshold of life forever with God. In the Gospel of John, written by the end of the first century, the message of life in Christ is closely linked to overcoming death and attaining "eternal life." Thus John 5:24 uses the present tense in an "absolute" sense to express the inseparable link between moral and sacramental life on the one hand, and eternal life on the other: "Whoever listens to my words and believes in the One who sent me *has* eternal life." (cf. 6:47). That this refers to the life of the Christian and to the condition of the dead is clear from related passages: "The hour is coming, indeed it is already here, when the dead will hear the voice of the Son of God, and all who hear it will live." (5:25), and, "Do not be surprised at this, for the hour is coming when the dead will leave their graves at the sound of his voice." (5:28). Even more clearly, the text insists on the classic Jewish convictions about the moral life: "Those who did good will come forth to life and those who did evil will come forth to judgment." (5:29).

In the sixth chapter of the Gospel of John, these themes culminate in the assertion that "It is my Father's will that whoever sees the Son and believes in him should have eternal life, and that I should raise that person up on the last day [6:40].... No one can come to me unless drawn by the Father who sent me and I will raise that person up on the last day." (6:44). The cause of this mysterious transformation is an intimate relationship mediated by eating the flesh and drinking the blood of the Lord: "Anyone who does eat my flesh and drink my blood has eternal life and I shall raise that person up on the last day [6:54].... Whoever eats my flesh and drinks my blood lives in me and I live in that person." (6:56).

Other passages, chronologically earlier than the Gospel of John, already teach that the Christian is assimilated into the person of Christ and thus shares his relationship with the Father: "The Spirit bears witness to our spirit that we are children of God." (Romans 8), and Colossians identifies sacramental baptism as the means for this assimilation: "Buried with him in baptism you have been raised up with him in virtue of your faith in the power of God who reawakened him from death." (Col. 2:8ff).

In the earliest decades of Christianity, questions quickly arose with regard to the death of the body, survival of the soul, and the relationship between the dead who die in Christ and the faithful who continue to live in this world.[12] What happens immediately after death to human souls, whether they are believers or not?[13] Is there a "sleep of the soul" (until we are reawakened) by the Second Coming of Jesus in glory?[14] Is there a way in which souls are "with the Lord" but free of their bodies?[15] What will the sanctified dead do in heaven[16] while awaiting reunion with their material bodies?[17] What will they do after they are so reunited and the world comes to an end?[18] In what body will humans rise at the end of time?[19] Are such bodies made of ordinary matter,[20] or are they made of a refined, spiritualized material? Do the material parts of the body necessarily have to be of the "same" matter that was present in the body when the person was alive? Or are the material elements interchangeable? What is the heavenly banquet and how can it be enjoyed without some kind of body?[21] What sort of body is adapted to the delights of the kingdom of heaven? Will there be bodily activities in heaven?

Also, the link between individual participation in eternal life and the final resolution of all justice and mercy in the return of Christ had to be worked out. Since the contents of the New Testament do not fully address these questions (some of which are, however, found in the New Testament itself), a long process of theological reflection began among the early Christians. For the sake of convenience, these points are taken up in the *Catechism of the Catholic Church* in the paragraphs cited; in interpreting the *Catechism*, the reader should keep in mind that each paragraph is a pithy summary of centuries of theological debate. The summary is a useful marker of doctrinal conviction, but the debate behind the conviction gives that very conviction its persuasive force.

One of the first phases of debate touching on our topic took place in the course of the second century, when a reaction set in against more radical tendencies toward Hellenization among Christians. The reaction took the form of a strictly literal interpretation of the resurrection, with renewed emphasis on the material body. The literal resurrection of the body is affirmed for Jesus in his resurrection already in the New Testament. The resurrection of believers unites themes of conversion and transformation in this life to the impact of the resurrection of Jesus on the life of the believer. Thus, some early Christians expressed their enthusiastic sharing in the resurrection of Jesus by asserting that "the resurrection has already occurred." (II Timothy 2:18, cf. 1002).

Others recognized the sacraments as a means by which Christians are empowered by the resurrection: "baptism is death and resurrection to new life." Paul himself, in I Corinthians 15:44-54, tried to explain how the resurrection occurs in terms of matter that is transformed, not repeated. Thus, we have the hope that "we will rise in a spiritual body" and other similar ideas. This was clarified by the assertion, given some of its classic formulation in the book of Revelation (20:12-15), that the human race would rise bodily from the dead at the end of the world; the unrepentant would be consigned to eternal punishment, while the repentant believers would be saved and would share the life of the heavenly kingdom forever. Christian preaching became quite insistent on the teaching that the resurrection was not going to be merely spiritual; rather, each person would rise in the same body in which they had lived and died.

In part, especially in the second century writings of St. Irenaeus and others, it seems that a de-emphasis on the "spiritual body" was a reaction against the so-called "Gnostic" movements whose views are articulated in works like the "Treatise on the Resurrection" in the Nag Hammadi Codices. This is a clear presentation of the theme that, with faith and spiritual knowledge, the "resurrection has already occurred." However, some sectarian teachers went even further. In some circles, the material world and the human body were understood in a profoundly negative light. The entire world system is not "good" at all, in spite of Genesis 1; rather, as part of the rebellion of primordial entities against the One True God, the material cosmos was created as a trap for souls. Embodied life and pleasures of the senses, regulated by a perverse set of false religious laws, keep humanity in moral bondage. Salvation requires an ascent out of this gigantic trap, including escape from the body and its demands. In reacting to this pessimistic assessment of the human condition, asserting the resurrection of the body became an indispensable rhetorical strategy.

In the third and fourth centuries, when scholars such as Origen of Alexandria, Didymus the Blind, Evagrius of Pontus, John Chrysostom, and others tried to elaborate upon the contents of I Corinthians 15, to affirm the resurrection of the transformed person as a soma pneumatikos (spiritual body), it was not long before other theologians such as Jerome, Epiphanius, and Theophilus of Alexandria, remembering the second-century debates, came down very hard on any modification of the strictly literal teaching on the resurrection of the same body. To these controversialists, the resurrection of the body was not only one of the revealed truths of the Bible, it was also an affirmation of the sacramental life of the Church, which communicated divine grace by means of material signs and rites.

Moreover, there is a moral component to their concern, because Jewish teachings on the resurrection insisted that resurrection in the positive sense was a resurrection of "the righteous" to the "life of the world to come." (cf. *Talmud*, Sanh. 10, 1). Thus, the mainstream of Christian theology maintained its tie to the Pharisaic school of thought, against the now virtually extinct Sadducees and the Samaritans, who insisted that Mosaic Law does not place much importance on whatever life there may be after death. For Sadducees and Samaritans, the only life worth living for a follower of the Torah is an embodied life in this world following the laws, observances, and ritual precepts.

Please note that some modern writers make the mistake of interpreting the Saducean viewpoint (cf. Mark 12:18-27 and Acts 23:6-9) as an out-and-out repudiation of the afterlife. However, it would be more accurate to understand their position as one focused on adherence to the strict requirements of ritual law in this world; in such a system of religious observance, one does not teach what lies outside the sphere of one's own competence. The Pharisaic position, on the other hand, recognized in some passages of the Hebrew scriptures, in particular the Psalms and the later writings including Wisdom and Maccabees (before these works were separated from the Jewish canon), that God's justice requires an afterlife, the "life of the world to come," in which deeds good and bad are fully rewarded and punished so that justice may finally be done by God's own intervention.

For Christians, this Pharisaic set of convictions was readily applied to the death of Jesus, whose resurrection was believed in as the vindication of his message and identity. The "cause" of Jesus is his proclamation of the reign of God, which unites an ethical life in this world with the hope of the eternal heavenly banquet. Disconnecting the eternal life of the saved and sanctified from one's own body seemed to distance the soul from the bodily matrix of all deeds, virtuous or not. As John Meier concludes in his third volume on the life of Jesus, with regard to Jesus' own teachings on the resurrection in Mark 12:18-27: "Jesus is not saying that humans will be transformed into angels, will become immaterial, or will cease to be sexual beings. Rather, at the resurrection, God's power will cause humans to undergo a radical transformation of their existence; they will receive refined bodies like the angels. Like the angels, these risen humans will be made immortal by God's power. Though sexual beings, they will not engage in sexual activity or marriage, since like the angels they will have no need to reproduce themselves in view of death."[22]

A careful examination of the biblical text makes clear that the imagery referring to the manner in which human beings will rise from the dead is extremely complex. It was not until the Scholastic theologies of the high Middle Ages that we have systematic treatises that take up most of the objections by attempting to devise a rational framework in which coherent answers can be given.[23] Theology in the Catholic tradition is, in the words of St. Augustine, "faith seeking understanding" (*fides quaerens intellectum*). In other words, having accepted the Christian revelation and having incorporated that revelation into our lives and views of reality, how can we respond to those who believe differently and make inquiries? How, too, may Christians teach what we believe in a coherent system that reconciles the basic worldview with liturgical and moral praxis? How should Christians respond to new challenges without losing the coherence of the central message of Jesus? Classic theological method takes into account the diversity present in the New Testament, but gives greater weight to the overall coherence of the message of the canon taken as a whole. In a sense, it is axiomatic to mainstream Christianity that the witness of these early documents taken together, as a whole, truly represents the apostolic faith. The canon is itself a statement of "catholic" faith (i.e., in Greek, *kath' holon*, meaning a consensus among those who believe).

In recent decades, so much effort has gone into sorting out the diversity of views present in the New Testament that it almost seems a radical novelty to assert the integrity of the canon as a whole. I think it would be fair to say that this "consensus" way of reading the early Christian writings is present in the writings of Clement of Rome (late first century) and Ignatius of Antioch (early second century). Even today, a Catholic Christian who is following the daily readings in the *Liturgy of the Hours* both from the Bible and from early Christian writings will be familiar with this "consensus" approach. At the same time, one will note in medieval conciliar decrees in the West, in the decrees of Trent and of the Second Vatican Council, and in the *Catechism of the Catholic Church*, a strong assertion of continuity in faith with Scripture and the early Christian writings.

At the same time, it is important to recognize that this theological conversation was accompanied by spiritual practices that were not restricted to the monasteries but often occupied a considerable part of the activities of lay Christians. No ancient branch of Christianity ever completely lost the connection between theology, liturgy, and spiritual practice. The Christian faithful have always been conscious of the spiritual meaning of death and have responded to the inevitability of death with moral and prayerful disciplines of various kinds.

In early Christianity, the meaning of a believer's death was intuited in light of the rituals of the sacraments of initiation: Baptism, Confirmation (or Chrismation), and Eucharist. Each of these sacraments enacted the inner meaning of the Death and Resurrection of Jesus Christ, also known as the "Paschal Mystery." Writers on the subject of Christian views of the afterlife often devote a great deal of attention to texts in the New Testament such as the First Letter to the Thessalonians in order to find out what early Christians believed. However, in the ritual texts that have come down to us, there is comparatively little assimilation of a text like First Thessalonians. The early Church read these letters as part of a larger picture of Church life and practice; the primary context for reflection on death was the death and resurrection of Jesus. In fact, the normative power of the Paschal Mystery extends into the sacraments, into preaching, into moral teaching, and above all into the stages of the spiritual life. Wherever suffering and loss are experienced as promoting spiritual transformation, there we find the application of the Paschal Mystery as the key to understanding what is actually going on.

In the experience of martyrdom, therefore, the early Church saw those who were executed for their faith as participating in the death of Jesus. By overcoming fear of death, the martyrs gave "witness" (the literal meaning of *martyr*) to their unconquerable faith in Jesus as Savior and Lord. Someone who was willing to die for his or her beliefs was a tremendous challenge to the cynical outlook of many inhabitants of the Roman and Parthian Empires, and in the course of time, their posture of courage began to wear down the resistance of these great international political cultures to the message of the Gospel. Thus, the Roman Empire eventually became a Christian culture; even earlier, Armenia became a Christian kingdom. In fact, a large part of the Roman Empire was probably majority Christian before the end of the persecutions. Significant Christian populations in Egypt, Palestine, Syria, and Asia Minor created a kind of Christian heartland in the Eastern Mediterranean.

In that heartland there arose a movement that brought together the ideals of the sacraments of initiation with the personal role modeling provided by Christian martyrs. This movement was called monasticism. The courage to die for Christ was combined with a willingness to live one's entire life in complete dedication to Christ and His teachings. The monk "died" every day spiritually, and every day lived the resurrection by dedicating himself or herself to a form of all-embracing prayer. Simple work, liturgical prayer, and formless contemplation transformed a person of faith into an enlightened saint, which was after all the goal of the sacraments of the Church for every Christian. The monk made this transformation into the project of a lifetime so that it would penetrate body, mind, and spirit completely. Thus, for such a person, death held no fear and few mysteries: The monastic life was a way of living in the presence of God at all times as if one were a member of Heaven's angelic realms.

The tombs of holy martyrs and ascetic monks became places of pilgrimage for Christian believers. A body that had been made holy by a dramatic death or by a lifetime of self-sacrifice retained the spiritual power of the sacraments that had been received during the lifetime of the one who had been "present" in that body. The Syriac Fathers taught that the sacred oil of Chrismation (i.e., chrism, the oil blessed solemnly by a bishop and used in baptism, confirmation, and the ordination of priests) penetrated even the bones of the Christian believer, and as a fruit of a life lived in holiness, those bones could work miracles even after the death of a saintly believer. Virtually all early Christians believed that the bone-relics of saints could produce miraculous effects. Moreover, the Eucharist was celebrated in the places where saints were buried. In some of the great basilicas built after Christianity became a legal religion the burial place of a saint is directly below the raised platform on which the altar for the Eucharist is erected, as if to dramatize the connection between the Eucharistic liturgy and the immediate presence of the holy person. At the Eucharist, the living community of believers is united with the deceased in the "communion of the saints."

This conviction is so strong that, for many centuries, Christians wanted to be buried in or near a church, particularly where martyrs were venerated. Archeology shows time after time that Christian burials along-side the walls of churches were the ideal, if not always the norm. This is called "burial *ad sanctos*"—burial near to holy persons and rites—and it signifies that the dead participate in the life of the whole Church, the living and the dead. This desire for the prayers of the faithful is already present in some early Christian epitaphs from the second century, such as that of the Bishop Abercius in Asia Minor, who asked for the prayers of passersby. It was understood that the bodies of the dead await in "hallowed ground" the return of Christ in glory at the end of time. The churchyard or the monastery or shrine crypt is a "safe" place in which a body awaits its resurrection because even the dead body in some way participates in the prayers of the community that worships there.

It was not until the Napoleonic period (early nineteenth century) that civil law, not Church law, forbade entombment in crypts for hygienic reasons. Even then, in continental Europe, the cemetery became a holy place outside the town walls, with its own funerary chapel, set apart by the mournful, fragrant cypresses planted there. The parish churchyard continued to be a feature of parish life, though, in those lands not touched by the Napoleonic obsession with hygiene and order.

Unfortunately, with the destruction of the majority of European monasteries in the Reformation and Enlightenment periods, this great tradition of liturgical spirituality was lost to the average Christian believer. For this reason, the very notion of a life lived in joyful preparation for eternal life seems as alien to modern Christian practice as the life of a hermit in the Himalayas. And even there, the violent imposition of modernity has had its moment of blood vengeance and destruction. It is a sad commentary on history that the past three or four centuries have witnessed a world war against monastic institutions, traditional societies, and the ancient wisdom of humanity in general.

In spite of the violence and polemics, some elements of continuity with the past persisted in some Christian environments. The contemplative life flourished in the course of much of the post-Napoleonic nineteenth century and contributed to liturgical renewal and a spiritual revival that has touched a large number of modern Christians. On the other hand, we live with an ongoing chastisement of the legacy of the past on the part of "Enlightenment" thinking and empirical science, elevated by modernity to the rank of a sort of cultural arbitrator. It is not easy to find an objective critical account of problematic aspects and distortions of pre-Enlightenment Christian practices. Secularist writers tend to condemn everything as a "dark age of dogmatism," or else, on the other side, there is a tendency to romanticize a sort of pre-Raphaelite mystical past of cowls, cloisters, and exquisite panel paintings.

Late medieval popular piety, under the impact of wars and plagues, became obsessed with death and dying. Whereas the thirteenth century was a time of a flourishing culture of faith, exemplified by the churchmanship of Innocent III, the sanctity of Francis and Dominic, the scholarship of Aquinas and Bonaventure, and the glory of the Gothic cathedrals, the fourteenth century was marked by the Black Death and the Hundred Years' War. The insecurity of the times contributed to the emergence of fanatical movements awaiting the millennium. Penitential fervor took the form of processions of the Flagellants. The veneration of relics seemed to have lost its early Christian sobriety and became an expression of superstition and even avarice. Fear of death gave rise to strange beliefs, such as the idea that by attending Mass, one held back the time of one's death. Popular preaching on death and the end of the world sought to bring people to conversion by making the fragility of human life and the rigors of divine judgment as dramatic as possible, without sufficient attention to the consequences of certain popular notions about divine wrath and chastisements.

The movement known as the *Devotio moderna* inspired a romanticization of Christian piety that seems to have become uprooted from the early Christian experience of the sacraments. As a result, the need for the Church, the priesthood, the Eucharist, and other sacraments was weakened across a broad swath of the pious public. The implications of that weakening were not fully appreciated until the Protestant Reformers of the sixteenth century began to attack Masses for the dead, chantry priests (priests ordained and paid exclusively to offer Masses for the dead), the doctrine of indulgences, and the doctrine of Purgatory. In a short time, deep-seated dissatisfaction with the Catholic teachings on spirituality and above all on life after death exploded in a multitude of reform efforts that permanently shattered the cultural and religious unity of Europe.

The Catholic Church responded to the challenge of the Protestant Reformation with its own version of reform. In fact, on the eve of the Reformation, the Fifth Lateran Council (1513 AD) had promulgated the formal definition of the dogma of immortality of the soul,[24] making it clear that there is no need for a belief in the "sleep of the soul" after death. By the middle of the sixteenth century, the Council of Trent gathered in several sessions to reaffirm the doctrines that had been challenged by Luther, Zwingli, Calvin, and other Reformers.

Yes, there is Purgatory for those who, having been forgiven their sins, still need to complete the purification process of the spirit that is needed because of the corrupting effect of sin on human consciousness. Yes, Masses for the dead are of help to souls undergoing postmortem purification. Yes, the Church has the power to extend indulgences that diminish the nature of the mysterious suffering that souls experience in Purgatory. Yes, there are saints who intercede for people before the Presence of God. Yes, the sacraments are the normal way of salvation intended by God and revealed in the Scriptures. Yes, Christians should live a sober and upright life, but no, Original Sin does not leave human beings utterly corrupt and depraved. Yes, salvation depends on grace alone, but grace is only efficacious if human beings respond to it and put it into practice. Implementation of the Council decrees took the form of the founding of new religious orders, the reform of older orders, the founding of the seminary system for training priests, the revitalization of religious instruction for the young, the founding of schools and institutions of charity, and greater rigor in diocesan administration.

Great saints of the period such as Catherine of Genoa elaborated the connection between an austere program of life and the purification of Purgatory. Prominent mystical saints, such as John of the Cross and Teresa of Avila, understood the need for the purgative way in this life and foresaw in moral illumination and the life of the virtues a dawning of holiness. In the unitive way, they experienced the transformation of body and soul leading to conformity to the image of God by grace. Thus, what Christ is by nature, we become by grace: children of God. Having established the norms of Catholic orthodoxy, the Church proceeded to focus on pastoral care in a worldwide network of parishes, with their cyclic celebration of the sacramental rites.

Before considering the funeral rites that are to be celebrated after death occurs, it is important to summarize what Catholic Christians believe about what happens spiritually once the soul has separated from the body.

In accordance with magisterial teachings, immediately after death the person experiences the "Particular Judgment"[25] and is consigned, on the basis of accepting or rejecting the divine grace that was offered to him or her in embodied life, to:

1. Hell for eternity, in recompense for negation of the gift of divine love; the punishment of hell is "eternal separation from God in whom alone man can have the life and happiness for which he was created and for which he longs."[26]
2. Purgatory for purification of the residues of sin remaining after sincere repentance; although assured of eternal salvation, they undergo a purification after death, so as to achieve the holiness necessary to enter the joy of God.[27]
3. Heaven and the beatific vision for all eternity, the original intention of God for all.[28]

The General Judgment will be preceded by "the resurrection of all the dead,"[29] the general resurrection.[30] (Acts 24:15; John 5:28-29; Matthew 25:31, 32, 46). At the judgment itself, in the presence of Christ "who is Truth itself, the truth of each man's relationship with God will be laid bare. The Last Judgment will reveal even to its furthest consequences the good each person has done or failed to do during his earthly life."[31] In this way, the very ancient biblical hope of final justice for both good and evil will be fulfilled. The Last Judgment is also the end of purgatory; the Kingdom of God will come in all its fullness.[32]

Proximate Preparation: *Lex orandi, lex credendi*

The Catholic Church has recently revised the rites of the dying, which include the sacraments of Anointing of the Sick, Reconciliation (Penance), Eucharist, and if necessary, Confirmation. From a catechetical point of view, these revised rites require prior preaching and instruction within the community of the parish, as in, for example, the homilies at Mass, in adult education programs, and in the practical ministry extended to the sick and dying. Of course, in the home or hospital setting, the sacraments are celebrated usually with great simplicity, with a small group of people present, taking into consideration the fact that the dying person may be able to participate with only limited attention. One also has to take health considerations into account. Nevertheless, it should be emphasized that every Catholic has the right to the final Holy Communion, known as *Viaticum*, as the sign of the culmination of a life lived in faithful preparation for eternal life.

Pastoral care, whether carried out by clergy or by lay volunteers, requires a considerable amount of psychological and spiritual sensitivity. In the course of an illness, whether long or short, there is a special moment that places a person very near to death.[33]

Known as the "death agony," once upon a time it was announced publicly, especially in the rural parishes of Europe, by a certain sequence of the ringing of church bells. The sacrament that signifies this unique situation, prelude to the irrevocable moment of death, is the Eucharist received as *Viaticum*—which is what the Eucharist received at this particular time is called. On the basis of earlier Latin usage of this term to signify provisions for a journey, the Early Church very quickly applied it to any and all spiritual support offered to the faithful as the time of their departure from this world drew near: Baptism, Confirmation, Extreme Unction, and above all the Eucharist, understood to be the nourishment *par excellence* for the great pilgrimage towards eternal life.

The first notice that history gives us for this perspective is a decree of the Council of Nicaea (325 AD), in which it is stipulated that "whoever is near death should not be deprived of the final and necessary *Viaticum*. If afterwards the person does not die, having been forgiven and admitted to Holy Communion, he/she will be given a place among those who only participate in the prayers [at Mass]. As a general rule, after an inquiry, the bishop is to give the Eucharist to anyone who is at the point of death and asks to receive." In the decree of Nicaea, one should note that *Viaticum* is considered a provision, a foodstuff for the great journey beyond death.

Above all, it is presented as a "final and necessary" rite that seals the continuity between sacramental communion in this life with participation in eternal life for a member of the community of the faithful. After Nicaea, this practice was the standard everywhere. The norm was in fact understood and put in practice quite literally: *Viaticum*—i.e., the consecrated Eucharistic wafer—was placed in the mouth of the dying person, even if this involved giving communion more than once in a day and even burying the sacrament with the deceased, an abuse condemned by numerous Church councils.

The Church was convinced after the period of the Roman persecutions that the dying Christian had the right under any circumstances to receive *Viaticum*. Pope Innocent I decreed in 405: "No one should leave this world without holy communion." Because the faithful have this right, the Church has the duty to carry out the rites by which communion is given to the dying. This motivation for pastoral practice appears clearly in the *Ordo Romanus* XLIX: "As soon as it is seen that a sick person is close to death, he is to be given communion from the Holy Sacrifice, even if he has eaten that day, because communion will be for him a defense and an aid in the resurrection of the just. It will, in fact, resurrect him."

Thus, sacramental practice made the clear connection between the Paschal Mystery in Christ and the Christian's participation in that Mystery. However, during times of plague and war, a certain tension arose between the administration of the Anointing of the Sick and the administration of *Viaticum*. In practice, the anointing, now called Extreme Unction (i.e., anointing at the point of death), became the highlight of the "last rites." It is interesting to note, however, that the Ritual Book of the Council of Trent continued to place *Viaticum* among the sacraments for the time of death. Instead of placing *Viaticum* in the chapter dealing with the

Eucharist, it is placed in the chapter that deals with the communion of the sick: "*Viaticum* of the most sacred Body of our Lord Jesus Christ is to be given to the sick in a timely manner, with extreme care and attention, so that it does not come about that, because of a lack of attention on the part of the parish priest, someone should die deprived of such a great good."[34] And further: "The parish priest will give communion in the form of *Viaticum* when there is a probability that [the sick person] will soon be unable to consume it. If afterwards the sick person, having received *Viaticum*, should live for several more days, or even escape the danger of death and wish to receive Holy Communion again, the parish priest should not fail to respond to this pious desire."[35]

In these old ritual books, the time of death is highlighted by a long series of prayers and readings, called the "Rite for the commendation of the soul."[36] These prayers continue up to the moment of the final breath, when the priest is to intone the famous responsory: "Come to his/her aid, O Saints of God ...,"[37] followed by the Apostolic Blessing composed for the moment of death.[38]

The ritual at the present time, shaped by the reforms of the Second Vatican Council, situates *Viaticum* among the sacraments of the sick, immediately following Anointing of the Sick. The Introduction to the rite of Commendation of the Dying clarifies the theological basis for this practice: "In *Viaticum* the dying person is united with Christ in his passage out of this world to the Father. Through the prayers for the commendation of the dying contained in this chapter, the Church helps to sustain this union until it is brought to fulfillment after death." (paragraph 212).

In the moment of death, when it seems that all is tragedy and defeat, in reality the true identity of the Christian, which had been acquired in the experience of Baptism, is being newly proclaimed. This Baptismal identity, this "resemblance" to Christ, reaches its fullness through sharing in the resurrection. Thus final Holy Communion expresses this tenet of faith and affirms it existentially by the presence of the Church, whose members do not abandon into solitude those who are about to conclude their earthly itinerary. The ministry of the care of the dying, now often entrusted to a layperson, expresses precisely the concern of the Church to nurture its members on the Body of the Lord right up to the threshold of their journey to eternity.

In the contemporary social situation, taking into consideration health care at the end of life, sensitivity is required in order to determine the right moment for final Holy Communion. That moment just before death needs to be a true sign of participation in the Paschal Mystery of Christ. Thus in the plan of a ritual, *Viaticum* needs to recover its place as truly the final sacrament, in close connection with the death that is soon to occur. Obviously, if the person is unconscious or unable to consume the consecrated wafer, the ritual gestures have to be restricted to anointing, prayers, and blessings. Anointing requires the presence of a priest.

However, final Holy Communion can be given by a lay minister. In any case, given our discussion of the need for a life led in preparation for eternal life, we would want to avoid the mentality in which the priest was considered the person "always ready" for these "emergencies," as if his intervention would determine the final salvation of the dying person, even influencing the decisions of God in judging the deceased. Even more absurd would be a kind of pastoral practice in which the dying person is "forced" to receive Holy Communion at a time in which this is impractical and distracting. In some cases, the consecrated wine is administered to a person too ill to receive the consecrated wafer; however, such practices seem to go beyond the requirements of authentic pastoral care. Any faithful Christian would be grateful for the prayerful presence of clergy, family, and friends at the time of death.

Still, an exaggerated emphasis on sacramental rites at such a time might not signify the grace that God wishes to confer. For example, in the ritual books currently in use, we can find the "Continuous Rite" for conferring the Sacrament of Reconciliation with the plenary indulgence for the time of death; in case of necessity even the Sacrament of Confirmation can be administered and after that the Anointing of the Sick and Eucharist in the form of *Viaticum*. Even the *Catechism of the Catholic Church* gives a theoretical support to this procedure when it asserts that "just as the Sacraments of Baptism, Confirmation, and Eucharist constitute a unity called the Sacraments of Christian Initiation, so also one can say that Reconciliation, Anointing of the Sick, and Eucharist as *Viaticum* constitute at the end of a Christian's life the Sacraments that prepare for our return to the Father's house or the Sacraments that conclude our earthly pilgrimage."[39]

However, any amount of pastoral experience in homes and hospitals would indicate that this rite should be used sparingly and judiciously. One might also ask if these sacraments, as a form of preparation for death, are being presented in adult education courses in the parishes. If not, it should be no surprise that misunderstandings arise.

In reality, a sacrament is not to be considered as a momentary act or series of ritual actions jammed together all at the same time. We need to keep in mind the vision of the document on the liturgy, *Sacrosanctum Concilium*: a sacrament, "in particular the Eucharist ... (no. 10), recapitulates one's past life and commits a human being to the future." The faithful person who receives a sacrament should be conscious of the fact that the Christ encountered in the sacrament is no different from the Christ who has been alongside him/her all through life. Thus, the response of faith that a Christian makes to Christ in the act of celebrating the sacrament should be the same response of faith that he/she seeks to make in his/her daily life. Moreover, the *lex orandi* of the liturgy is the overarching *Viaticum* of the Church, since it is always celebrated in connection with the wellspring of Paschal grace conferred by Christ himself, not only at the end of life, but in the continuity of time throughout a life.

The document of Vatican II, *Gaudium et Spes*, considers all of human activity in the light of the Paschal mystery, which purifies it and heals it in reference to the *eschaton*, that is *the end toward which it is directed*: "Constituted Lord by His resurrection, He, the Christ, continues to work in the hearts of people by the power of His Spirit, not only awakening a desire for the world to come, but in itself also inspiring, purifying and fortifying the generous proposals with which the human family seeks to make its own life more human, applying this to the whole world. In all things a process of liberation is working to the extent that egoism is renounced and all terrestrial forces are taken up into human life, so that all is projected into the future, when humanity itself will become an acceptable offering to God."[40]

This is the reality, rooted in our human existence, which is proclaimed to everyone who receives the Eucharist, reminding us of our final hope: "He will preserve you for eternal life."[41]

CONSIDERATIONS ON FUNERAL RITES

The three parts of the funeral rites are at the home, in church, and at the cemetery.[42] In my own pastoral experience in rural Southern Italy during the 1990s, I found that it was still possible to live these three parts of the liturgy of the dead—involving home, church, and cemetery—in full. It was still customary to die at home, although it is more and more common for deaths to occur in the hospital. The rites of commendation, rosary, the vigil for the deceased, and so on can be done in either setting; in the hospital a morgue with chapel facilities is available. By law, burial must take place within 24 hours of death; even so, since the family has usually gathered—in the case of a lingering illness—it is possible to celebrate all the liturgical moments with pastoral effectiveness. The body of the deceased can be carried to the parish church by pallbearers, or in a hearse; distances are not too great as to preclude a formal procession, with chanting, hymns, and psalmody.[43]

Ancient customs such as throwing rice and almonds on the path of a child or unmarried adult are preserved; death is a nuptial day for the pure. The regular funeral rites are performed in the parish church with the body present along with a substantial presence of family, friends, and fellow citizens in solidarity. Immediately after the incensation and blessing of the body with holy water, the procession to the cemetery takes place. The cemetery is outside of town; the faithful and the clergy accompany the body in a slow-moving hearse to the place of burial.

Final rites are performed in the cemetery chapel, and the grave or niche is blessed in accordance with the ritual book. In the American setting, the body is usually embalmed and two or three days of the "wake" or funeral vigil are observed in a "funeral home." It is recommended that the body be brought with solemnity to the church, but it is often impractical to hold a procession from the funeral home to the church. The Eucharistic liturgy is celebrated; in America white vestments are prevalent as a sign of the resurrection; in Europe, purple or even black vestments are still used. After the final blessings, the body may be taken to the cemetery for graveside rites or to the crematory. At a later date, the cremated remains may be interred in the ground or in a niche of a columbarium, with a simple rite of blessing.[44]

In my pastoral experience in the United States, I have been disappointed to note how the funeral rites in Catholic and Protestant local communities are being disrupted. Under the influence of television and cinema images that, for the sake of humor or drama, exploit the great moments of transition in life for entertainment purposes, both clergy and laity have become susceptible to a distasteful shift in attitude toward the death rituals of human beings. There is already a societal conspiracy of silence about death. This extends itself into the pastoral care of the dying. Some families are reluctant to welcome clergy into their homes to celebrate the rites appropriate to illness and dying, such as the rite of final reception of Holy Communion (*Viaticum*) or the anointing of the sick. With the loss of a close pastoral relationship with the dying, it is a logical next step to see the rites of death itself undergoing corruption.

In some places, it has become fashionable to allow the funeral rites to be infiltrated with triviality, secular posturing, worldliness, inappropriate gestures, decadent ceremonies, and manifestations of theological doubt. This crucial rite of passage, which is meant to affirm the close relationship between the spiritual life of a Christian believer with the life, death, and resurrection of Jesus Christ, is now in many instances irreparably marred. Funerals ought to be a time in which bonds of fellowship and faith are enhanced; instead, they have come to reflect the degraded esteem that this culture holds for every human being, living or dead. No one is holy; no one is a source of luminous inspiration; no one is a valid role model—except perhaps those celebrities whose careers of transgression are chronicled in the tabloids. The decline in quality that we observe in too many parishes is a reflection of the rampant selfishness of our materialistic culture. As a culture we have truly failed to find in the fact of death a motivation for seeking new ways to live and to love in solidarity and in faith.

On the basis of pastoral experience, I also recommend the abolition of eulogies. It is significant that the *Catechism* objects to eulogies.[45] The obvious reason is that they sometimes become an occasion to glorify the deceased in inappropriate ways. Often they take the form of recalling disedifying episodes in the person's life. There are lame attempts at humor that would be more appropriate in a private setting than in the context of the liturgy. If trivialization is a sufficient reason to abolish the eulogy, there is also the grave consideration of outright abuse. I am referring to the astonishingly common exploitation of the lay eulogy (sometimes given after Holy Communion at the funeral Mass) by a family member who seizes upon the opportunity to "harangue" the crowd with the intention of gaining converts to alien religious groups. Some of the most egregious examples of this include telling people that the deceased, who "failed" to join the sect being touted, is now residing in hell, and "so will the rest of you unless you convert!" I have actually presided over such episodes in three Catholic churches on the West Coast: in each instance, the Catholic Church was the target of the eulogist, whose assigned task, completely ignored of course, was to share a short appreciation of the deceased.

I understand that such egregious breaches of common decency are part of a consistent strategy across a spectrum of sectarian movements. Usually it is the Catholic faith or an Asian traditional religion that is the target of eulogy abuse. Clergy and families should be aware of this phenomenon. There is nothing like something offensive to make us rethink some of our sloppy habits, in particular our unwillingness to preach solid Christian doctrine at funerals and other times of crisis and transition. I would also suggest that Christian churches and ecclesial communities work out rules for funeral etiquette among themselves, and with leaders of other religions, to guarantee better relations in our communities of faith.

It is not difficult to prepare funeral homilies with appropriate content.[46] The Rite of Christian Funerals gives a large selection of biblical texts that allude to various aspects of the human experience of death and dying. The meaning of suffering and death, life as a preparation for entry into eternal life, the promise of heaven as life with God, the Eucharist as the nutriment of immortality, and the meaning of grace and redemption are all themes corresponding to the readings assigned for funerals.

Funerals, in my experience, are one of the most effective settings for preaching the Gospel of Jesus Christ. Often there are people present who have no idea what the Church believes about life, death, grace, holiness, and redemption. It is a pastoral opportunity not to be missed. The homily should be not more than fifteen minutes, sensitively tuned to the circumstances of the deceased and the family, and not overly emotional. A serene, doctrinally sound exposition based on Scripture and the faith of the Church can be of enormous comfort to the grieving family and friends. At such a time, people need to feel grounded in recognizable traditions of faith.

With regard to the celebration of the Eucharist at funerals, the *Catechism* offers very sound pastoral guidance: "In the Eucharist, the Church expresses her efficacious communion with the departed: offering to the

Father in the Holy Spirit the sacrifice of the death and resurrection of Christ, she asks to purify his child of his sins and their consequences, and to admit him to the Paschal fullness of the table of the Kingdom. It is by the Eucharist thus celebrated that the community of the faithful, especially the family of the deceased, learn to live in communion with the one who 'has fallen asleep in the Lord,' by communicating in the Body of Christ of which he is a living member and, then, by praying for him and with him."[47]

Belief in the need for prayers for the dead goes back to the *Second Book of Maccabees* 12:38-46; the epitaph of Bishop Abercius of Phrygia, from the second half of the second century, also asks passersby for prayers. The Eucharist is the "source and summit" of Christian life and prayer and should be offered not only at the funeral, but at memorial services in subsequent years and months. Such celebrations contribute to a healthy and spiritually meaningful grieving process for family and friends of the deceased and should not be neglected.

In recent decades, the expense of embalming and burial has increased to the point that many families are practically obliged to adopt the more economical practice of cremation. Cremation has always been a problematic sign for Christians because it seems to deny the reality of the resurrection of the body. Since 1963, permission has been granted for Catholics to make use of cremation, even if various norms are specified for avoidance of doctrinal misunderstandings.

CONCLUSION

In this essay, I have adopted as normative the practices of the Catholic Church, since that is the Christian tradition with which I am most familiar. The majority of Christians are Latin Rite Catholics throughout the world. Some Orthodox Christian writers have recently made the claim that their distinct approach to life after death is more authentically apostolic than the Catholic approach (see Select Bibliography); in particular, they object to Catholic teachings on Purgatory. A less contentious understanding of these teachings should be worked out in ecumenical theological exchanges.[48] At the present time, after more than forty years of ecumenical dialogue, it is possible to say that the various branches of Christianity have stimulated one another to reexamine their beliefs and, in some cases, to make revisions in mode of presentation and even in content.

For example, the Catholic International Theological Commission has just published a document, "The Hope of Salvation for Infants Who Die without Being Baptized,"[49] which examines the teachings on the postmortem state known as "limbo," finding this theological theory inadequate to the full content of the Church's doctrine of salvation. Significantly, the document recognizes many indications that the faith of Catholics, moved by the action of the Holy Spirit, has developed significantly with regard to the salvation of persons who die without baptism. "It must be clearly acknowledged that the church does not have sure knowledge about the salvation of unbaptized infants who die.... [T]he destiny of the generality of infants who die without baptism has not been revealed to us, and the church teaches and judges only with regard to what has been revealed. What we do positively know of God, Christ and the church gives us grounds to hope for their salvation...."[50]

It should be recognized that the writings of German Protestant authors W. Pannenberg, D. Bonhoeffer, and K. Barth continue to resonate in Christian discussions of the afterlife. All three of these theologians judge the doctrine of the "immortality of the soul" extraneous to the Christian confession of faith in the resurrection. In the 1990s, the German Catholic bishops also responded with great caution, mindful of the debate on immortality raised by these Protestant theologians, to remind Catholics that the immortality of the soul depends entirely on the sustaining will of God, a teaching already found in the writings of St. Augustine.

However, on the level of popular belief, there is much more resistance to the notion of the resurrection of the body than to the immortality of the soul. This is in part the result of a general impression that the resurrection of the body is an irrational dogma because assembling the decomposed bodies with the identical material elements would be, from a biochemical point of view, literally impossible. At the same time, a high percentage of Christians of all denominations (possibly as high as 25 percent) believe in some form of reincarnation. This can be attributed in part to the wide dissemination of literature from Buddhism, Hinduism, Theosophy, and Western occult traditions.

As a form of popular spirituality, these worldviews seem at first to reflect a distinct drift from standard biblical reflection. At the very least, such beliefs call for a more coherent response on the part of theologians, particularly since they give evidence of the persistence of literal belief in an afterlife in societies that, in other aspects, seem completely secular and materialistic. I have suggested elsewhere that a psychological approach might be helpful in bringing together popular belief in the survival of death with other intimations of "immortality" in human behavior. The latter might include the way we "construct" literary or "career" immortality; the apotheosis of various celebrities; widespread claims of contact with the dead; trends in funerary monuments and ceremonies; occult interest in out-of-the-body travel; and scientific research on near-death experience. These topics rarely attract the attention of theologians, with the unfortunate consequence that a large segment of the generally religious or "spiritual" public ignores the work of theologians.

Taking another approach to the question of popular trends related to belief in the afterlife, we should note that non-mainstream conservative

Catholics, Orthodox, and Protestants have been writing or reprinting works asserting more "traditional" beliefs to the attention of contemporary readers. In the Catholic traditionalist milieu, for example, teachings on Purgatory have been revived. Reading this literature, even with a degree of prudent skepticism, it is nonetheless impossible to deny that these are testimonies of persons of integrity. The literary forms in which they express themselves may be marred by a rhetoric of persuasion showing clear signs of political or social context.

However, so many accounts by holy lay people, clergy, monks, and mystics cannot be ignored. After all, even in the setting of mainstream Catholic mysticism, reporting such experiences of contact with the dead would not have been considered advisable or normative. There would have to be a more compelling reason to reveal such experiences than social or political ideology in a climate hostile to mystical self-aggrandizement. In a secularized cultural milieu, even admitting to belief in such phenomena is likely to provoke disparagement, so reporting personal contact with the dead outside a circle of close friends is tantamount to an admission of mental unbalance.

Without going into a long excursus on the limits of empirical observation, I would like to report on several episodes that I experienced, or which I researched in the field. The first is simply a short-lived visionary experience that occurred during the recitation of the Our Father at Mass one morning in the 1990s; I had a clear spiritual vision of the ascent into a sphere of light of a priest who had been my spiritual director and who had died in 1975. The experience seemed to be a kind of message: that this holy priest was liberated from Purgatory and would now be living the joyful life of heaven. His face was radiant with benevolence, and there was no difficulty in recognizing him.

Another episode involved a layman who died of cancer in the mid-1990s in Italy. In order to help him cope with his physical pain, I had taught him some relaxation techniques based on guided meditation and had made him a recording that he used on a daily basis for several months before dying. The night of his death, in a completely darkened bedroom, I saw a dim sphere of light about fifteen to eighteen inches in diameter. The sphere was able to communicate that this was the person who had died (I had been waiting for a call that he had died, but had not had confirmation of his actual death) and that he had not actually believed in life after death, but had "tolerated" the prayers and instructions of his wife and myself; now he wanted to thank me for my efforts because, thanks to the guided meditation, he had quickly adjusted to his postmortem condition. Later, his wife and other people recounted episodes of contact with this man. Both of these episodes suggest that spiritual preparation for death is not a waste of time, since conscious survival and some kind of purification process does occur after death.

One aspect of the fear of death that these two experiences may resolve at least for some readers is that concern that medical progress will occur such that one's death from a particular disease can be prevented. Thus people are afraid to die a "wasted" death. In reality, life after death is a landscape all its own and there is nothing lost in opening ourselves to the exploration of the "life of the world to come." St. Gregory of Nyssa's notion of an ongoing growth in love seems to require exploration, deepening, and growth in dimensions of existence that an earthly life cannot accommodate. My personal view is that this embodied life is itself a preparation for that vaster mode of living; living well and wisely here, we will be ready for what awaits us. Living badly here will, naturally, have the opposite result.

NOTES

1. *Catechism of the Catholic Church.* 2nd. ed. Washington, DC: Libreria Editrice Vaticana–United States Conference of Catholic Bishops, 2000, paragraph 1013. Hereafter referred to as CCC along with paragraph number.

2. *The Roman Ritual: Order of Christian Funerals Approved for Use in the Dioceses of the United States of America by the National Conference of Catholic Bishops and Confirmed by the Apostolic See.* Appendix 2: Cremation: Reflections on the Body, Cremation, and Catholic Funeral Rites (Totowa, NJ: Catholic Book Publishing Co., 1997), 13.

3. See CCC 1013.

4. See CCC 1014.

5. Particularly helpful is "Holy Living, Holy Dying," from the 1986–88 Roman Catholic–United Methodist Dialogue. See Joseph A. Burgess and Jeffrey Gros, F.S.C., eds., *Ecumenical Documents V: Growing Consensus: Church Dialogues in the United States, 1962–1991* (Mahwah, NJ: Paulist Press, 1995), 529–42. This work contains much practical guidance in pastoral care.

6. See S. Alfonso M. De' Liguori, *Apparecchio alla Morte* (Verona, Italy: Libreria Salesiana Editrice, 1912), 51.

7. Ibid., 49.

8. Ibid., 78–80.

9. Even St. Martin of Tours saw the devil before him at the time of death; granted, he easily rejected the feeling of fear. St. Alfonso's own dear companion in the Redemptorists, his procurator general Fr. Francesco Maria Margotta, went through terrible trials before receiving consolation at the time of his death on the Nativity of the Blessed Virgin; see Sant' Alfonso Maria de' Liguori, *Opere Ascetiche, Pratica di Amar Gesu Cristo,* vol. I (Redentoristi Roma, 1933), 66–67.

10. See CCC 994; 995; 989; 999.

11. Karl Rahner, *Theological Investigations,* vol. IV. Translated by Kevin Smyth. (Baltimore, MD: Helicon Press, 1966), 352.

12. See CCC, paragraphs 997; 366; 382; 1055; and 2635, respectively.

13. CCC 1021–22.

14. CCC 366; 991; 1001.

15. CCC 1023–28.

16. CCC 954–59; 962.

17. CCC 2796.

18. CCC 1029; 1042–43; 1045; 1046; 1049.

19. CCC 998–1001.

20. CCC 999.

21. CCC 1027; 1642; 1036; 1344; 1244; 1335. John P. Meier, *A Marginal Jew: Rethinking the Historical Jesus,* vol. 3. In: *Companions and Competitors* (New York: Doubleday, 2001).

22. Meier, 424; cf. 423–24.

23. See especially the *Summa Theologica* of St. Thomas Aquinas, part III, Supplement: "Treatise on the Resurrection" and "Treatise on the Last Things."

24. CCC 366.

25. CCC 1012; 1021–22.

26. CCC 1022; 1861; 1033–37; 1057.

27. CCC 1028; 1030–32; 1054.

28. CCC 1023–27; 1058.

29. CCC 1001; 1038–41; 1059.

30. CCC 988; 990; 992; 998.

31. CCC 1039.

32. CCC 1060.

33. This section is in part a paraphrase translation of an essay by Gianni Cavagnoli, "Il Viatico e il Rito Continuo della Penitenza e dell'Unzione degli Infermi," pp. 163–67 in *Guida Liturgico Pastorale 2006–2007 Regione Ecclesiastica Abruzzese-Molisano* (Pesaro: Editore Arti Grafiche Stibu Urbania, 2006).

34. See the Ritual Book of the Council of Trent (Tit. IV, cap. 4, n. 1).

35. Ibid. (Tit. IV, cap. 4, n. 3).

36. Ibid. (Tit. V, cap. 7).

37. Ibid. (Tit. V, cap. 8).

38. Ibid. (Tit. V, cap. 6).

39. CCC 1525.

40. See the document of Vatican II, *Gaudium et Spes,* section 38.

41. See also CCC 2299; 1682; 1683.

42. CCC 1686.

43. See CCC 1690, symbolism of processions, cf. pilgrimage; journey.

44. CCC 2300; 1684.

45. CCC 1688.

46. CCC 1684; 1687.

47. CCC 1000; 1689.

48. An example that could be cited is the agreement on "Eschatology" between the Old Catholic Church and the Eastern Orthodox, Kavala, Greece, 17 October 1987, published in Jeffrey Gros, F.S.C., Harding Meyer, and William G. Rusch, eds., *Growth in Agreement II: Reports and Agreed Statements of Ecumenical Conversations on a World Level, 1982-1998* (Grand Rapids, MI: WCC Publications, 2000), with William B. Eerdmans, 264–66. See also the common document between Lutherans and Roman Catholics, "Church and Justification," from September 11, 1993, especially Section 5.2 on The Eschatological Consummation of the Church, in William G. Rusch and Jeffrey Gros, eds., *Deepening Communion: International Ecumenical Documents with Roman Catholic Participation* (Washington, DC: USCCB Publications, 1998). And "Holy Living, Holy Dying" *op. cit.*

49. International Theological Commission, "The Hope of Salvation," *Origins* 36 (45, April 26) (2007): 725–46.

50. See the Catholic International Theological Commission document, "The Hope of Salvation for Infants Who Die without Being Baptized." Ibid., Section 79.

SELECTED BIBLIOGRAPHY

St. Thomas Aquinas. *The Summa Theologica*. Translated by Fathers of the English Dominican Province, Revised by Daniel J. Sullivan. In *Great Books of the Western World*, vol. II, Supplement to the Third Part (QQ. 69–99), Treatise on the Resurrection and Treatise on the Last Things, edited by Robert Maynard Hutchinson. Chicago, IL: Encyclopedia Britannica, 1952.

Beulay, Robert, O.D.D. *La Lumière Sans Forme: introduction a l'etude de la mystique chretienne syro-orientale*. Chevetogne, Belgium: Editions de Chevetogne, 1987.

Episcopal Church. *The Book of Common Prayer*. New York: The Church Hymnal Corporation and The Seabury Press, 1979.

Brown, Peter. *The Body and Society: Men, Women and Sexual Renunciation in Early Christianity*. London: Faber and Faber, 1989.

Bynum, Caroline Walker. *The Resurrection of the Body in Western Christianity, 200-1336*. New York: Columbia University Press, 1995.

Catechism of the Catholic Church. 2nd ed. Washington, DC: United States Catholic Conference–Libreria Editrice Vaticana, 1997.

Châtellier, Louis. *The Religion of the Poor: Rural Missions in Europe and the Formation of Modern Catholicism, c. 1500–1800*. New York: Cambridge University Press, 1997.

Clark, Elizabeth A. *The Origenist Controversy: The Cultural Construction of an Early Christian Debate*. Princeton: Princeton University Press, 1992.

De' Liguori, S. Alfonso M. *Apparecchio alla Morte*. Verona, Italy: Libreria Editrice Salesiana, 1912.

Sant' Alfonso Maria de' Liguori. *Opere Ascetiche, Pratica di Amar Gesu Cristo*, vol. I. Redentoristi Roma, 1933.

Delumeau, Jean. *Sin and Fear: The Emergence of a Western Guilt Culture 13th–18th Centuries*. New York: St. Martin's Press, 1990.

Durrwell, F. X., C.S.S.R. *The Resurrection: A Biblical Study*. Translated by Rosemary Sheed. New York: Sheed and Ward, 1960.

Goehring, James E. *Ascetics, Society, and the Desert: Studies in Early Egyptian Monasticism*. Harrisburg, PA: Trinity Press International, 1999.

St. Gregory of Nyssa. *From Glory to Glory: Texts from Gregory of Nyssa's Mystical Writings*. Selected, with an introduction by Jean Danielou, S.J. Translated and edited by Herbert Musurillo, S.J. Crestwood, NY: St. Vladimir's Seminary Press, 1995.

———. *The Soul and the Resurrection*. Translated by Catharine P. Roth. Crestwood, NY: St. Vladimir's Seminary Press, 1993.

Guida Liturgico Pastorale, 2006–2007 Regione Ecclesiastica Abruzzese-Molisano. Pesaro: Editore Arti Grafiche Stibu Urbania, 2006.

Metropolitan of Nafpaktos Hierotheos. *Life After Death*. Translated by Esther Williams. Levadia, Greece: Birth of the Theotokos Monastery, 1996.

Huizinga, Johan. *The Waning of the Middle Ages: A Study of Forms of Life, Thought, and Art in France and the Netherlands in the Dawn of the Renaissance*. Translated by Fritz Hopman. London: Edward Arnold & Co., 1924.

Hurtado, Larry W. *Lord Jesus Christ: Devotion to Jesus in Earliest Christianity*. Grand Rapids, MI: William B. Eerdmans Publishing, 2003.

International Theological Commission. "The Hope of Salvation." *Origins* 36 (45, April 26) (2007): 725–46.

Meier, John P. *A Marginal Jew: Rethinking the Historical Jesus*, vol. 3. In: *Companions and Competitors*. New York: Doubleday, 2001.

The Order of Christian Funerals: Appendix: Cremation. International Commission on English in the Liturgy and Bishops' Committee on the Liturgy. Chicago: Liturgy Training Publications, 1997.

The Order of Christian Funerals. International Commission on English in the Liturgy and Bishops' Committee on the Liturgy. Chicago: Liturgy Training Publications, 1989.

Ott, Ludwig. *Fundamentals of Catholic Dogma*. Edited in English by James Canon Bastible. Translated by Patrick Lynch. St. Louis, MO: B. Herder Book Company, 1960.

Archimandrite Panteleimon. *Eternal Mysteries Beyond the Grave: Orthodox Teachings on the Existence of God, The Immortality of the Soul, and Life Beyond the Grave*. Jordanville, NY: Holy Trinity Monastery, 1996.

Pastoral Care of the Sick: Rites of Anointing and Viaticum. International Commission on English in the Liturgy. Collegeville, MN: The Liturgical Press, 1983.

Padre Pio of Pietrelcina, O.F.M.Cap. *Letters: Volume II Correspondence with Raffaelina Cerase, Nobelwoman (1914–1915)*. Edited by Melchiorre of Pobladura and Alessandro of Ripabottoni. English Version edited by Gerardo Di Flumeri, O.F.M.Cap. San Giovanni Rotondo, Italy: Editions Padre Pio of Pietrelcina, 1997.

Rahner, Karl, S.J. *Theological Investigations*, vol. IV. Translated by Kevin Smyth. Baltimore, MD: Helicon Press, 1966.

The Rite of Christian Initiation of Adults. International Commission on English in the Liturgy and Bishops' Committee on the Liturgy. Chicago: Liturgy Training Publications, 1988.

Robinson, James M., General Editor. *The Nag Hammadi Library*. 3rd ed. San Francisco: Harper, 1990.

Schouppe, F. X., S.J. *Purgatory: Explained by the Lives and Legends of the Saints*. Reprint edition. Rockford, IL: Tan Books and Publishers, 1986.

The Syriac Fathers on Prayer and the Spiritual Life. Introduced and Translated by Sebastian Brock. Kalamazoo, MI: Cistercian Publications, 1987.

Tugwell, Simon, O.P. *Human Immortality and the Redemption of Death*. Springfield, IL: Templegate Publishers, 1990.

3

Death and Dying in Islam

Hussam S. Timani

> Everyone shall taste death. Wheresoever you may be, death will
> overtake you even if you are in fortresses built up strong and high!
> —Qur'an 3:185; 4:78

AN INTRODUCTION TO ISLAM

Islam refers to that state of perfect harmony between God and His creation. It also means submission to one God. Thus, anyone who submits to
the One and only God is called a Muslim. And because of this submission, Muslims are in a state of perfect harmony with their God. This state
of harmony was established immediately after God created the souls of
human beings and made them testify that there is no god but God. "And
when your Lord brought forth from the Children of Adam, from their
loins, their seed (or from Adam's loin his offspring) and made them testify as to themselves (saying): 'Am I not your Lord?' They said: 'Yes! We
testify'" (Qur'an 7:172). Therefore, with the state of harmony established
between God and human beings, the Christian concept of original sin is
quite problematic for Muslims, and this impacts their view of death and
dying.

The God of Islam is unique, beyond comprehension, genderless, all-
powerful, and merciful. He is merciful because He never ceased to sustain
His creation. His mercy is reflected in the guidance he has sent to human

beings throughout history via prophets from Adam and Abraham to Moses, Jesus, and finally Muhammad (d. 632 CE). Muslims believe that Muhammad was the last and final prophet to receive guidance from God. This last message, which was revealed first to the Arabs and later to all human beings, came in the form of a revelation received by Muhammad via the angel Gabriel. Muhammad received the message of the Qur'an (Arabic for "recitation")—composed of 114 Suras (chapters) and over 6,000 Ayas (verses)—over a period of twenty-two years from 610 to 632 CE. This Qur'an came as a form of mercy, and as a gift, from God to the Arabs.

The Qur'an's main message is the oneness of God. Thus, the Qur'an was revealed to the Arabs to lead them back to the straight path and to reestablish the state of harmony between them and God. This harmony can be maintained by performing the Five Pillars: (1) *Shahadah*: to testify that there is no god but God and Muhammad is His servant and messenger; (2) *Salat*: to pray five times a day; (3) *Zakat*: to pay alms to the poor; (4) *Sawm*: to fast for the entire month of Ramadan from dawn to dusk; and (5) *Hajj*: to go on pilgrimage to Mecca once in a lifetime, if affordable.

Also, the Qur'an gave the world a new set of beliefs that are central to Islam, such as unique perspectives on Judgment Day, the resurrection of the dead, and life after death. "They swear by God to the very limit of their oaths that God will not raise him who dies.... They say, Are we to be returned to our former state when we have become decayed bones? They say, that would be a detrimental return" (16:38; 79:10–12). These passages reflect the disbelief in the Qur'an and its message that, on Judgment Day, every human being will be resurrected and will be destined for eternal life.

Regarding the theme of the book you now hold in your hands, death and dying are important concepts in the Islamic tradition. Today, there is a vast literature (mostly in Arabic) on these topics written by early Muslim scholars and theologians who based their works on the Qur'an and *Hadith* (the "sayings" of the Prophet Muhammad). There are 165 Qur'anic verses and thousands of prophetic *hadiths* pertaining to dying and death in Islam. This chapter explores Islamic rituals and beliefs on these subjects based on primary sources and the interpretations of early and modern Muslim scholars.

DEATH IN ISLAM

How should a Muslim prepare for death, and how does death take place? What is the role of the Angel of Death, and what happens to human beings in the grave? According to Islamic tradition, these events can be both frightening and comforting, depending on how one understands them or approaches them. The Qur'an tells us that the soul of a dying man comes up to his throat while he gazes on (56:83–84). It is also revealed in the Qur'an that dying people see the angels of death stretching out their hands, saying, "Give up your souls" (6:93).

Although the Qur'an attests to the punishments and rewards of human beings on Judgment Day, little is mentioned about the punishments and rewards that take place before resurrection. For instance, the Qur'an states that martyrs (those who die in the cause of God) are not dead, but they are alive with God (22:58-59; 3:170–71), which means that they do not experience the horrors of the grave. Instead, they shoot straight to Paradise. The Qur'an also speaks of angels tormenting the soul while it sits in the grave (8:50; 46:27). These are the only Qur'anic accounts of what happens immediately after death before the coming of "the Hour."

According to the Islamic tradition, God created death after He created Adam and his offspring (i.e., the souls of human beings). The creation of death is narrated by Jalal al-Din al-Suyuti in his *Hal al-Mawta wa al Qubur* ("The State of the Dead and the Grave"; fifteenth century):

When God created Adam and his offspring, the angels said: "The earth is not big enough to contain them." God replied: "I will give them death." The angels then said: "Knowing that they will die, they will not enjoy life." God replied: "I will give them hope." When Adam descended to earth, God said to him: "Build for there will be destruction, and multiply for that you will perish."[1]

The Prophet once said:

God communicated to Adam the following: "O Adam! Go on your pilgrimage before something happens to you." Adam replied: "What is going to happen to me, O God?" Then God answered: "Something that you are not aware of, that is death." "What is death?" Adam replied. God said: "You will taste it."[2]

Hence, the following Qur'anic verse:

Everyone shall taste death. And only on the Day of Resurrection shall you be paid your wages in full. And whoever is removed away from the Fire and admitted to Paradise, he indeed is successful. The life of this world is only the enjoyment of deception. (3:185)

This verse indicates that there is life after death and that death should not be feared. But, this next life is either in hell or in paradise, and that depends on how humans conduct their affairs in this world. Therefore, Muslims try their best to please God by following His guidance and the examples of His prophet, Muhammad. Following the right path is the only way to salvation. Unlike the Christians, Muslims do not believe in a God-sent divine being to save humanity and to wash away the original sin. In Islam salvation depends totally on the individual, and no person is responsible for the deeds of another. For this reason, Muslims take the teachings of their religion very seriously as the only way to ensure entry into Paradise.

Although life after death in the Islamic tradition is a life of eternity and comfort, Islam teaches that believers should not long for death or look forward to dying. Al-Suyuti narrates the following *hadith*: "O Muslims, do not long for death and do not look forward to it. Even if you were destined to Paradise, having a long life is much better for you. And for those who are destined to the fire of hell, why the rush."[3] Al-Suyuti narrates another *hadith*: "Long for death only when it is about to take you, or when you are sure about your good deeds."[4] Moreover, the Islamic tradition sees a benefit in a longer life. And those with short lives may be at a disadvantage.

People who live longer will have the opportunity to correct wrongdoings. It is reported that the Prophet said: "The longer the Muslim lives, the more rewarding life will be. There is nothing better to God than a long lived Muslim who spent all his life praising Him."[5] Thus, for this reason alone, killing an innocent life (including the self) is strongly condemned in the Qur'an: "Do not kill anyone whose killing God has forbidden" (17:33). "Surely, the killing of them is a great sin" (17:31). These verses show the extent of God's loath to cutting a life short. The Prophet also commented on the killing of the self in the following *hadith*: "Whoever killed himself, he is surely destined to the eternal fire of hell. And with whatever object a person used to kill himself, that same object will be used for his torment in hell."[6]

Al-Suyuti also discusses the various definitions of death according to a number of Muslim scholars, who tell us that "death is not pure annihilation or perishing but a disconnection of the soul from the body. It is the parting of two entities, a change in status, and a movement from one abode to another."[7] According to one *hadith*: "This life is the believer's prison. Once he passes away, he parts with his prison."[8]

Therefore, according to the above definition, death is not the end but a transition from one life to another. Death sets the believers free and should not be feared. Muslim scholars, however, add that for the unbelievers this life is heaven for they are destined to their prison in the hereafter. The Prophet also said many positive things about death. For instance, the tradition narrates that Muhammad once addressed God saying: "O God: Make death a pleasure for those who know that I am your messenger."[9] Another *hadith* addressing the Muslims: "If you keep my tradition (examples and teachings), there will be nothing more beloved to you than death."[10]

In *Al-Anbiya' wa Malak al-Mawt* ("The Prophets and the Angel of Death"; 2002), Egyptian scholar and theologian Ali Ahmad al-Tahtawi discusses the concept of death based on Qur'an and *Hadith* commentaries. In the first chapter, he tells us that death is the antilife. He defines life as this connection between the soul and the body but for a limited period. Death is the state when the soul and the body part ways. Death, like life, is God's creation. In the Qur'an, God said: "Who has created death and life that He may test you which of you is best in deed" (67:2). Al-Tahtawi adds that death is one of four lives that human beings go through. These four lives are (1) the life in the womb, (2) the life in this world, (3) the life in the grave, and (4) the eternal life in hell or heaven. Al-Tahtawi contends that humans experience pain and difficulty in the womb, but are relieved when they are born in this life. Similarly, when people die and enter the grave they are relieved from this world. In the words of one Muslim scholar:

The believer in this world is like the fetus in his mother's womb. When it is born and sees the light and is fed from his mother's breast, it admires what it experiences and does not want to return to its previous life. Similarly, the believer after dying feels God's presence and does not wish to return to this world.[11]

Also, in the Islamic tradition, visits to the grave are encouraged so that believers are consistently reminded of death. It is said that the Prophet Muhammad, who first banned grave visitation, ultimately allowed such rituals and even encouraged them. The following *hadiths* illustrate the benefit from visiting the grave as narrated by al-Suyuti: "Visit the graves for they remind you of death.... I had prohibited you from visiting the graves, but you may visit them now for they make you detach yourself from this world and focus on the hereafter.... Visit the graves for your visit will increase your good deeds."[12]

The preparation for death is a lifelong commitment in the Islamic tradition. However, Muslims who are advanced in age and whose death is nearer every day are required to follow the teachings of the Qur'an and the examples of the Prophet so they will ensure a smooth transition from life to death. According to the tradition, there is no excuse for those who reach the age of sixty and have not repented. At this age (a likely age for passing away, according to one *hadith*), people should turn to God and repent for their sins by following Islamic teachings. Adhering to the teachings of the Qur'an and the examples of Muhammad make life in the grave less difficult and less painful. The predeath preparations include the following: (1) repentance; (2) writing of the will; (3) patience in all matters; (4) constant remembrance of God by excessive recitation of the Qur'an; (5) praying to the Prophet; and (6) acceptance of death with pleasure and joy.

Repentance requires that the dying person change his behavior, if he has deviated from Islamic principles. According to religious scholars, Muslims can repent by the following four actions: (1) Refrain from vice, (2) regret one's vices, (3) make a vow not to engage one's vices again, and (4) settle all disputes justly with other people. Repentance is mentioned in many verses in the Qur'an: "O you who believe! Turn to God with sincere repentance! It may be that your Lord will expiate from you your sins, and admit you into Gardens under which rivers flow (Paradise)" (66:8).

Leaving a will is especially important for a dying person. It is pleasing to God, says the Islamic tradition, because it leads to a just conclusion. Justice is the ultimate goal in Islam. A person who dies without leaving a will may cause problems after his death, and some people may also end up deprived of what is truly theirs—thus injustice would be committed. If injustice is committed because of the unfair distribution of a person's will, the dead person will be held responsible for his negligence in front of God. To this effect the Qur'an says:

It is prescribed for you, when death approaches any of you, if he leaves wealth, that he makes a bequest to parents and next of kin, according to reasonable manners. [This is] a duty upon Al-Muttaqun (the pious). Then whoever changes the bequest after hearing it, the sin shall be on those who make the change…. But he who fears from a testator some unjust act or wrongdoing, and thereupon he makes peace between the parties concerned, there shall be no sin on him. (2:180–82)

The Qur'anic verses pertaining to the will indicate that God made the writing of a will a duty to be performed by all Muslims. In these verses, God requires that parents and close relatives should be the immediate beneficiary in the will. It is also required that the person writing the will must be fair in the distribution of his wealth in which no close relative who is entitled to a portion of the wealth should be deprived from it. The unfair distribution of said wealth is an act of injustice and is considered a sin in Islam. Distant relatives should not be included in the will if close relatives are still alive. Those who change the terms of the will following a person's death will be responsible for their deeds. The dead person will not be held accountable for the changes.

A fatal illness, according to Islamic teachings, should not be a cause for fear and sorrow. Muslims who are dying because of their illness must attempt to accept death with patience and joy. Those who receive their death with patience will be rewarded in the next life. Having a deadly illness may be considered a blessing for many Muslims because it is a wake-up call to make amends for wrongdoings, to remember God more often, to increase the quantity of one's praying, and to readjust life to serve God before it is too late. Thus, a dying person who is aware that his death is quickly approaching should accept his fate with extreme patience. Here is the Qur'anic proclamation on the matter:

And certainly, We shall test you with something of fear, hunger, loss of wealth, lives and fruits, but give glad tidings to the patient. Who, when afflicted with calamity, say: "Truly! To God we belong and truly, to Him we shall return." They are those who are blessed and will be forgiven from their Lord, and they are those who receive His Mercy, and it is they who are the guided ones. (2:155–57)

In the Islamic tradition, a dying person will dedicate most of his time to the remembrance of God and the recitation of His words from the Qur'an. These two acts have the capacity to wash his sins and to earn him God's mercy and forgiveness. It is reported that the Prophet once said: "No believer dies without remembering God."[13] Muslim religious scholars encourage dying Muslims to increase their recitation of the Qur'an because, as it is said, "those who remember God while dying, God will remember them." Scholars also assert that the constant remembrance of God and the recitation of the Qur'an by dying Muslims is a sign of happiness and salvation in eternity. "Verily, those who recite the Book of God (this Qur'an)... they hope for a (sure) trade-gain that will never perish" (35:29). "Therefore remember Me, I will remember you, and be grateful to Me and never be ungrateful to Me" (2:152).

The Islamic tradition also opines that praying to the Prophet Muhammad and having an accepting attitude toward death will save the dying person from the torment of the grave. The Qur'an says:

God sends His Graces, Honors, Blessings, and Mercy on the Prophet, and also on His angels. O you who believe! Send your prayers on him [Muhammad], and you should greet him with the Islamic way of greeting. Verily, those who annoy God and His Messenger God has cursed them in this world, and in the Hereafter, and has prepared for them a humiliating torment. (33:56–57)

The true believer is the one who accepts death with satisfaction and joy, knowing that through death he will meet God. The dying person who accepts death with such a mood of acceptance and anticipation is a true believer because he knows for certain what awaits him. Rejecting death is a sign of disbelief. According to the Prophet: "Whoever longs to meet God, God longs to meet him. And whoever hates meeting God, God hates meeting him."[14]

Moreover, the dying person will be saved from the humiliating torments of the grave if on his deathbed he testifies that there is no god but God and that Muhammad is His servant and messenger. The mere recitation of this testimony is sufficient. Thus, believers who are in the presence of a dying or an already dead Muslim are required to recite these words over and over as a way to remind all present of the oneness of God. The Prophet Muhammad even proclaimed: "Whosoever's last words were 'there is no god but God' will surely enter Paradise."[15]

When death is about to take place, the dying person sees the angels of death and realizes that his time has expired and that he is about to be taken to a different world. According to one *hadith*, Satan also appears before the dying person and makes one last attempt to engage the individual in evil before departing this world.[16] The commentaries, however, rarely mention this account; they focus instead on the "Angel of Death," who is mentioned in both the Qur'an and the *Hadith*. In the Qur'an, the Angel of Death is mentioned in the following verses: "They say, 'What? When we have disappeared into the earth, shall we really be created anew?'" In fact, they deny the meeting with their Lord. Say, "'The Angel of Death put in charge of you will reclaim you, and then you will be brought back to your Lord'" (32:10–11). The Prophet Muhammad also spoke briefly of the Angel of Death: "Then comes the Angel of Death and sits by his (the dying person's) head."[17] Early Islamic sources discuss in detail the authority of the Angel of Death, usually called 'Izra'il, who is described by the other angels as the mightiest thing of all creation. To this description, God replies: "I have created it and I am greater than it, and all creation will taste of it!"[18] Before submitting to 'Izra'il, death cries out to its own power:

I am death who separates all loved ones! I am death who separates man and woman, husband and wife! I am death who separates daughters from mothers! I am death who separates sons from fathers! I am death who separates brother from his brother! I am death who subdues the power of the sons of Adam. I am death who inhabits the graves.... Not a creature will remain who does not taste me....[19]

According to well-known eschatological accounts, 'Izra'il has no knowledge of the time of the person's death. Only God has this knowledge. When death occurs, 'Izra'il receives this information from God who instructs the angel to deliver the death. Four angels are entrusted with the task of announcing the news to the dying person that his life has expired. Other angels, known as the noble scribes, come to his left and to his right. The following account describes the encounter between the angels and the dying person:

The one on the right says, "Peace be upon you. I am the angel entrusted with your good works." He takes out a white piece of paper, spreads it open and says, "Look at your deeds." And at that he is joyful. And the angel on the left says, "I am entrusted with your evil deeds." He takes out a piece of black paper and spreads it out, saying, "Look!" And at that the sweat pours from him and he looks right and left in fear of reading the page.[20]

Every human being experiences ten difficulties upon death: the first is the experience of death itself and the departure of the soul from the body; second, the ritual washing, the shrouding, and the carrying of the body to the grave; third, the burial; fourth, the questioning of the angels; fifth, the resurrection from the grave on the Day of Judgment; sixth, facing God on the Day of Judgment; seventh, the weighing of the deeds; eighth, the receipt of the book of deeds in the left hand or the right hand;[21] ninth, the passing of a bridge to hell; and tenth, the fire of hell.[22]

The early sources describe in graphic detail the process of the soul's removal from the body. According to one fourteenth-century account narrated by Ibn Qayyim al-Jawziya (in his *Kitab al-Ruh,* "the Book of the Soul"):

And when [one's] destiny approaches, that is, his earthly death, then four angels descend to him: the angel who pulls the soul from his right foot, the angel who pulls it from the left foot, the angel who pulls it from his right hand, and the angel who pulls it from his left hand.... The good soul slips out like the jetting of water from a waterskin, but the profligate's spirit squeaks out like a skewer from wet wool.[23]

If the dying person was a nonbeliever, he should hope for a delayed death, so that he could perhaps correct his wrongdoings, but, he must realize that there is no return and that the book that recorded his deeds is folded forever. God said: "When death comes to one of them, he cries, 'My Lord, let me return so as to make amends for the things I neglected.' Never! This will not go beyond his words: a barrier stands behind such people until the very Day they are resurrected" (23:99–100). Thus, according to these verses, there is no return from death and the dead are in a suspended state (life in the grave), between this world and the next, where they remain as such until the Day of Judgment, when they are condemned for eternal life in hell or heaven.

Upon death, Muslims prepare the body for proper burial according to the teachings of the Qur'an and the Prophet Muhammad. The teachings require that the body be washed and put in a white shroud. After that, Muslims gather around the body to pray for the dead person by reciting Qur'anic verses. Once the prayers are over, the body is lowered to the grave and placed on its right side facing Mecca, Islam's holiest city. After burial, and when the mourners have left, the dead person's family and close friends may remain by the grave for a short period of time to say additional prayers. The traditional narratives tell us that the moment the last person leaves the grave, the dead person's soul begins to experience the suffering of the cemetery environment. The suffering is so intense that Muhammad once spoke of it by saying: "I seek refuge in God from the torment of the grave."

The Islamic tradition forbids loud lamenting, but there is no harm in crying over the dead. Muslim theologians relate a *hadith* in which the Prophet was found weeping for his dead son. When he was asked: "Did not you forbid weeping over the dead?" He replied: "What is objectionable is loud lamenting, singing, the tearing of one's flesh, and ripping of clothes."[24] It is believed that lamenting will increase the suffering of the dead and can be considered a sign of disbelief in God and objection to His will. The following story attests to this idea:

It is related that when a man dies, the lamenters gather in his house, and the Angel of Death stands at the door of his house [and he says to these people], "What is this crying? By God, I have not reduced the life of any one of you. If your crying is on account of me, surely I am [only] a servant under orders. If it is on account of the dead man, surely he is under constraint. If it is on account of God Most High, then you are not believers in God Most High! By God, I shall return time and again among you!"[25]

LIFE IN THE GRAVE

What happens to human beings after death? Some verses in the Qur'an attest that God gave us life, causes us to die, and then gives us life again so we return to Him (2:28). Commentators have interpreted the second rebirth as our resurrection on Judgment Day. Some have understood it as a reference to the life in the grave while awaiting resurrection on Judgment Day. Although the Qur'an is so explicit about the particulars of Paradise and Hell, it is left to early Muslim commentators to describe in detail what actually happens in that life in the grave, the stage between death and resurrection, often referred to in the Qur'an as the *barzakh*. The latter is also described as the absolute separation between the living and the dead, with no chance of return, as mentioned earlier, to straighten out past wrongdoings or to communicate with the living. The events that take place in the grave, as expressed in the Qur'anic tradition, are fully accepted by traditional Muslims today. "The great majority of contemporary Muslim writers," according to Jane I. Smith and Yvonne Y. Haddad, "choose not to discuss the afterlife at all ... [because] of embarrassment with the elaborate traditional detail concerning life in the grave...."[26] For instance, modernist scholars and theologians deemphasize the traditional affirmations that death is a fearsome ordeal. They instead stress the notion that death is merely a transitional stage and is as natural as sleep. According to Smith and Haddad: "In general the modernist interest is to illustrate the continuum of human life from birth in this world to the final birth or resurrection...."[27]

The Prophet spoke of the difficult and painful experience a person encounters upon death. After death, the disembodied soul is aware of the washers performing the ritual wash and preparing the body for burial. One narrative describes how the soul reacts to such a scene:

O washer, by God I swear to you, take off my clothes gently, for I have gone out from the devastating power of the angel of death. By God, O washer do not make the winding around me tight, so that I can yet see the faces of my people and my children and my relatives; this is the last time I can look at them, for today I will be separated from them and will not see them until the Day of Resurrection.[28]

Traditionalists believe that the person's deeds throughout his life are exposed in front of him soon after he is buried. In the grave, the soul becomes aware of its fate on the Day of Judgment. Therefore, the grave is the first station on the road to eternity. If the person were a believer, he would enjoy his life in the grave and is promised the utmost happiness and comfort in heaven. On the contrary, the unbelievers will start suffering in the grave and are promised further and more severe punishment in hell. Once the Prophet said: "The grave is the first station of life after death. If the person survived the grave [i.e., if he were a believer], then he will live in peace and happiness forever. But if he did not survive the grave, he should expect more suffering in hell."[29]

Early traditional accounts describe the events in the grave in more details. The following account is frequently narrated in early sources:

When the dead person is put into his grave and the earth is poured on him, the grave calls to him, "You used to enjoy yourself on my surface, but today you will grieve in my interior; you used to eat all kinds of delicacies on my surface, but today the worms will eat you while you are inside me."[30]

The Prophet also describes the grave in graphic detail:

When the servant of God is buried and his family and friends leave the grave, he hears the sound of their footsteps as they walk away. Immediately after everyone leaves, two angels, called Munkar and Nakir, descend to the grave and start the process of questioning the dead person. They say: "What do you say about this man, Muhammad?" The believer would say: "I testify that he is the servant of God and his messenger." Then they say to him: "Look at your place in the grave. God has changed it from fire to a garden." At this moment, the grave will be expanded for the dead person to enjoy. As for the unbelievers and the hypocrites, they are also asked the same question about Muhammad. They answer: "We do not know. We just reiterated what we heard the people say." The two angels reply: "You did not know and you did not testify." For them, the grave is tightened against their bodies.[31]

Although the questioning of the grave pertaining to children is never mentioned in the Qur'an, some Muslim scholars have argued that children do experience the torment of similar questioning. The scholars reached their conclusion based on the following *hadith*: "The Prophet Muhammad once prayed in the funeral of a young boy and said: 'O God save him the suffering of the grave.'"[32] Another *hadith* relates the following: "The dead person suffers because of the weeping of his parents."[33] Some Muslim scholars have challenged the above *hadith* narratives and contended that the questioning of the grave is for those who could reason while on earth. They argued that a child is not able to distinguish between right and wrong, so how would he be asked about who Muhammad was? These scholars conclude that the child cannot be asked about something that he was unaware of.[34] There is another twist to this issue. According to the tradition, children are not responsible for their acts until they reach the age of puberty. It is the duty of the parents to make sure the children pray five times a day and that the girls abide by the codes of Islamic dress. Thus, the larger issue of if and how children are addressed in the grave remains unclear and is still debated in the Islamic tradition.

The early sources mention that the spirits of the deceased maintain some contact with their families by returning to the places where they lived on earth. The reports suggest that the spirits keep returning to earth until they finally make a complete break with the world of the living. According to one report:

When a [believer] dies his spirit circles around his house for a month, observing how his possessions are divided and his debts paid off. When the month has passed it returns to the grave, circling around until a year has gone by. It sees whoever prays for him and who grieves for him. After a year has passed his spirit ascends to [the place] where the spirits are gathered together for the day of resurrection, the day when the trumpet will be blown.[35]

The early commentaries also speak of an immediate reward for the soul for performing its religious duties. This is illustrated in a journey on which the soul is taken to the presence of God and then returned to the body. One version of the narratives describes the journey as the following:

After death, the dead person meets angels with faces so bright as if they are the sunlight. These angels carry with them heavenly winding-clothes and embalming fluid. Then the Angel of Death joins them and asks the soul to leave the body. The soul slips easily from the body and ascends with the angels to the seventh layer of the heavens where God Himself is to be found. Then God reveals the fate of the soul to the angels saying: "Write the name of my servant in the uppermost heaven and then return him to earth to his body."[36]

The unworthy soul on the other hand faces fearsome angels who are blackish in appearance. The Angel of Death joins them and demands the soul to leave the body. The unworthy soul squeaks out like a skewer from wet wool and is carried upward. The gates of heaven, however, do not open to it. God communicates to the Angel of Death the fate of the unworthy soul, saying: "Write its book in the underground." The Angel of Death flings the soul from his hands, sending it back to the body. Immediately following its arrival in the body, the two angels begin their questioning of the soul.[37] It is not clear whether the soul's ascent to the heavens and its return to the body takes place before or after burial. Some accounts indicate that all of these events happen while the body is being washed; others cite the Prophet describing the events as if they happen after burial.

The eleventh-century doctor of theology Abu Hamid al-Ghazali describes four categories of dead people to whom the angels and the personification of deeds come in the grave. The first category is the religious scholars who are considered the best in performance of their religion. The angels are severe in their questioning about "who is your Lord, what is your religion, and who is your Prophet." Of course, the religious scholars are expected to give correct answers and they are automatically granted a reward for the good deeds they have done.

The next category includes those who performed good deeds while on earth, even if they were not as pious or informed in the religion as the religious scholars. The personification of deeds warns the dead person of the impending visit of Munkar and Nakir and then instructs the soul in its own defense. When the angels are about to ask their questions, the soul will be ready with the correct answers: "God is my Lord, Muhammad my Prophet, the Qur'an my guide, Islam is my [religion], the Ka'ba[38] my [prayer direction], and Abraham my father and his community my community."[39] The souls who fall into this category are not automatically rewarded. The angels, however, open a door for them, showing them the terrors of hell, but they are told that this Fire is not for them. "God has exchanged your place in the Fire for a place in the Garden."[40]

Al-Ghazali's third category consists of those who know the answers but find it difficult to profess that God is their only Lord and that Islam is their religion. This is usually because of waywardness or insincerity. This group tastes some kind of punishment in the grave. The fourth and last category is the category of the profligates. These persons not only find it difficult to profess the Lordship of God, but also they simply do not know the answers. These persons are severely beaten and the personification of their deeds takes the shape of an animal. This kind of punishment may also be applied to a believer who committed bad deeds while on earth. The following account is frequently mentioned in the tradition:

The story is told that someone who had died was seen in a dream and was asked, "How are you?" He replied, "I prayed one day without performing the ablutions, so God put a wolf in charge of me to frighten me in my grave. My situation with it is a most terrible one!"[41]

Al-Ghazali's fourfold division is an indication that all persons are held responsible for their deeds on earth. He further suggests that each individual is subject to some kind of punishment in the grave, slight or heavy, dependent on his or her deeds on earth.[42] The faithful and the faithless alike will suffer the torment of the grave. It is reported that the Prophet was in pain as he described how even the believer must undergo such questioning:

The voice of Munkar and Nakir in the hearing of the believer are like antimony in the eye and the pressure of the tomb to the believer is like the compassionate mother whose son complains to her of a headache and she strokes his head gently. Woe to those who doubt God—how they will be squeezed in their graves like the pressure of a boulder on an egg.[43]

According to the Islamic tradition, souls sometimes communicate with each other in the grave. Says Ibn Qayyim's *Kitab al-Ruh*, souls visit each other and remember their affairs in the previous life. There are different levels of souls that dwell in the grave, and each communicates with those on its own level. The soul's level is determined by the dead person's deeds while on earth. For instance, pious souls may not visit with souls of lesser piety. The extremely pious souls are destined to visit the souls of the Prophets. Early Muslim commentators reached this conclusion based on the following Qur'anic verse:

And whoso obey God and the Messenger, then they will be in the company of those on whom God has bestowed His Grace, of the Prophets, those followers of the Prophets who were first and foremost to believe in them ... like the martyrs, and the righteous. How excellent these companions are! (4:69)

This above-mentioned verse was revealed following a conversation between Muhammad and one of his followers. The narrative is cited in Ibn Qayyim's *Kitab al-Ruh* using these words:

A man amongst Muhammad's supporters came crying and said to the Prophet: "O Messenger of God, my love for you surpasses that for my own family and wealth. I love you more than I love myself. I just realized that when we die, we will never meet again. I am not as worthy as you are, and my soul is not worthy of the Paradise of a Prophet."[44]

Muhammad remained quiet. Suddenly, the above-mentioned verse was revealed, attesting that those who obey God and His Messenger will earn a place in the highest heaven and will enjoy the company of the Prophets.

It is reported that, according to the *hadiths,* the dead can hear the words of the living, know who inquire about them and who visit them at the grave, and are aware of their own state in the grave as well as the state of their relatives and loved ones on earth. In *Kitab Ahwal al-Qubur* ("the Book of the Torments of the Grave"), the fourteenth-century Ibn Rajb narrates that the Prophet once stood at the grave of some people he knew and asked: "'Did you find what God had indeed promised?' Then those who stood with him asked: 'O Prophet: Are you talking to dead people?' He replied: 'They can hear me but cannot talk. They can hear what I am saying.'"[45] Other *hadiths* suggest that the "dead person recognizes the individuals who wash and wrap his body [in his winding clothes] and who lower it to the grave."[46] According to one *hadith*: "No man visits the grave of his brother and sits near him but that the dead person greets him."[47] Also, one source relates that the Messenger of God said: "No servant of God passes by the grave of a Muslim man whom he knew on the earth and greets but that the dead person recognizes him and returns the greeting."[48]

These *hadith* narratives, however, are doubted and challenged by many Muslim scholars as they contradict the following Qur'anic verses: "Verily, you cannot make the dead to hear.... So verily, you [O Muhammad] cannot make the dead hear" (27:80; 30:52). To remedy this contradiction, Muslim scholars have suggested that any communication between the living and the dead takes place through the medium of dreams. The following story is one of many related to dream communication:

Someone has related this story: Our father engaged for us a teacher to teach us our lessons at home. Then the teacher died. After six days we went to this grave to visit him, and began to discuss with each other the matter of God's command, may He be exalted. Someone passed by us selling a plate of figs, which we bought and ate, throwing the stems onto the grave. When night came, the Shaykh saw the dead man in a dream, and said to him, "How are you?" "Fine," he replied, "except that your children took my grave for a garbage pile and talked about me, with words that are nothing but infidelity!" The Shaykh reprimanded us, and we said [to each other], "Glory be to God! He continues to bother us in the hereafter just as he did on earth."[49]

The idea that the interaction between the dead and the living is not "real" but happens in sleep is supported by the following verse: "It is God who takes away the souls at the time of their death, and those that die not during their sleep. He keeps those [souls] for which He has ordained death and sends the rest for a term appointed" (39:42). Ibn Qayyim cites historical reports explaining the verse to mean that the souls of the dead and the living meet in sleep, and they question each other. The soul of the living returns to its body, whereas the soul of the dead is prevented from returning to earth. Early commentators give further explanation to the above-mentioned verse saying that God keeps the soul that experienced actual death—although it wished to return to its body— and sends the soul that experienced death in sleep so it will die the actual death in its appointed time. Thus, Ibn Qayyim suggests that God makes human beings experience two types of death: The greater death, which is actual death, and the lesser death, which is the death in sleep. Ibn Qayyim adds that God, therefore, created two types of souls: One type that He prevents from returning to its body and another type that He sends back to continue living until its appointed time. Muslim commentaries frequently make references to sleep as the small or lesser death and that in the grave the believer will "sleep the sleep of a bridegroom!" Thus, the likening of sleep to death is a recurrent theme in Islamic tradition and literature. Such a theme can be illustrated in the following story about the famous eighth-century mystic Rabi'a al-Adawiyya:

Rabi'a used to pray all night, and when the day dawned she allowed herself a light sleep in her place of prayer, until the dawn tinged the sky with gold, and I used to hear her say, when she sprang up in fear from that sleep, "O soul how long wilt thou sleep and how often wilt thou wake? Soon wilt thou sleep a sleep from which thou shalt not wake again until the trumpet call on the Day of Resurrection."[50]

In his *Kitab al-Ruh*, Ibn Qayyim discusses the *hadiths* that deal with the activities and location of the soul, and then he provides his own interpretations. For instance, Ibn Qayyim debates whether the soul dies or remains alive upon the death of the body. He tells us that Muslim scholars have debated this issue. For instance, one group argued that the soul actually dies. They supported their argument based on the following Qur'anic verses: "Everything will perish save His Face" (28:88). Another group argued that the soul does not die for it was born to remain. Only the body perishes. Ibn Qayyim interjects his opinion saying that the death of the soul means its separation from the body. The soul does not perish but remains after its creation in a state of happiness or suffering until God returns it to its body.[51]

Another issue Ibn Qayyim touches on is the location of the souls between death and resurrection. He asks: "Are they in heaven or on earth? Are they in Paradise? Are they reborn in bodies other than their own, or do they remain souls without bodies?" According to Ibn Qayyim, some authorities say that the souls are at the gates of Paradise receiving its breezes and enjoying its fruits. Another group tells us that the souls are in the grave. Others contend that the souls are free and that they roam the skies and the earth. Some argued that the souls of the unbelievers are in the Fire of Hell and the souls of the believers are in Paradise.

According to Ibn Hazm, an eleventh-century Muslim theologian and man of letters, the souls are where they were before the creation of their bodies, meaning that they are with Adam until the Day of Judgment.[52] Ibn Hazm bases his conclusion on the following verse: "So those on the Right Hand—how [fortunate] will be those on the Right Hand! [This is respect for them, because they will enter Paradise]. And those on the Left Hand—how [unfortunate] will be those on the Left Hand! This is a disgrace for them, because they will enter Hell" (56:8–9). Thus, for Ibn Hazm, this verse meant that the believers are with Adam on his right hand and the unbelievers are on his left hand. These are the various interpretations of what happens to the soul between death and resurrection on the Day of Judgment. Some of them are based on Qur'anic verses, while others are merely speculation.

DEATH AND MARTYRDOM IN ISLAM

Martyrdom, or death for the sake of God, is considered one of the noblest deeds in the Islamic tradition. The Qur'an speaks very highly of martyrs, placing them in the same grouping with the Prophets. According to the Qur'an:

And whoso obey God and the Messenger, then they will be in the company of those on whom God has bestowed His Grace, of the Prophets, the followers of the Prophets who were the first and foremost to believe in them, the martyrs, and the righteous. And how excellent these companions are! (4:69)

In Islam, all the prophets from Adam and Abraham to Moses, Jesus, and Muhammad are not dead but alive with God. In other words, they are not dead in the grave awaiting resurrection to face God on the Day of Judgment like everyone else. The Islamic tradition holds that the Angel Gabriel carried Muhammad on a night journey from Mecca to Jerusalem, and from there he ascended to heaven, into the very presence of God. On his journey through the "seven heavens," he met Prophets from the past. Thus, this account suggests that these Prophets are already in heaven. Martyrs, according to the Qur'an, have the same privilege. Martyrs do not go to the grave; rather, they shoot straight to Paradise. Furthermore, the *hadith* tells us that the first drop of the martyr's blood washes his sins,[53] and seventy people from his family are automatically rewarded with a place in heaven.[54] The following Qur'anic verses attest to this:

And say not of those who are killed in the Way of God, "They are dead." Nay, they are living, but you perceive [it] not. Think not of those who are killed in the Way of God as dead. Nay, they are alive, with their Lord, and they have provision. They rejoice in what God has bestowed upon them of His Bounty, and they rejoice for the sake of those who have not joined but are left behind, that on them no fear shall come, nor shall they grieve. (2:154; 3:169–70)

Muslim commentators have interpreted this verse to mean that martyrs need not fear for their families on the Day of Judgment; instead, they will rejoice because their martyrdom has earned their families a place in heaven.

According to Islamic tradition, Muslims do not wash the bodies of martyrs, nor do they pray for the martyrs' souls. One who has sacrificed his life for God's purposes is buried in his clothes with the blood on him, as a proof of his noble deed. It is reported that it was Muhammad who gave the instructions neither to wash the body of the martyr, nor to pray for his soul.[55] Thus, Muslims today do not perform the traditional prayer on the martyr because his soul, which bypasses the grave and goes straight to heaven, no longer needs the intervention (i.e., the prayers) of the living to lessen the torments of the grave.

It is important to mention, as an addendum, that martyrdom is conferred only on those who are killed for a noble cause, i.e., a soldier who dies fighting to defend his country or a firefighter who dies trying to save a human life. The killing of an innocent life as well as the ending of one's own life is condemned in the Qur'an as the ultimate sin, and the person who commits such acts will burn in hell for eternity. As the Qur'an tells us:

O you who believe! ... do not kill yourselves (nor kill one another)... whoever commits that through aggression and injustice, We shall cast him into the Fire.... If you avoid the great sins [one of the great sins is the killing of an innocent life including the self], we shall admit you to a Noble Entrance (i.e., Paradise). (4:28–31)

Verse 5:32 makes it clear that the killing of even one innocent life is equivalent to the killing of all humans: "... if anyone kills a person ... it is as if he kills all mankind, while if anyone saves a life it is as if he saves the lives of all mankind." Therefore, according to the verses above, those young Muslims who, in contemporary times, blow themselves up and take with them innocent lives are sinners, not martyrs. For the martyrs (those who die saving lives), the Qur'an promises them an eternal life in heaven: "And [there will be] *Hur* [fair females] with wide, lovely eyes [as wives for the pious]. Verily, We have created them of special creation, and made them virgins, full of love, equal in age, for the Companions of the Right Hand" (56:22; 56:35–38). Some Muslim commentators have interpreted the Arabic word *Hur* to mean a pure being or an angel of whom seventy-two are promised to each martyr. The number seventy-two, which is never mentioned in the Qur'an, is based on a prophetic *hadith*. The underlying principle is that true selflessness, in the form of martyrdom, is always rewarded by God.

All this being said, Islam justifies waging the lesser jihad ("armed struggle to defend the community") only when Muslims are attacked. In such a case, the Muslims are permitted to kill their attackers who are committing an aggression and are no longer considered innocent. Along these lines, Islamic extremists see America as an aggressor in the Muslim world, and the American "war on terror" in the eyes of the extremists is an aggression against Islam. Moreover, Muslims who support America in this war are also deemed aggressors. Thus, for the extremists, the West and its allies (Muslim and non-Muslim) are no longer innocent people, and the verse "if you kill an innocent life," no longer applies to them.

The good news is that a majority of Muslims do not read such Qur'anic verses in this extreme way and look aghast at the atrocities committed in the name of Islam. A more moderate reading of Islam's aggressors might be seen in the following: "...If they cease hostilities, there can be no further hostility.... Be mindful of God, and know that He is with those who are mindful of Him. Spend in God's cause: do not contribute to your destruction with your own hands, but do good, for God loves those who do good" (2:193–95). The passage "do not contribute to your destruction with your own hands" is understood by the majority of Muslims to outlaw suicide and other forms of self-harm, and "do good, for God loves those who do good" is generally understood to mean that Muslims should persuade their attackers, if possible, to reach peaceful settlements before going to war.

DEATH AND DYING IN SUFISM

Sufism is the mystical dimension of Islam that takes the practitioner on a spiritual quest for a direct experience or communion with God. The term Sufism is derived from the Arabic word *suf*, meaning "wool," in reference to the wool garment worn by monks. The meaning of the term may also come from the word *safa'* (Arabic for "purity"), which reflects the idea of purification. The Sufi understanding of God and their worldview are within the Islamic tradition, being based on the Qur'an, the *hadith*, and the *shari'a* (Islamic law). As mystics, they focus on the Qur'anic command to remember God without ceasing, making meditation on God an intense devotional practice. They opine that repeating the name of God is one of the first steps to union with God, and thus they tend to focus on His many names.

For Sufis, death is a reawakening for a life that offers a "spectrum of opportunities, that, if taken, allow one to recover awareness of one's full identity."[56] In mainstream Islam, everyone will face God on the Day of Judgment, but the Sufis are "the impatient ones. They want God now— moment by moment, day by day, in this very life."[57]

The Sufis accept death as a gift from God. Based on this belief, death is no longer a source of fear. A Sufi teaching says: "Die before you die." The interpretation of this teaching is that we should learn what death has to teach us before it is too late. In Sufi tradition, the wisdom and knowledge we gain at death reveal the true value of life. Day-to-day activity becomes so much richer if we are able to gain this wisdom and make use of it before we die.

The tradition "Die before you die" also meant the inner death of one's lower qualities and spiritual resurrection in this life. Thus, death means the annihilation of the lower qualities that separate the beloved (God) from the lover (God's creation). For the Sufis, "There is nothing good in love without death."[58] In this case, death may be understood as "dying to one's own qualities or even as corporeal death, since this leads the lover toward the beloved."[59]

Sufi literature talks about the upward movement of the soul, a borrowing from the Neoplatonic idea of the return of the soul to its divine origin. Some might even say there is a hint of reincarnation. The following Sufi poetry seems to point in this direction:

> I died from minerality and became a plant,
> And from plant I died and became animal,
> I died from animality and became human.
> Why fear death?
> Next time I shall die as human,
> to soar higher than angels,
> all will perish except His [God's] face.
> Oh, let me not exist!
> for non-existence
> proclaims in organ tones, "To Him we shall return."[60]

For the Sufis, the statement "to Him we shall return" does not mean the actual return of the soul to God as is the belief in mainstream Islam. Rather, it means the state of Nonexistence, the indescribable divine essence, which is "beyond every possible mode of expression or imagination."[61] The above poetry speaks of the development of man from mineral to plant and then to animal. This lowly state is a prerequisite for the soul to move upward to the divine. The Sufis see death as a spiritual resurrection to a higher life. In the words of one Sufi poet:

> Kill me, o my trustworthy friends,
> for in my being killed is my life.[62]

Furthermore, the Sufis believe in constant development even after death. This idea is illustrated in the following lyrics:

> Only when man becomes deprived of outward being like winter,
> there is hope for a new spring to develop in him.[63]

This spring is a day of resurrection, a new life. Jalal al-Din Rumi, a thirteenth-century Sufi poet, said:

> Go and die, go and die,
> in this love, go and die,
> when you die in this love
> souls will fly.

> Go and die, go and die,
> And from death have no fear,
> for from earth you will rise and seize the heavens.

Go and die, go and die,
and leave this lower soul,
for you are as prisoners and this lower soul is as a chain.[64]

Sufis welcome and accept death as a gift and blessing from God. The following story reflects this belief: "When the angel of death came to take Abraham's soul, Abraham said: 'Have you ever seen a friend take his friend's life?' God answered him, 'Have you ever seen a friend unwilling to meet or go with his friend?'"[65] According to Rabi'a the mystic: "Death is a bridge whereby the lover rejoins the Beloved."[66] In the words of Muhyi al-Din ibn al-'Arabi, a twelfth-century mystic:

One dies when, by God's will, one's borrowed time ends. One's material being—which is called life—ending at an appointed hour, loses all its character and qualities both good and bad, and nothing remains. In their place God comes to be. One's self becomes God's self; one's attributes become God's attributes. That is what the Prophet ... meant when he said, "Die before dying."[67]

The notion of "Die before your die" is a common expression in Sufi poetry.

THE DAY OF JUDGMENT, THE RESURRECTION, AND HEAVEN AND HELL

On the Day of Judgment, according to the Islamic tradition, all those who are alive will die. The Angel Israfil will sound the trumpet to announce the resurrection. On that day (also referred to in the Qur'an as the Last Day; the Day of Standing Up; Day of Separation; Day of Reckoning; Day of Awakening; the Encompassing Day; and the Hour) the world will be shaken to its foundations, and all the dead will rise from their graves and will be sorted out into three sorts: those nearest to God (the Prophets, those who were the first to believe in them, and the martyrs), Companions of the Right Hand (the believers), and Companions of the Left Hand (the unbelievers). All will be clothed in new bodies that are beyond human comprehension. "We have decreed death to you all, and We are not outstripped, to transfigure you and create you in [forms] that you know not" (56:60–61).

Then, according to the Qur'an, each one will stand alone and naked before God and "no bearer of burdens shall bear another's burden; and if one heavily laden calls another to (bear) his load, nothing of it will be lifted even though he be near of kin" (35:18). Thus, no one will be responsible for the sins of another. Also, no one can hide anything from God for He knows everything. The Books of Life, which are kept by the Recording Angels, will be presented to witness against the person's actions. God warned in the Qur'an: "And We have fastened every man's deeds to his neck, and on the Day of Resurrection, We shall bring out for him a book which he will find wide open. (It will be said to him): 'Read your book. You yourself are sufficient as reckoner against you this Day'" (17:13–14). The Prophets also will line up before God, and they too will have to answer to their actions. Each soul will be weighed in the balance of God's justice, and each will be sent to heaven or to the fire of hell.

Heaven and hell are physical places, according to the Qur'an. Heaven is referred to most in the Qur'an as the *firdaws*, or the seventh heaven, and *Janna*, or the Garden, a place of physical and spiritual pleasure. The Qur'an states: "But it is for those who fear their Lord, that lofty mansions, one above another, have been built. Therein can they call for fruit in abundance, and drink, and We shall bestow on them, of fruit and meat, anything they desire" (39:20; 38:51; 52:22).

Hell is referred to in the Qur'an as *al-Nar*, literally "the Fire," *al-Hawiya*, the Abyss, and *Jahannam*, literally "the Depths," among other names. Hell is a physical place of unimaginable torment and suffering, but some Muslim scholars have argued based on Qur'anic verses (11:107-108) that some of those who end up in Hell will be there for only a period of time. In other words, for some, hell is a place for purgation, and with God's mercy, they will be forgiven and admitted to Heaven. However, the Qur'an clearly states that those who commit *shirk*, that is to associate "partners" with God, i.e., believe in other gods, will dwell in the eternal fire of Hell: "Verily, God forgives not that partners should be set up with Him (in worship), but He forgives except that to whom He wills: and whoever sets up partners with God in worship, he has indeed invented a tremendous sin" (4:48).

CONCLUSION

This chapter has largely discussed the concept of death and dying in Islam from the Sunni orthodox point of view. The sources consulted for this project represent the views of traditionalist Muslim scholars and theologians. As this chapter has demonstrated, these traditionalists, who produced the most extensive works on this subject, discussed their topic in detail and emphasized the literal interpretations of Qur'anic verses and *hadith* reports. For these traditionalists, the accounts of death and the graphic detail of the torments of the grave serve as a reminder and warning for believers to follow the teachings of the Qur'an and the *hadith*. They focus mainly on the range of events from death to the resurrection and pay less attention to life in hell and heaven. Furthermore, traditionalists tend to see death as a transitional stage from one life to another, and, for them, life in the grave is the initial step to eternal punishment or reward.

NOTES

1. Jalal al-Din al-Suyuti, *Sharh Hal al-Mawta wa al-Qubur* ("The State of the Dead and the Grave") (Beirut, Lebanon: Dar al-Kitab al-Arabi, 2004), 13–14.

2. Ibid., 143.

3. Ibid., 14.

4. Ibid., 15.

5. Ibid.

6. Abd 'Allah al-Talidi, *Mashahid al-Mawt* (The Flashes of Death) (Beirut, Lebanon: Dar Ibn Hazm, 2000), 16.

7. Al-Suyuti, *Sharh Hal al-Mawta*, 19.

8. Ibid., 20.

9. Ibid.

10. Ibid.

11. Ali Ahmad al-Tahtawi, *Al-Anbiya' wa Malak al-Mawt* (The Prophets and the Angel of Death) (Beirut, Lebanon: Dar al-Kutub al-'Ilmiyya, 2002), 24.

12. Al-Suyuti, *Sharh Hal al-Mawta*, 25.

13. Hassan Ayub, *Rihlat al-Khulud* (The Flight to Eternity), 4th ed. (Cairo: Dar al-Salam, 2004), 29.

14. Ibid., 36.

15. Ibn Qayyim al-Jawziya, *Kitab al-Ruh* (The Book of the Soul) (Beirut, Lebanon: Dar al-Kitab al-Arabi, 2005), 17.

16. Al-Tahtawi, *Al-Anbiya'*, 27.

17. Ayub, *Rihlat*, 93.

18. Jane I. Smith and Yvonne Y. Haddad, *The Islamic Understanding of Death and Resurrection* (Oxford: Oxford University Press, 2002), 35.

19. Ibid.

20. Ibid., 36.

21. In the Islamic tradition, receiving the book of deeds in the left hand is a sign that the soul is condemned to the fire of hell.

22. Al-Tahtawi, *Al-Anbiya'*, 39.

23. Smith and Haddad, *The Islamic Understanding*, 36.

24. Ibid., 59.

25. Ibid., 60.

26. Ibid., 100.

27. Ibid., 105.

28. Ibid., 37.

29. Ayub, *Rihlat*, 99.

30. Smith and Haddad, *The Islamic Understanding*, 39.

31. Ayub, *Rihlat*, 99.

32. Ibn Qayyim, *Kitab al-Ruh*, 94.

33. Ibid.

34. Ibid.

35. Smith and Haddad, *The Islamic Understanding*, 50.

36. Ayub, *Rihlat*, 100.

37. Ibid., 101.

38. The Ka'ba, a cuboid building in the center of Mecca, is believed to have been built by Abraham and his son Isma'il. Being the first monotheistic place of prayer, Muslims from all over the world face the Ka'ba when they pray.

39. Smith and Haddad, *The Islamic Understanding*, 44.

40. Ibid.

41. Ibid., 45.

42. Ibid., 46.

43. Ibid.

44. Ibn Qayyim, *Kitab al-Ruh*, 23.

45. Ibn Rajb, *Kitab Ahwal al-Qubur* (The Book of the Torments of the Grave) (Beirut, Lebanon: Dar al-Kitab al-Arabi, 2003), 133.

46. Smith and Haddad, *The Islamic Understanding*, 51.

47. Ibn Rajb, *Kitab Ahwal al-Qubur*, 143.

48. Ibid., 142.

49. Smith and Haddad, *The Islamic Understanding*, 52.

50. Margaret Smith, *Rabi'a* (Oxford: Oneworld Publications, 1994), 48.

51. Ibn Qayyim, *Kitab al-Ruh*, 40.

52. Ibid., 98.

53. Ibn al-Nahhas, *Fi al-Jihad wa Fada'ilihi* ("On Jihad and its Virtues") (Beirut, Lebanon: Dar al-Basha'ir and Islamiyya, 2002), 697.

54. Ibid., 739.

55. Muhammad 'Amara, *Qissat al-Nihaya* ("The Story of the Final Hour") (Beirut, Lebanon: Dar Ibn Hazm, 2002), 33.

56. Robert Frager and James Fadiman, *Essential Sufism* (New York: HarperSanFrancisco, 1997), 251.

57. Ibid., ix.

58. Annemarie Schimmel, *Mystical Dimensions of Islam* (Chapel Hill, NC: The University of North Carolina Press, 1975), 135.

59. Ibid.

60. My own translation from Rumi's *Divan-e Shams*.

61. Schimmel, *Mystical Dimensions of Islam*, op. cit., 322.

62. Ibid.

63. Ibid., 323.

64. My own translation from Rumi's *Divan-e Shams*. See also A. J. Arberry, *Mystical Poems of Rumi 1* (Chicago and London: The University of Chicago Press, 1991), 70.

65. Frager and Fadiman, *Essential Sufism*, 253.

66. Ibid.

67. Ibid., 254.

4

Awakening to Mortality: Buddhist Views of Death and Dying

John M. Thompson

> Furthermore, ordinary worldly persons are troubled and embarrassed by the sight of death in others and seek to avoid it, forgetting that they themselves are subject to it. But I know that I myself cannot escape death, so it would not be proper for me to avoid the sight of it in others.... Mulling things over in this way, my live infatuation with my life completely disappeared....
>
> —The Buddha, from the Pali, *Anguttara Nikaya*

If you ever find yourself in a conversation you want to end, try asking a simple question: "What happens when we die?" Chances are the chatting will cease and you will find yourself on the receiving end of some very confused stares. No one likes death—it remains one of the last surviving taboos in the twenty-first century. The seemingly universal avoidance of death in everyday social interaction is fraught with irony since all of us know someone who has died and all of us are going to die as well. Not surprisingly, religion has a lot to say about death: why it occurs, what happens after it, even how (perhaps) it can be overcome. In fact, several prominent scholars, such as E. B. Tylor, Herbert Spencer, and even

Sigmund Freud, have speculated that religion originates in humanity's attempt to deal with our mortality.[1]

Few religious traditions, however, have as much to say about death as Buddhism. In Buddhism, death is a fascinating topic—the subject of diverse, even contradictory teachings and practices. Yet despite such variety we can discern a general Buddhist message about death: Death is a fact of existence that we must face and come to terms with. Furthermore, because of its importance, death calls for great care in how we handle it, both individually and collectively.

BUDDHISM 101: A BASIC OVERVIEW

As with any religion, the history of Buddhism is a mixture of fact, myth, and legend. Traditionally, Buddhists claim their faith is eternal, synonymous with reality itself. However, in our particular cosmic epoch, the Buddhist path (*marga*) was established by one man: Siddhartha Gautama (ca. 560–480 BCE), the son of a tribal chief who ruled a region encompassing northeastern India and Nepal.

We know little of Siddhartha's life outside of legend, but he belonged to the warrior (*kshatriya*) caste and, as such, was groomed to lead his father's kingdom. His father took pains to shower him in luxury, sheltering his son as much as possible from the pains of ordinary life. In this, however, he failed, and sometime before Siddhartha's thirtieth birthday, he realized the inevitability of disease, old age, and death.

Overwhelmed, he abandoned his luxurious home to become a wandering ascetic seeking the solution to the suffering inherent in life. He studied with several gurus, mastering their various teachings and yogic techniques. Yet he found none led to liberation. He even embarked on a path of harsh asceticism, starving himself to the point of death in an attempt to overcome desire, but he ultimately realized that such a path did not lead to liberation. Rather, Siddhartha understood that he needed to find a "middle way" between the extremes of luxury and asceticism.

Determined to find enlightenment, Siddhartha vowed to sit under a *pipal* tree (now referred to as the "bodhi tree") until he achieved liberation. Legends tell of his temptation by Mara (the Indian "devil"), with the Earth herself testifying to his virtue. Yet through it all, Siddhartha remained steadfast, entering into a series of meditative states and attaining ever-deeper insights into reality. Finally, one day, just as the sun was breaking the horizon, he awoke to the true nature of existence—he had become the Buddha.

Realizing that he needed to share his insights, the Buddha began a life of teaching, attracting many followers over the years as he traveled through the Ganges region, finally passing on at the age of eighty. Accounts of his death are quite moving, with the Buddha remaining calm and composed, comforting his followers and reminding them to "be lights unto themselves" as they strove to achieve their own awakening.

In the following centuries Buddhism spread throughout India, into Central and Southeast Asia (including Indonesia), and from there to China, Korea, and Japan, as well as into the Himalayan region of Bhutan and Tibet. Thus, what began as a small protest movement in India in the 6th century BCE spread all over Asia. More recently, Buddhism has made inroads into Europe, North and South America, and Australia. Current estimates are that there are some 330 million Buddhists worldwide, comprising approximately 6 percent of the world's population.

The term "Buddha" is an epithet meaning "awakened one"—the Buddha "woke up," whereas the rest of us are basically asleep, ignorant of true reality. A Buddha is one who has attained *nirvana* (literally being "blown out"), a state beyond suffering. Although the Buddha declined to describe *nirvana* in detail, saying that it was incomprehensible for those enmeshed in delusion, it seems to be a way of existence marked by clear understanding and acceptance of the human condition. Buddhists maintain that the historical Buddha (also known as Sakyamuni, the "enlightened sage of the Sakya clan") was not the only one to attain such a state—others preceded him and exist in other world systems. In a sense, "Buddha" names the truth Siddhartha came to realize and embody. Theoretically, we *all* can follow his lead and become Buddha, an idea stressed particularly in later schools.

Much controversy surrounds the exact content of the Buddha's teachings (Dharma). The Buddha himself did not write anything, and his teachings were not written down until after centuries of oral transmission. There are some discrepancies in current records but overall we can be fairly sure of some things. First and foremost, the Buddha's teachings were pragmatic and experiential—they were supposed to be put into practice by those whom he taught. Moreover, they were not based on speculation or wishful thinking. The "knowledge" that Buddha sought to impart was not so much a body of information as a series of insights concerning the nature of existence. In essence, he laid out a method of knowing reality and coming to terms with it, thereby freeing us from sufferings and anxieties. His was a therapeutic tradition, a guideline for how to live.

Not surprisingly, Buddhist teachings are rooted in traditional Indian views of the universe, albeit with some important twists. According to basic Indian teachings, the world we know is in constant motion, a continuous cycle known as *samsara* (lit. "wandering through"). *Samsara* is far larger and more complex than our immediate existence; it includes all beings throughout the universe and stretches from the distant past into the foreseeable future. Thus, we can speak of *samsara* as the beginningless round of birth-and-death in which all beings find themselves. Most beings, ignorant of their true nature and enslaved to passion, are pushed along blindly by *karma* (action), wandering from life to life, continually subject to assorted joys and pains, death and rebirth. However, Indian traditions also teach that one can break free of *samsara* through spiritual training, attaining a radical freedom often called *moksha* (liberation).

Operating within this basic Indian framework, Buddha laid particular stress on the notion of change. When we actually pay attention to experience, we see that everything is impermanent, constantly changing from moment to moment. Buddha also stressed the interconnection between all factors within this ever-changing cycle. That is, all phenomena rely on each other for their being; nothing stands apart from the cycle of existence. Such interconnectedness means that all beings are bound together in an intricate web of relationships.

Mostly, however, we are ignorant of this basic situation and instead labor under a sense of ourselves as separate, as distinct individuals thrown into the midst of innumerable "others." Invariably, such self-(mis)understanding means that we desire to preserve and protect ourselves. Such fundamental "selfishness," in turn, manifests in actions motivated by hatred, delusion, and greed. According to Buddha, if we "wake up," we will truly understand how things are and *not* act out of blind habit or selfishness. Indeed, our actions will be "free," not born out of neurotic compulsion but marked by a deep compassion for those around us. Attaining *nirvana* can only come from a careful life of good conduct and moral intention (for Buddhists *karma* has more to do with volitional actions rather than mechanical "doings"), as well as meditative training in which one learns to pay attention to the present situation and discern what is actually the case.

A few things are important to keep in mind about Buddhist teachings that will help us in understanding the Buddhist views of death. While the teachings may seem abstract, they come from specific, concrete situations that all human beings can relate to. As such, they do not comprise a systematic philosophy so much as a body of guidelines meant to lead to greater understanding of the world and ourselves. As one Buddhist scholar has noted, "Buddhist teaching is transformation manifesting as information."[2] Buddhists often use the metaphor of the finger pointing to the moon: It is useful to have such pointers, but once we find the moon, we don't need to keep using our fingers to find it.

GENERAL BUDDHIST VIEWS OF DEATH

The pragmatic, nonspeculative focus of the Buddha's central teachings extends to the subject of death. While it may seem morbid to contemporary Westerners (who tend to avoid or deny death), Buddhism faces death head on.

Death is a regular occurrence in any society. Buddhist teachings stress the inherently fragile and impermanent nature of existence and try to promote acceptance and understanding so that we may transcend the suffering that comes with life and its inevitable end. In itself, death is neither inherently good nor inherently bad—it is merely a fact of existence. Siddhartha himself was well acquainted with death: His mother died soon after his birth and, despite his father's best efforts, one of the four sights that prompted him to embark on his religious quest was a corpse.

To this day, Buddhists look to Buddha's own passing as a "model death," and monks often meditate on decaying corpses in order to gain insight into the nature of reality. Overall, Buddhism provides an assortment of skillful methods of acknowledging and working through death, both for the benefit of the deceased as well as for the bereaved. Like most religions, such approaches vary depending on the social and cultural context. In fact, one reason Buddhism was able to spread to so many cultures is that it has had more to say about death and the hereafter than most indigenous traditions.

Perhaps the primary Buddhist teaching about death is that it is inevitable and unpredictable. For most of us, this is hard to face and we try to avoid it at all costs. From a Buddhist perspective, there are three basic responses we can have to the fact of death: rejection, attraction (both of which are motivated by passion), or acceptance (neutral).[3] Most commonly, we reject death and get caught up in a cycle of fear or anger. At times, however, we may be attracted to death and entertain thoughts of suicide or engage in reckless, suicidal behavior.[4] According to Buddhist teachings, a neutral response of acceptance is preferable, as it enables us to live more fully and compassionately.

Moreover, for Buddhists death is intimately tied to birth. Anything that is born will inevitably die. Life is, in this sense, a "perpetual perishing," a complex process of varying durations moving through time. Every moment, thus, is essentially marked by death, and it leads inevitably to another birth, another death, and so on. Buddhists speak of this process as "becoming" (bhava), analyzing it into various stages, each depending upon the others. The Buddha himself dubbed this interdependent network pratitya-samutpada ("conditioned arising"), and it essentially describes the nature of samsaric existence: Every phenomenon we encounter arises and departs in relationship to other phenomena. Thus, samsara is a thoroughly interdependent and interconnected cycle.

As previously noted, the interconnectedness of birth, life, and death was a cornerstone of traditional Indian cosmology. Buddhists often depict the cycle of samsara as a "wheel of becoming" (bhavachakra), illustrating each phase with a scene and placing the entire process in the jaws of Yama, the god of death. Unlike other Indian schools, though, Buddha denies that the beings bound up in samsara are actually "souls" that take on different bodies. For Buddha there is no permanent abiding "self" or "soul." Instead, the Buddha analyzed the human being into a nexus of intertwined processes that change moment by moment.

The most common Buddhist analysis breaks the "person" down into five aggregates (*skandhas*): materiality, raw feelings, perceptions, volitional habits, and conscious awareness. A "person," in this view, is merely a conventional name for the conglomeration of these five aggregates, which themselves are constantly interacting and changing in response to each other and the greater environment. This nexus is propelled along by *karma*, more or less mechanically. The aggregates themselves are temporary, and the grosser material ones are dispersed at biological death. When the requisite supporting conditions (volition, desires, selfish habits—all founded on basic ignorance of reality) are present, rebirth occurs. Rebirth does not require a physical body in the ordinary sense. There is no unified, systematic explanation of the rebirth process in Buddhism, although it appears that consciousness plays a particularly decisive role. Buddhists generally agree, though, that rebirth does not occur in the case of *arhats* (enlightened monks) or *buddhas*. There is no discernible beginning to this cycle and, barring awakening, no true end. Death does not end this cycle but is merely one phase within it.

The decisive feature of the cyclical Buddhist cosmos is the pervasive experience of suffering (*duhkha*). Life in *samsara* means that no being is immune to loss, pain, sadness, bodily degeneration, and death. Note that suffering refers not just to the gross matters of pain, sorrow, and anguish but also to the fact that even joy and happiness are unsatisfactory because they are only temporary and often are rather disappointing. Furthermore, it is important to bear in mind that *duhkha* refers to the typical way we *experience* reality, not necessarily that reality itself. In our radically contingent and impermanent world, all beings inevitably suffer because nothing lasts, and much that occurs is beyond our control.

As the Buddha said in his first sermon, "Now, monks, what is the Noble Truth of suffering? Just this: Birth is suffering, old age is suffering, sickness is suffering, death is suffering. Involvement with what is unpleasant is suffering. Separation from what is pleasant is suffering. Also, not getting what one wants and strives for is suffering."[5] To put it another way, we could say that we suffer because life in *samsara* is a continual series of "mini-deaths." However, according to the Buddha, this suffering is our unenlightened *experience* of existence, not existence in and of itself.

Buddhist teachings also detail various forms or "realms" of rebirth within *samsara*. Most scholars agree that in such matters Hinduism and other religions have heavily influenced Buddhism. Traditionally, Buddhists have recognized six realms of rebirth—humans, heavenly beings (gods), animals, hells, hungry ghosts, and titans (*asuras*, demonic beings). After death one is reborn in one of these realms, depending upon one's karmic inheritance. Buddhists usually consider the first two realms (human and heavenly) as being fortunate, with the other four being unfortunate. All six realms of rebirth, though, lie within *samsara* and are marked by constant change and suffering to varying degrees.

Of particular interest among the realms of rebirth are the various heavens and hells. As is so often the case, there are no uniform schemes of these heavens and hells across Buddhist traditions, but typically existence in these realms is far longer than an ordinary human life. Standard accounts enumerate some eight "hot hells" in which beings are subjected to horrific torture in recompense for their karmic debts, along with sixteen or so "minor hells." There are also several heavenly realms wherein one who has a positive karmic balance may be reborn. Among these are six heavenly realms of desire (*kama*). These include the Tushita Heaven, wherein Maitreya, the Buddha of the next cosmic epoch, and various celestial *Bodhisattvas* ("*buddhas* to be") reside.

There are also the heavenly realms of form and nonform (both of which are beyond desire). Different schools of Buddhism give different numbers of heavenly realms and typically maintain that they are accessible here and now by highly accomplished meditators. Unlike in other religions, however, existence in the Buddhist heavens and hells is still a temporary (albeit long-lasting) state. One is born, lives, and dies in these realms, with death merely marking a transition to a different state. Enlightenment, the attaining of *nirvana*, takes one beyond all aspects of *samsara*, even the most joyous heavenly realms.

For most Buddhists, these realms of rebirth are quite real and not the product of speculation. Indeed, they have been presented as tangible realities by Buddhist teachers going all the way back to the historical Buddha himself, who, it is said, claimed on the night of his enlightenment that he had surveyed the entire universe with his divine vision and perceived all beings everywhere as they were dying out of and being reborn into the many realms of rebirth.

In addition, Buddhists maintain that in this life we can experience these realms in visions, dreams, meditative states, or through memories of previous lives. While secular Westerners may scoff at such "superstitious nonsense," Buddhists traditionally accept them as true. However, while many, perhaps most, Buddhists understand these realms of rebirth as literal places, many Buddhists view them more or less psychologically. In fact, the idea that *samsara* is best understood as a cycle of consciousness (rather than "existence" in the grossest sense) is fully consistent with most canonical texts and is especially common among advanced practitioners of meditation.

COMMON MISUNDERSTANDINGS REGARDING BUDDHISM AND DEATH

Clearly, death is of paramount importance in Buddhism, and the religion has much to say about it. Despite (or perhaps because of) its many

teachings concerning death there are a number of common misunderstandings about the subject and its place in Buddhism. To begin with,
because Buddhist teachings stress suffering and the inevitability of death,
people often conclude that Buddhism itself is a negative, pessimistic religion. While such a conclusion may make sense from a contemporary mid-
dle-class perspective conditioned by a life of comfort, for most people
throughout history the Buddhist assessment would be obviously true. Pre-
modern societies worldwide have typically been plagued by famine, disease, and warfare, with high infant mortality rates and relatively short
life expectancies. Death, disease, and suffering are common in modern
industrialized societies as well, although we prefer to ignore this fact.

As we have already pointed out, contrary to popular belief Buddhism
does *not* teach reincarnation. Rebirth (*punrabhava*, properly translated as
"re-becoming") is not reincarnation in the usual sense, nor does it hinge on
the end of biological functioning. The physical death of a biological orga-
nism (e.g., a "person"), of course, is a real event, but it is only the most
obvious sign of an ongoing process. In actuality, the life of any being is
part of a series of "mini-lives," each conditioned by its predecessors and, in
turn, conditioning the next. Thus, rebirth (along with "re-death") is a continuous, moment-by-moment phenomenon. As the Buddha told his fellow
monks, "When the aggregates arise, decay, and die, O *bhikku*, every
moment you are born, decay, and die."[6] Ordinarily, we are blind to this
fact, but from a Buddhist perspective, we are dying and being reborn at every moment.

Samsara ends when one attains *nirvana*, but this is not the same thing
as death. Certainly one does not have to die to attain *nirvana*; the
Buddha himself spent forty-five years teaching *after* attaining *nirvana*. In
the Buddhist perspective biological death is an event within *samsara*
brought about through various causes and conditions and marked by suffering. *Nirvana* is the absence of suffering and unlike *samsara* is uncondi-
tioned and unchanging. The Buddha repeatedly stressed that *nirvana*
could not be accurately described because language applies only to conditioned things. However, he did use negative terms to hint at what *nirvana*
might be, often referring to it as "deathless."

This did not mean, however, that his physical being was permanent.
Like all compounded things, the "person" of the Buddha was impermanent and subject to decay. According to Buddhist tradition, at the age of
eighty, the Buddha underwent his "extinction," or *parinirvana* ("final *nirvana*"). Technically we can speak of this as the Buddha's "death" (he was
no longer alive, after all), so long as we keep in mind that he was not
dead in the usual sense, i.e., reborn in some other realm. During his lifetime the Buddha declined to answer questions about what happened to a
Buddha after his extinction, stating that such questions were "not conducive to edification."

Although Buddhism teaches acceptance of death rather than rejection of or attraction to it, we can also say that the monastic path involves a type of death, figuratively speaking; a monk or nun is, after all, theoretically "dead" to ordinary worldly pleasures and ways of life. Such a person is also removed from his or her family lineage and thus in a sense "dead" in the strict familial sense. This fact is symbolically underscored by the ritualized nature of the ordination process. In traditional Buddhist societies, this event has intriguing parallels to a funeral service. An ordination ceremony typically entails the postulant leaving home and taking up residence in a monastic community, shedding his/her family name and receiving a new religious name. The novice will also have his/her head (including eyebrows) shaved and will don a monastic robe (according to tradition, the latter were originally made from funeral shrouds). Moreover, some aspects of monastic training entail "mortification of the body" (enduring mental and physical discipline and hardship) as a way of deadening the passions.

Finally, it often comes as a shock to some people to learn how important the dead themselves are in Buddhism, particularly at the popular level. Nowhere do we see this more clearly than when it comes to the role of relics, particularly fragments of the Buddha's actual body. As in many other religions (e.g., Roman Catholicism) in Buddhism relics of sacred figures retain traces of their holy aura and provide a means of attaining a type of spiritual "grace." Relics are usually housed in special memorial structures (burial mounds and/or tombs) and such memorial mounds (usually called *stupas*) are found throughout the Buddhist world.

According to ancient sources, the various relics left after the Buddha's cremation were divided into eight portions, each of which was placed in a special *stupa* erected at a location associated with a major event in the Buddha's life. These sites became major places of worship, and to this day *stupas* housing relics of the Buddha or especially saintly monks and nuns are common destinations for pilgrims seeking to earn "merit" (*punya*, "good karma") as a way to overcome hardship or gain a better rebirth for themselves or their loved ones. This reverence for relics further attests to the fact that in Buddhism death is not the end nor need it be a source of grief. Rather, it should be acknowledged and ultimately transcended.

TAKING LIFE IN BUDDHISM: SOME CONTROVERSIES

One of the hallmarks of the Buddhist path is adherence to the principle of *ahimsa* ("no harming"). Buddhists, both lay and monastic, are enjoined to avoid causing harm to all beings, including themselves. By and large this principle has given Buddhism an overall peaceful air. Naturally, a life of *ahimsa* would preclude the taking of life (i.e., bringing about a being's death), and generally speaking this has been the case. However, Buddhist adherence to *ahimsa* has never been absolute. For instance, contrary to popular belief, not all Buddhists are vegetarian, and even monastics are allowed to eat meat so long as it has not been slaughtered solely for their purposes.

More to the point, according to Buddhist teachings, under certain conditions actually bringing about a death may be permissible, although this is a complex matter that requires making some important and subtle distinctions. For example, manslaughter, the inadvertent causing of another human's death, is by definition unintentional, thus not technically an "action." Therefore, it carries no karmic consequence (although those responsible should demonstrate repentance and take appropriate action to make up for their negligence).

Murder, the intentional taking of a life, is another matter. As a rule, murder is a grave offence and is never permitted for anyone. Yet even here there are some exceptions, most notably in the case of the Buddha himself. For instance, in "The Skill in Means Sutra," a scripture dating perhaps to the first century BCE, the Buddha relates how in a previous life as a sea captain named "Great Compassion," he slew a robber on his vessel who was plotting to murder the other passengers (all devout Buddhist merchants progressing along the spiritual path) and steal their possessions. The Buddha explains that he murdered the man to prevent both the robber from falling into the great hells as a result of his dastardly deed, as well as the merchants, who would have killed the robber themselves as they learned of his plans.[7] The key factor in judging such an extreme action is the intention motivating it; a violent act, even one involving the taking of life, is permissible in rare cases and may, in fact, be laudatory as long as it is motivated by compassion.

Because killing is such a grave action, there are also Buddhist teachings on how to kill. In this regard it is particularly helpful to recall that Siddhartha himself was of the warrior caste and was trained in the arts of war. Buddhist art is also rife with depictions of sacred figures who are heavily armed, often in combat positions. Moreover, there have been various martial arts techniques (e.g., *gongfu*) taught by Buddhist masters throughout history. Generally such training is a means for instilling discipline, concentration, and detachment from various passions. Often, martial arts instructors could create a vivid sense of impending death in their students as a way to bolster their training. Theoretically, the idea behind such practices is that when violence is necessary, one should act quickly and decisively, causing as little pain and suffering as possible. One of the most mysterious and intriguing of all Buddhist killing techniques was the *maha suklaja* ("great white shattering"), an esoteric rite employing a secret *mudra* (hand gesture) and the uttering of a *mantra* (secret spell). Allegedly by performing these actions an adept could activate the intrinsic energy within an opponents' body, quickly leading to unconsciousness and death.[8] Again, however, the violence and suffering are minimized as much as possible.

Not surprisingly, the role of intention is crucial in how Buddhist tradition deals with abortion and euthanasia, both of which seemingly run counter to the practice of *ahimsa*. In general, Buddhists understand both abortion and euthanasia to involve the taking of life (causing a death), and thus such actions are discouraged. Yet even here there is no universal agreement across the board. Several Buddhist texts seem to speak against abortion (as well as infanticide), yet it is practiced in various Buddhist societies. Perhaps the most well-known (and controversial) example of Buddhist treatments of abortion is the contemporary Japanese practice of *mizuko kuyo*, a formal ritual for aborted fetuses (as well as those that have been miscarried or are stillborn) aimed at appeasing the dead and helping it along to a better rebirth as well as assuaging the guilt and sorrow of the mother.[9] As for euthanasia, it may also be permissible under certain circumstances (e.g., terminal illness). Ideally, the act will be done with the person's consent and full awareness when he or she is not under the sway of cravings.

Suicide, the taking of one's own life, is an especially complicated matter in Buddhism. Generally, it is forbidden but again there are exceptions. Once again, the most notable example is the Buddha himself, who, according to tradition, sacrificed himself for others innumerable times in his previous lives. In fact, most Buddhists view sacrificing one's life to save others from harm as bringing great "merit," and devout Buddhists may even vow to make such sacrifices when they are embarking on the *bodhisattva* path. Clearly, suicide can be a sacred act in Buddhism. One of the most famous canonical examples occurs in the *Lotus sutra*, where the Buddha commends one monk for giving his own body in a previous existence as a sacred offering to the Dharma.[10] Several historians have pointed out that this scriptural passage inspired various fervent Buddhists in medieval China and Japan to sacrifice themselves in imitation of this monk. Even more famously, several Vietnamese monks committed suicide by setting themselves on fire during the Vietnam War, an action justified according to Buddhist teachings because it aimed at drawing world attention to the horrendous suffering of people victimized by the conflict.

There are also other examples of exemplary suicide in Buddhist history. Sporadically, for instance, there have been cases of monks who have committed "*samadhi* suicide" by entering rarified meditative states and remaining in them while calmly observing their bodies starve and eventually cease to function. This practice, although exceedingly rare and more often associated with Jain monks, has occurred even in recent years, with the practitioners being held up as models of monastic discipline.[11] There are also examples in Japanese history of "self-mummified Buddhas,"

mountain priests who vowed to be buried alive. Typically large crowds
would gather to watch as the monk was buried (temporarily being kept
alive by a bamboo tube for breathing). The crowd would keep vigil, beat-
ing drums and chanting, until the monk had died. Afterwards, the dead
priests became objects of intense popular worship. In addition, during
Japan's tumultuous medieval period, it was common practice for *samurai*
warriors to engage in rigorous Zen training, often meditating on death as
part of their preparation for battle. *Samurai* also trained to commit *seppuku (harikari)*, a highly ritualized form of suicide, in order to avoid dis-
honor. Such actions, however, were rarely motivated by altruism. Taking
all these examples together, we can say that at times a Buddhist "cult of
death" has arisen, albeit somewhat outside of the mainstream.

TRADITIONAL BUDDHIST APPROACHES TO DEATH

Because of its admonitions to accept death as inevitable, Buddhism
teaches that death must be prepared for. As death approaches, friends and
relatives join to help the dying person have a "good death" and so ease the
transition to the next life. Most of the time in traditional Buddhist communities this will take place in the home, although sometimes the dying
person will be transported to a nearby temple. Usually monks will be
called in and fed on the dying person's behalf and in return the monks will
chant passages from *sutras* or other ritual texts. The ideal death, for a
Buddhist, is to pass on in a calm, even joyful state, recollecting one's blessings and good deeds to ensure the best possible rebirth.

Over the years, Buddhism has developed a number of ways of handling
death, devising special rituals to both aid the deceased and comfort the
bereaved. Funerals are particularly important rites in Buddhism as a way
of reminding people of basic Buddhist truths while guiding those present
through the inevitable grief and shock that death brings. Most Buddhist
funerals involve cremation, reflecting the religion's Indian roots. Generally speaking, the physical body has no real relevance after death. It is
common in Buddhist societies to hold a memorial service in honor of the
deceased shortly after the funeral (usually forty-nine days, the period traditionally thought to exist between a person's lives) and each year on the
anniversary of the person's death. As might be expected, funerals for
monks and nuns differ from those for lay people and often call for special
ritual observances by the entire monastic community.

Most Buddhist death rites revolve around the concept of "merit" and
involve ancestors. Indeed, in most Buddhist countries both of these are
the primary concerns of the laity. Typically, a family will sponsor funerals
and memorial services, hiring monks to officiate in exchange for donations (food, robes, money, property, etc.). The idea is that sponsoring
such a ritual creates merit (spiritual "capital," we might say) that the

living donate to aid in the deceased gaining a good rebirth. In addition, most Buddhist rites feature some way to commemorate the ancestors, either to honor them or placate them, should they be upset. In satisfying the ancestors through such rituals, the living hope to remain in their good graces and enjoy their protection and blessings.

Although death is a natural and inevitable occurrence, in most Buddhist societies it marks a disruption to daily life and brings pollution. Traditional Buddhist funerals include numerous avoidance rites to contain the pollution and minimize its spread. Only certain designated people actually handle the corpse, and they will undergo special purification rites. Usually, the relatives of the deceased (particularly immediate family) are regarded as polluted as well, and traditionally they undergo a period of mourning that also is designed to isolate them from the larger society. In cases where a holy person dies, however, there is no pollution. Popular Buddhist lore is filled with tales of holy people whose corpses did not decay but instead gave off a wondrous perfume. Furthermore, the relics of such people are thought to have magical healing powers, typically becoming the focus of intense veneration once they are enshrined in *stupas*.

TREATMENT OF DEATH IN VARIOUS BRANCHES OF BUDDHISM

In the years after the Buddha's passing, a series of schisms in the *sangha* (Buddhist community) led to the rise of various distinct schools. Most died out but some continued, resulting in the establishment of three major branches: Theravada, Mahayana, and Vajrayana. All three venerate Sakyamuni Buddha and share the same core teachings but are marked by differences in practice, organization, etc. As might be expected, all three branches have somewhat different teachings and practices regarding death.

Theravada

Theravada, the "Teaching of the Elders," is the oldest and most conservative of the three main branches and is, perhaps, closest to the form of Buddhism established by Sakyamuni. Found mainly in Sri Lanka and Southeast Asian countries such as Thailand, Cambodia, and Myanmar (Burma), the sacred scriptures of Theravada are written in Pali, an ancient language related to Sanskrit. Although most Theravada Buddhists are lay people, monks are the key players in the religion. The ideal figure in Theravada is the *arhat*, an elder "wise man" who through diligent practice has attained *nirvana*.

Most teachings and practices concerning death in Theravada are carryovers from the earliest forms of Buddhism. Among these, funerary observances are of central importance. In Theravada, funerals often have a festive atmosphere, except in extraordinary circumstances, and grief is rarely displayed. As in all religions, Theravada funerals both honor the deceased and mourn their passing while also comforting those left behind, assuring them of their continued survival. Thus, funerals both commemorate the dead and celebrate the living.

A typical Theravadin funeral takes place in the home or (rarely) at a nearby temple. The family makes the basic preparations, providing candles, flowers, a bowl for cleansing the body, and an image of the Buddha. The body is washed (symbolizing the cleansing necessary for the deceased's consciousness to ascend to heaven) after which the hands will be clasped together over the chest and bound three times by a thread symbolizing passion, anger, and ignorance—the "three poisons" binding us to *samsara*. Later these bonds will be removed to represent the final release (*nirvana*) to which all good Buddhists aspire.

In keeping with the norms of early Buddhism, most Theravada funerals and memorial services involve sharing "merit" with the deceased. This is typically done by pouring water into a bowl until it overflows while monks chant verses stating that, just as water flows downward, so may the "merit" being offered reach the departed. Just as with other forms of Buddhism, so, too, do Theravadins believe that this merit will help the deceased in his or her next life. However, in Theravada the official view is that the deceased goes on to an immediate rebirth rather than lingering in an intermediate state between lives. The body is then placed in a wooden coffin and taken in procession to a nearby cremation ground, although several days may elapse before the actual cremation ceremony, which marks the finale of the funeral. Local monks will chant passages from the *Abhidharma* ("higher teachings," the section of the Buddhist canon devoted to metaphysical topics) while a senior monk delivers a sermon stressing impermanence and the inevitability of death. A typical funeral sermon will include something along the following lines:

Death is a common event that will come to everyone without exception. Nobody can live forever, but everybody must die sooner or later.... The only things left by a dead person are his good deeds, which we can remember.... Everybody must remember that we all have to die, not only the person whose funeral we are attending today.

Before death comes, we must prepare ourselves for it. The Lord Buddha did not cry when death was approaching because he knew the meaning of death. We cry when we see death because we do not have the knowledge of a Buddha.[12]

During the cremation itself, monks will lead those assembled in prayers declaring forgiveness for the deceased and asking for the same on behalf of those left behind.

One of the most important functions of funerals in traditional Theravadin society is to afford protection from the spirits of the dead. This aspect of Buddhism is often overlooked in academic discussions or dismissed as "superstition." Yet it is vital at the popular level and reveals much about basic conceptions of death and the afterlife. Spirits of people who have died violently or unexpectedly (e.g., by accident) are particularly dangerous, prone to causing all sorts of misfortune or illness, and so must be propitiated or kept at bay. To this end, an entire collection of sacred chants (*parittas,* lit. "protections") have been compiled over the centuries that are still widely used in Theravada countries (*dharanis,* sacred "spells," are the Mahayana counterparts). Monks will chant *parittas* at almost all major ceremonies to secure blessings or ward off evil. The idea, however, is not to harm the spirits but to generate loving-kindness from all those assembled and then to donate such positive influences to any malignant forces present. Often *parittas* will be integrated into rituals commemorating departed ancestors, which are a staple in the Theravadin liturgical year.

Mahayana

The Mahayana ("Great Vehicle") branch of Buddhism arose near the beginning of the Common Era as a critical response to certain forms of Buddhism that had become increasingly focused on arcane scholastic pursuits rather than spreading the teachings of Sakyamuni to ordinary people. Concentrated mainly in East Asia (China, Korea, Japan) as well as Vietnam, Mahayana is considered to be more liberal and inclusive of the laity than Theravada, affording more room for popular devotion and emphasizing compassion for others. Mahayana teachings downplay the attaining of *nirvana* as the goal of spiritual striving, speaking instead of becoming enlightened, that is, achieving a mystical wisdom (*prajna*) that cuts through dualities. The spiritual ideal in Mahayana is the *bodhisattva* (lit. "wisdom being"), one who aspires to become Buddha and who, out of compassion, vows to aid *all* sentient beings to attain enlightenment, even if it takes eons.

In Mahayana we see an increasingly transcendent view of Buddha. Rather than a being who taught the way to overcome suffering and whose life serves as a model for us to follow, in Mahayana the notion of Buddha evolved over time, gradually becoming a glorious deity who can manifest an earthly body where and when needed, and yet, in essence, remains the personification of the True Cosmic Reality. In this transcendent sense, Buddha is truly deathless, yet his earthly manifestations (e.g., Sakyamuni Buddha) do die. According to Mahayana teachings, this eternal Buddha uses "expedient means," provisional teachings pitched to different audiences, to help sentient beings overcome their particular forms of ignorance. By having recourse to the notion of "expedient means," Mahayana Buddhists have been able to reconcile seemingly contradictory teachings, creating systems of doctrine that go far beyond the original Dharma of Sakyamuni.

Although the deified Buddha is the focus of great devotion, many followers of Mahayana have special reverence for the various *bodhisattvas*. These compassionate "Buddhas-to-be," who aid others (similar to the saints of Christianity), play a large role at the popular level, lending a decided air of "grace" to this form of Buddhism. *Bodhisattvas* take specific vows dedicating themselves to the welfare of all sentient beings. The path of a *bodhisattva* is another example of how Buddhist tradition provides a means of accepting and transcending death, as it essentially allows one to take control over one's direction within *samsara*; it is said that the *bodhisattva* way stretches across many lifetimes and that the sacred vows propel one through various rebirths. Veneration of particular high-level *bodhisattvas* such as Maitreya (the Buddha of the next cosmic epoch) and Avalokiteshvara became very big in Mahayana circles, and popular lore is filled with stories of these god-like beings manifesting in different forms to save people from injury, illness, attack, and even death.

No *bodhisattva*, though, is as associated with death as Ksitigarbha, the "one who encompasses the Earth." Known as Dizang ("Earth Store") in Chinese and Jizo in Japanese, Ksitigarbha vowed to be reborn in all the hells until no beings are there, thus he is sometimes called the "*Bodhisattva* of Hell beings." Closely associated with Yama, the Indian god of death, Ksitigarbha is continually reborn in the hells where he preaches Dharma and ushers beings into better lives. Renowned for his exceptional character, Ksitigarbha is extraordinarily popular in East Asia as a guide for those wandering through *samsara*. With his pilgrim's staff he guards travelers by land, aids women in labor, and is the special guardian of young children. In his Japanese form of Jizo, he plays a central role in rituals of *mizo kuyo*.

Practitioners of Mahayana are actively encouraged to take *bodhisattva* vows and dedicate themselves to following the *bodhisattva* path. Generally the motivation for such actions is feelings of compassion for other beings (often because of their sufferings and the prospect of their deaths) or faithful dedication to the Buddha, or even as a way of honoring departed loved ones. Yet one may also take *bodhisattva* vows out of fear of death itself. Some texts advise aspiring *bodhisattvas* to "think of death and the inevitable retribution after death. Death and dissolution are everywhere around us.... All happiness ends in sorrow, and life ends in death.... the fierce and irresistible foe of all living beings. Realising [sic] the peril of death and suffering after death, a wise man should feel fear and trepidation (*samvega*) and resolve to become a *bodhisattva*."[13] Regardless of the motive, vowing to become a *bodhisattva* is highly meritorious and commonly it is marked by an official ceremony in which the *bodhisattva* dedicates the merit accrued to his or her deceased family members. Once again, we clearly see here the deep connection between spiritual striving and death in Buddhism.

As noted above, Mahayana arose near the beginning of the Common Era and spread widely as Buddhism entered areas outside of India, leading to the formation of various popular school and sects. Among the most interesting Mahayana schools, particularly when it comes to death, are Chan (in Japanese, Zen), the great meditation school, and Pure Land. Although we will turn to the former later in this chapter, it is the latter that has most influenced popular views and practices surrounding death.

Pure Land Buddhism is essentially a salvation faith, one that focuses on devotion to the Celestial Buddha Amitabha, the Buddha of Infinite Light and Life. According to legend, while still a *bodhisattva* he vowed to establish a Paradise where all those who had faith in him would be reborn after death. This Buddhist Pure Land closely resembles popular Christian views of "Heaven," and likely derived from early (pre?) Buddhist ideas concerning the heavenly realms, wherein those with good karmic inheritances would be reborn. Pure Land *sutras* give graphic descriptions of this heavenly realm, speaking of it as a pleasant and beautiful place, devoid of all pain and suffering. The Pure Land is adorned with precious gems, the air is filled with wondrous music and is pervaded by perfumes, and is so beauteous that no one there can entertain evil or hellish thoughts. However, unlike the Christian Heaven, Amitabha's Pure Land is only a temporary abode. It was established as a place for the faithful to practice Buddhism as it was meant to be practiced and from there to go on to attain *nirvana*.

Although it began in India, Pure Land proved very popular in Central Asia and gained many adherents when Buddhism went to China, Korea, and Japan. To this day, most Buddhists in the world follow some form of Pure Land and even those who do not formally belong to the Pure Land school have been influenced by Pure Land teachings and practices. Pure Land has been so influential throughout East Asia that it is common for almost all Buddhists to adopt some of its rites concerning death. For example, in many Buddhist households where someone is nearing death, the dying person may hold a string attached to the hands of an image of Amitabha Buddha. This not only comforts the dying person and the assembled family members, it reminds them of Amitabha's promise that they will be reborn in his Pure Land.

There are several other common practices concerning the dead in Mahayana. For example, many followers of Mahayana make special donations in honor of the deceased and may have monks perform rites for the dead a number of times during the forty-nine-day between-life period. Monks will repeatedly chant the name of the Buddha or certain *sutras* and then transfer the "merit" from such services to the deceased. Monks also make special requests on behalf of the living that heavenly *bodhisattvas* and Buddhas remember the departed with compassion and aid in transferring any "merit" given by relatives on his or her behalf.

Historians generally agree that a major reason that Mahayana became so ingrained in East Asian societies had to do with the centrality of ancestor cults. Since prehistoric times veneration of clan ancestors has been a prominent feature of East Asian societies, and Buddhism, with its elaborate body of teachings and practices concerning death and the afterlife, seems a natural "fit" for such cultures. Certainly Buddhist elements appeared rather quickly in ancestral rituals once Buddhism entered East Asia, and the association between Buddhism and the dead is so strong that today some Buddhists fear their faith is being reduced to "funeral Buddhism."

One of the key functions of ancestral cults is to provide a ritualized transition whereby the recently deceased family member can become a venerated ancestor. Typically, this means that the dead are assimilated into the ancestors over stages. We can easily see this when we look at the example of Japan. When a family member dies, the corpse is cremated in traditional Buddhist fashion, and the ashes are buried in the family plot in a nearby cemetery. At this point the officiating priest will conduct a posthumous naming ceremony wherein the deceased receives a new name, which the priest inscribes on a wooden tablet. In popular belief, by writing the name of the deceased, the priest actually installs the spirit in the tablet itself, where it will linger for some time. The tablet is then placed in the domestic altar (*butusudan*), usually located in the main room of the house, marking the lingering presence of the spirit among the living. The tablet then becomes the focus of various memorial rites for a specified time (traditionally the forty-nine-day period between rebirths, although it may be a year or more). At the end of this period, there is a special service during which the tablet is burned (a symbolic "second cremation"), marking the final departure of the deceased spirit and his/her transformation to official ancestor status. Over time (two to three generations on average) the individual deceased are gradually incorporated into the group of anonymous ancestors. As previously noted, the rites of the ancestral cult are a central part of East Asian culture even today, and they remain one of the primary examples of Mahayana influence. It is also among East Asian Mahayana Buddhists that we find the most elaborate festivals in honor of the dead, as we shall see.

Vajrayana

Vajrayana, the "Diamond/Thunderbolt Vehicle," is the most recent of the three major branches of Buddhism. As the most ritually oriented form of Buddhism, Vajrayana has a mysterious, even magical air about it, differing quite a bit from the simple way of awakening originally taught by Sakyamuni. It grew out of Mahayana and essentially accepts basic

Mahayana teachings and, like Theravada as well, aims at awakening; however, it places more emphasis on attaining and making use of spiritual power by harnessing the passions of anger, lust, etc. In a sense, the Vajrayana path is a spiritual way of "fighting fire with fire." Thus, Vajrayana involves potentially dangerous practices that promise great power if done correctly.

Because of its dangerous practices, Vajrayana tends to be rather secret. Many of its rites are based on *tantras* (cryptic ritual texts); hence this branch of Buddhism is sometimes called "Tantric Buddhism." The *tantras* are deeply mysterious, and require extensive oral explanations by a guru ("lama" in Tibetan).

Like Mahayana, Vajrayana includes lots of deities (*buddhas, bodhisattvas*, various other spirit beings), who are here often depicted in fierce and/or highly erotic fashion. Vajrayana practitioners typically make use of *mantras* (magic verbal formulas), *mudras* (special gestures), and *mandalas* (elaborate diagrams of spiritual universe) in rituals and complex visualizations, often "joining" with the particular *bodhisattva*/deity who has been summoned for a specific ritual. The ideal Vajrayana figure is the *siddha*, an adept who gains spiritual power through ritual performance and uses his powers to aid others. Today, Vajrayana is found mainly in the Himalayan region (Nepal, Bhutan, Tibet, and among exiled Tibetans living in India) but is also prominent in Mongolia and certain places in Japan, as well as in various places in the West.

Vajrayana is sometimes called "Tibetan Buddhism" because it has long dominated the vicinity of Tibet, where it first arrived from India in the eighth century. Scholars generally agree that upon arriving in Tibet, Buddhism mixed freely with the indigenous shamanistic religion of Bon, which, like many indigenous religions, was very concerned with contacting spirit realms. Yet there is no doubt that Vajrayana is *Buddhist*, and it shares similar attitudes towards death that we see in other forms of Buddhism. Indeed, an old Tibetan proverb states that one who does not remember the inevitability of death is like a queen—someone who maintains an outer image of poise and composure while inwardly trembling with innumerable secret desires and fears.

One of the most famous tales in Vajrayana lore is the saga of the legendary wizard Milarepa (1040–1123), a story which, like most folk tales, is replete with violent death. In his youth, Milarepa slays many people through black magic in order to avenge the abuse he and his mother received earlier. However, the most famous scene in the story relates Milarepa's personal confrontation with death in the form of his mother's corpse lying forgotten in the ruins of their former house. This event, echoing as it does the story of the historical Buddha, becomes the catalyst for Milarepa's own spiritual quest. In his "autobiography" (a highly fictionalized retelling compiled long after the great *siddha*'s lifetime), Milarepa himself relates:

The ruins of the hearth mingling with dirt formed a heap where weeds grew and flourished. There were many bleached and crumbled bones. I realized that these were the bones of my mother. At the memory of her I choked with emotion and, overcome with grief, I nearly fainted.... I seated myself upon my mother's bones and meditated with a pure awareness without being distracted even for a moment in body, speech, or mind. I saw the possibility of liberating my father and mother from the suffering of the cycle of birth and death.[14]

Milarepa's story and this scene in particular underscores for many Tibetan Buddhists the necessity of facing death and coming to terms with the sorrow and loss it entails.

Tibetan Buddhism has drawn heavily on the shamanic aspects of Bon when it comes to the handling of death. Shamans, "medicine men" who serve as healers and ritual specialists among indigenous peoples the world over, commonly aid the deceased in passing over to the spirit world. The influence of such shamanic activity is particularly strong in traditions involving the legendary work entitled "Liberation through Hearing in the Bardo" (*Bardo Thol Dro*, commonly translated as *The Tibetan Book of the Dead*). This work constitutes a veritable "science of death," detailing the various stages of the *bardo*, the forty-nine-day period between lives. In Vajrayana tradition, a dying person has the *Bardo Thol Dro* read to him (or, in the wake of his funeral, before a picture of the deceased) in order to guide him through the *bardo*. Such readings are intended to help the deceased overcome attachments to his body or family and gain further insight into reality or provide clarity through the series of visions the deceased is thought to experience based upon his *karma*.

According to the *Bardo Thol Dro*, during the *bardo* the deceased faces a bewildering array of apparitions (including ghosts, demons, and gods) and may also glimpse a marvelous, pure light, heralding enlightenment itself. Particularly advanced yogins may become enlightened during this stage, essentially realizing that the visions they see are manifestations of their own minds, to be accepted and joined with rather than rejected. However, more often than not, the deceased will recoil in fear and confusion, and, desperate for a new body, be drawn to a new rebirth. It is possible, however, that through insight gained in previous lives or through the aid of others, the deceased can progress along the *bodhisattva* path or attain rebirth in a Pure Land.

Funerals in areas where Vajrayana predominates are similar to those in other Buddhist societies albeit with some intriguing features that reflect indigenous Himalayan beliefs. After death, the corpse is usually cremated but it may be dismembered and fed to vultures so that they might benefit. The latter rite (often referred to as "sky burial") is particularly arresting, having distinct parallels to funerary rites among followers of Zoroastrianism, the ancient religion of Persia, and various Native American peoples. A "sky burial" is so sacred that it requires a specially trained yogi (*tomden*) and cannot be performed before outsiders. The *tomden* will engage in special rituals involving secret prayers and *mantras* before dismembering the corpse and strewing the pieces on a stone platform encircled by prayer flags. This rite is really a type of sacrifice in which the flesh of the deceased is offered to benefit other beings, following the example of Sakyamuni Buddha in his previous lives. The recipients, usually vultures, are often regarded as manifestations of *dakinis*, fierce female spirits who serve as "Dharma protectors."

MEDITATIONS ON DEATH

In one of Plato's dialogues, the Greek philosopher Socrates speaks of the life of a philosopher as "training for death," and that could certainly also be said of Buddhist monks. As we have already noted, renouncing lay life and joining the monastic order is a sort of "social death" in Buddhism that hearkens back to the very earliest stage of the religion. In ancient India, renouncing one's home for the life of a wandering ascetic was tantamount to embracing death in a very real sense. The dangers of the world outside of the protecting confines of home and hearth were all too real in the form of predators (wild beasts and bandits), starvation, illness, and the buffeting of the elements themselves. Early Buddhist practices seem to have emphasized this fact, requiring monks to clothe themselves in robes stitched together from the shrouds of corpses and even to congregate at cremation grounds. To this day in Southeast Asia, forest monasteries are often established near cemeteries to ensure the quiet and seclusion necessary for monastic training.

From the start, the Buddha deemed meditation as essential for his monastic followers, and he outlined various practices of mental discipline. Some of the most potent involved the "cultivation of the foul" (*asubha-vana*), which is the close contemplation of corpses in varying states of decay. These quickly proved to be very effective at counterbalancing the sensual (especially sexual) desires that so often plague renunciates; instilling aversion can be quite useful, even necessary, on the path to liberation. Some canonical texts outline as many as ten categories of corpses, including bodies that are newly dead (showing little sign of decay), bloated, "gnawed" (by scavengers), and "bleeding" (smeared with blood), ending up with the bleached bones of a skeleton.

Such practices can have powerful albeit often unintended effects. One story in the *Samyutta Nikaya* relates that after teaching this form of meditation, the Buddha withdrew for a few weeks of solitude. Upon returning, the Buddha found that membership in the *sangha* had shrunk considerably during his absence, and so he inquired as to the reason. Ananda, the Buddha's devoted attendant, explained that many monks who had mastered the meditation became so disgusted with their *own* bodies that they committed suicide! At once, the rather chastened Buddha summoned his remaining followers and taught them how to meditate on the breath, a somewhat less drastic method for realizing the constantly changing nature of existence. From then on, meditating on decaying corpses became optional.[15]

Theravada still maintains such practices in the form of "corpse meditations" that monks will engage in periodically. The famous *Vissudhimagga* ("Path of Purification"), a meditation manual compiled by the fifth-century monk Buddhaghosa, describes in meticulous (and lurid) detail the various categories of corpses suitable for meditation. A good example is this description: "There is a *worm-infested* corpse when at the end of two or three days a mass of maggots oozes out from the corpse's nine orifices, and the mass like a heap of paddy or boiled rice as big as the body, whether the body is that of a dog, a jackal, a human being, an ox, a buffalo, an elephant, a horse, a python, or what you will."[16]

Some scholars have pointed to a rather unwholesome fascination with the macabre here, even if such extreme austerities are not central to Buddhist training. In fact, these practices are somewhat marginal, reserved only for the most ascetically inclined members of the *sangha*. Interestingly, some monks opt for a more contemporary version of this practice by observing autopsies.

Sometimes, Theravadin monasteries will house other graphic reminders of death. In his account of his time at a Wat (monastery) in Thailand, Tim Ward describes how the skeleton of a suicide was prominently displayed in a case next to a central altar, upon which pride of place was afforded a photograph of the corpse of a monk who had committed "*samadhi* suicide." In addition to the obvious attempt at instilling aversion to the pleasures of the flesh, the rationale here seems to be that such vivid reminders of *duhkha* as well as to the inevitable end of life will spur members of the community to greater attention in their spiritual practice. A similar purpose seems to be served in other branches of Buddhism by the presence of graveyards and ancestral halls (for deceased abbots) on monastery grounds.

Vajrayana has some intriguing death meditations as well. Many of these rely on powerful visualizations that harness the mind's abilities to picture all manner of horrors rather than actual corpses. The intention, however, is the same: to force us to deal with that which we normally seek to avoid. As with the various apparitions detailed in the *Bardo Thol Dro*, these visualization exercises allow us to confront the negative aspects of our own *psyches*. Some of these visualization practices may, for example, entail staring into a mirror and seeing one's reflection grow old, become a corpse, and eventually wither away.[17]

BUDDHIST FESTIVALS COMMEMORATING THE DEAD

Like other religions, Buddhism marks time with a number of holidays and festivals. These observances are usually happy events, occasions for most people to "cut loose" and enjoy themselves. Ironically, however, many of these festivals are associated with death, either commemorating the death of the Buddha or other holy figures, ancestors, and others who have passed on. Still, considering the importance that Buddhism places on accepting death, the fact that many Buddhist festivals commemorate the dead is not that surprising. Here are a few such festivals, and though there are many others, these show focus squarely on death in Buddhist tradition.

Vesak/Nirvana Day

Primarily a Theravadin festival, Vesak comes when the full moon enters the constellation of Taurus, usually during the month of May. It is the largest religious festival in Southeast Asia, commemorating as it does the Buddha's entire life story (birth, enlightenment, teaching career, and final passing), and typically lasts several days. Despite its celebratory nature, however, the themes of death and decay pervade all aspects of Vesak. In this the holiday clearly demonstrates the inextricable links between the Buddha's life, teachings, and passing.

During Vesak, devotees flock to temples, offering flowers, candles and incense to the Buddha images. These offerings are particularly significant, as the wilting of the flowers and the burning out of the candles and incense are vivid reminders of the continual presence of decay and destruction. During Vesak, lay Buddhists take extra care to refrain from all types of killing as well. Finally, Vesak is often marked by the ritual cleansing of temples' sacred relics.

Unlike Theravada, Mahayana marks the Buddha's birth, enlightenment and death with three separate festivals. The Mahayana observance of the Buddha's passing is known as Nirvana Day. It is generally observed on February 15 and commemorates the occasion of the Buddha's final entry into *nirvana* and his earthly death. According to traditional accounts, after wandering the Ganges region for some forty-five years, preaching the Dharma and acquiring thousands of followers, the Buddha succumbed to illness (perhaps dysentery or food poisoning). After calmly addressing the *sangha* one last time during which he reminded them that all things were impermanent and that they should continue to follow the path with great diligence, he passed out of existence. His remains were cremated, and the relics were distributed across the region, eventually being enshrined in *stupas* that became important sites of pilgrimage.

Like Vesak, Nirvana Day is a festive occasion. Although it marks the Buddha's passing from this world, it is not a time of sadness but a reminder of the Buddha's continuing presence among his followers. Typically, Nirvana Day is a time when devout Buddhists flock to temples and shrines to make offerings and receive further religious instruction. Kushingara, the traditional site of the Buddha's decease, becomes a major destination for pilgrims on this day, as do other *stupas* throughout the Buddhist world.

"Festival of the Hungry Ghosts"

Probably the most widely observed Mahayana festival is the "Festival of Hungry Ghosts." Known in Sanskrit as *Ullambana*, it has become such a large part of East Asian society that it is even celebrated by many non-Buddhists as a demonstration of devotion to their ancestors. During this time it is thought that the ancestors are reborn in this world as "ghosts" to wander the earth as potential sources of danger and misfortune. Monks and nuns will typically transfer the "merit" they have accrued from observing their summer retreats, put out food, and chant *sutras* to help the spirits attain a better rebirth. Laity tends to sponsor these rites and may also participate by burning paper boats or lanterns to help "ferry" the ghosts to a better world, similar to the Thai festival of Loi Krathong. Often, celebrants perform rituals before two altars: one for offerings to feed the ancestral spirits and one for offerings to feed "hungry ghosts," spirits of people who died in violent or untimely fashion or who do not receive homage from their descendents. There are many parallels between the "Festival of the Hungry Ghosts" and Halloween as well as the "Day of the Dead" (*Dia de Los Muertos*) observances in Mexico and throughout Latin America.

There are several stories explaining the origins of the "Festival of the Hungry Ghosts." The most famous centers on Mulian, a disciple of the Buddha and a previous incarnation of the *bodhisattva*, Ksitagarbha. After his mother died, Mulian was distressed to discover that she had been reborn in one of the "hell realms" or, in some versions of the story, as a "hungry ghost," condemned to wander the world without rest. Mulian consulted the Buddha who, gratified at the young monk's appropriate feelings, directed him to perform the rituals of "merit-transfer," so that his mother would attain a better rebirth. Because of its strong familial themes, this story and its accompanying festival quickly caught on in China and other areas of East Asia.

In Japan, *Ullambana* is known as *Obon*, and is celebrated in either July or August, depending on the region.[18] Lasting from the 13th to the 15th, this is a time when most Japanese return to the home in which they grew up. Graves are tended, often being sprinkled with water by each family member, and offerings of flowers, herbs, and incense are placed on the ancestral altar. Candles are lit to welcome the ancestral spirits home, and a Buddhist priest may be invited to chant a *sutra* before the altar. In the evenings most temples put on lavish performances of dances and plays. The climax of *Obon* comes on the evening of the 15th when bonfires are lit to usher the spirits back to their realm. Festivities in Kyoto are especially colorful, with crowds of people dressing in traditional *kimonos* and flocking to local rivers and parks for evening picnics. At nightfall, large bonfires in the shape of Japanese letters light up the surrounding mountainsides.

On August 15, at the conclusion of *Obon,* there is a special observance among Japanese who live in Hawaii. Held in Honolulu, this "Floating Lantern Ceremony" commemorates the end of World War II. In many respects this is an American adaptation of traditional Japanese observances in that small lanterns are lit and floated on rivers and streams. They are said to symbolize the spirits of the deceased as they cross the river of existence.

"Other Shore" (*Ohigan*)

Primarily a Japanese observance, *Ohigan* is celebrated twice yearly around the spring and autumn equinoxes. The term means "other shore," and refers to the common belief in Buddhism that the spirits of the dead reach *nirvana* by crossing the river of existence. The idea of "crossing over" also serves as a metaphor for the spiritual move from suffering to Enlightenment. *Ohigan* is a day for remembering the dead, particularly ancestors. Families celebrate by visiting graves, cleaning and decorating them, and reciting prayers and *sutras*. Most likely it is a Buddhist adaptation of ancient ancestral rites as it bears a strong resemblance to annual ancestral observances in Chinese culture, such as "Clear and Bright Festival" (*qing ming*), which is also held during the third lunar month near the spring equinox.

ZEN VIEWS OF DEATH

Chan/Zen Buddhism includes some of the most striking teachings and practices concerning death. Known for stressing the intense practice of meditation in order to attain a "sudden realization," Zen traces itself through a series of legendary masters to the historical Buddha himself. Even more so than other forms of Buddhism, Zen's decidedly *this* worldly focus challenges our usual views of life and death. Indeed, Zen rhetoric often seems to make death beside the point. One Zen story relates how a student asked his master what happens after death. The master gruffly replied, "How should I know?" Taken aback, the student stammered, "But ... but ... but you're a Zen master!" To this, his master retorted, "Yes, but I'm a *live* Zen master, not a *dead* one!"

In addition, Zen also stresses the "deathless" aspects of realization; when we awaken to our true identity as "one" with all things, we realize that we do not really die.

Yet this by no means fully covers how Zen handles death. Much traditional Zen monastic training entails learning to accept that death is an ever-present specter throughout life. Often, masters use all sorts of techniques to remind their students of this fact. Morinaga Soko, a contemporary Zen master, provides a good example from his own training. As he was being sent off for a period of intensive meditation, his master gave him three one-thousand-yen notes. Morinaga protested that he had some spending money left to him by his father, only to be informed that this was "*nirvana* money." With a stern face, the master then explained, "You're heading out now for the training hall where you will lay down your life. If fortune goes against you, you'll fall out and die by the wayside during training. So that you don't become a burden to anybody, this money is for the disposal of your body."[19] Such constant admonitions about the necessity of facing death on a personal level are one of the reasons why Zen practice became such a large component of *samurai* training during the Middle Ages.

Death is also present in a more prosaic sense in Zen. Although Zen has an irreverent reputation, monastic training is a highly ritualized affair. Also, as in other forms of East Asian Buddhism, much of Zen "ministry" involves presiding over funerals and, throughout the centuries, most schools of Zen have developed an elaborate body of funerary rituals. Moreover, contrary to common stereotypes, Zen places great importance on the veneration of deceased patriarchs, often incorporating the worship of relics into the regular monastic regimen. A good example is the cult surrounding the "mummy" of Huineng (638–713), the legendary "Sixth Patriarch." According to tradition, after his death Huineng's corpse became a source of miraculous power, and to this day it still holds a place of honor in his home monastery in Southern China.

It is important, however, to understand that much Zen discussion of death is more metaphorical than literal. Thus, when Zen texts speak of the "Great Death," they are typically speaking symbolically of the death of the ego, our sense of "self" as a separate individual being. From a Zen standpoint, it is this notion of a distinct "I," along with its concomitant fears and attachments, that is the source of our suffering. To that end, Zen masters instruct their students "to die while alive," so that they might truly live.

One of the most intriguing Zen practices is the tradition of masters composing poems as they sensed the approach of death. The idea was to provide a model of detachment and acceptance, much like that of the historical Buddha at the point of his *parinirvana*. Zen literature is filled with such "death poems," many of which display a haunting beauty. One example comes from Shaiku Sho'on, a Zen warrior forced to commit *seppuku* (ritual suicide) out of loyalty to his lord. Before taking up the knife he wrote,

The sharp-edged sword, unsheathed,
cuts through the void—
Within the raging fire
A cool wind blows.[20]

These lines, like so much of Japanese poetry, show a mixture of sorrow and joy at the fleeting experience of life. Here Sho'on expresses the longing for one clear, sharp insight to cut through suffering and thus bring peace. Yet such focus on the moment of death is somewhat misleading, for Zen, like all Buddhism, stresses that in its very arising *every moment* shares in death. As Matsuo Basho, the great *haiku* master, incisively notes, "Each moment is all being, is the entire world. Reflect now on whether any world or any being is left out of the present moment."[21]

CONCLUSION: ISSUES FOR CONSIDERATION

It may seem that all of this focus on funerals and death gives Buddhism a gloomy demeanor, and, as already suggested, some Japanese Buddhists, for instance, are concerned about the religion being reduced to "Funeral Buddhism" (*shoshiki bukkyo*) as their society becomes increasingly secularized. Nonetheless, facing death is an important part of Buddhism. After all, the Buddha taught that one overcomes suffering by understanding and acceptance rather than avoidance. By and large, cultures where Buddhism has flourished are resigned to death, regarding it as the basic accompaniment to life. As we have seen, funeral rituals are a regular part of the Buddhist life cycle. Moreover, because life is a constant process of change, grief, too, as part of life, shall ultimately pass. Buddhist teachings and practices, by promoting depth of understanding, attest to one of life's great paradoxes: that joy can be found even in the midst of suffering.

Certainly Buddhism from its inception has insisted that death must be accepted rather than denied or ignored. Such acceptance, though, should not be confused with a morbid, necrophiliac curiosity (as, for example, in the growing popularity of the Website "MyDeathSpace.com"). In this, perhaps, Buddhism is no different from other major world religions. Moreover, like other religions, Buddhism offers a host of ritual practices for handling death, and its teachings offer hope and consolation for both the deceased and the bereaved. At the very least, then, Buddhism would seem to be a source of great psychological and sociological wisdom when it comes to dealing with our inevitable mortality.

Yet Buddhism offers more than this. In its focus on death, Buddhism paradoxically prompts us to ask ourselves whether we are really living. Since death is inevitable and could happen at any moment, life is precious. In truth, it is in *this* moment and this moment alone that we live, and we should embrace it here and now in all its awful glory.

In addition, Buddhism reminds us that we really *do* exist beyond this life; whatever our fate, our actions clearly live on. Even more importantly, our connections to others (friends, family, and foe alike) remain despite death, binding us to each other even in the midst of continuous change. One contemporary Pure Land priest observes, "Humanity is one single body, one living Buddha body.... My life and yours are completely autonomous. Yet we each exist only in total resonance with all other beings. We all celebrate the birth of a child. Likewise we all mourn the passing of a child. We rejoice and grieve as one living body."[22]

Most of all, Buddhist teachings on death and dying can awaken within us a profound compassion for ourselves and for our fellow suffering beings. Nowhere is this better illustrated than in the story of Kisa Gotami, a poor wife whose only son dies while still a child.[23] Blinded by grief, she clings to his body, begging everyone she meets to give her medicine for her son. Finally, a wise man directs her to the Buddha. When she comes into his presence, she repeats her plea. Understanding her situation at a glance, the Buddha assigns her a task before he gives her the medicine: she is to make the rounds throughout a nearby city, asking for mustard seeds from any house where no one has died.

Buoyed by hope, she rushes to the city and begins knocking on doors. Unfortunately, at each house she finds the same thing: all have had someone in the household die. At this point she realizes the Buddha's lesson and leaves the city. Coming to the burning ground, she says to her dead boy, "Dear little son, I thought that you alone had been overtaken by this thing which men call death. But you are not the only one death has overtaken. This is a law common to all mankind."[24] She then lays his body down where it will be properly taken care of and returns to the Buddha, who accepts her into his order.

Not everyone, of course, has a monastic vocation nor is everyone inclined to follow the Buddhist path. But we can still take to heart some of its teachings—teachings offered from the Buddha himself to help us live more mindfully and compassionately.

NOTES

1. For a detailed history of the field of comparative religions see Eric J. Sharpe, *Comparative Religion: A History* (La Salle: Open Court, 1987).

2. Roger J. Corless, *The Vision of the Buddha: The Space Under the Tree* (New York: Paragon House, 1989), 217.

3. Note that this Buddhist analysis holds for any aspect of existence; typically we are repulsed, attracted, or neutral toward any and all stimuli.

4. There is a strong parallel between the Buddhist analysis of our typical responses to death and Sigmund Freud's discussions of *eros* (the life instinct) and

thanatos (the death instinct), both of which are the source of much subconscious conflict.

5. Quoted in John S. Strong, *The Experience of Buddhism: Sources and Interpretations*, 3rd ed. (Belmont, CA: Thomson Wadsworth, 2002), 43.

6. Quoted in Walpola Rahula, *What the Buddha Taught*, revised edition (New York: Grove Press, 1974), 33. The term *bhikku* is Pali for "monk."

7. Mark Tatz, trans., *The Skill in Means (Upayakausalya) Sutra* (Deli: Motilal Barsidass, 1994), 73–74.

8. Shifu Nagaboshi Tomio, *The Bodhisattva Warriors* (York Beach, ME: Samuel Weiser, 1994), 269.

9. See William R. LaFleur, *Liquid Life: Abortion and Buddhism in Japan* (Princeton: Princeton University Press, 1992). Recently various temples have increased offering such services, and indeed, several new temples have been founded for the express purpose of providing *mizuko kuyo* services.

10. See Leon Hurvitz, trans., *Scripture of the Lotus Blossom of the Fine Dharma (The Lotus Sutra): Translated from the Chinese of Kumarajiva* (New York: Columbia University Press, 1976), 291–98.

11. As related by Tim Ward in his autobiographical narrative of his stay in a Thai monastery. See Tim Ward, *What the Buddha Never Taught*.

12. Donald K. Swearer, *Buddhism and Society in Southeast Asia* (Chambersburg, PA: Anima Publications, 1981), 30–31.

13. Har Dayal, *The Bodhisattva Doctrine in Buddhist Sanskrit Literature* (London: Routledge & Kegan Paul, 1932), 60.

14. Lobsang P. Lhalungpa, trans., *The Life of Milarepa* (Boston and London: Shambhala Publications, 1977), 102.

15. Liz Wilson, *Charming Cadavers: Horrific Figurations of the Feminine in Indian Hagiographic Literature* (Chicago: The University of Chicago Press, 1996), 41–42.

16. Bhikku Nanamoli, trans., *The Path of Purification (Visuddhimagga) by Bhadantacariya Buddhaghosa*, 5th ed. (Kandy: Buddhist Text Publication Society, 1991), 185. Italics in the original.

17. Such practices can be very powerful, even for those who are not necessarily Buddhist. A professor with whom I worked, for instance, once related to me her experience of undergoing one of these visualizations under the direction of a Tibetan *lama*. She literally saw her reflection grow old and wrinkled, and it left a vivid and lasting impression on her of the ongoing process of life and its inevitable end.

18. August is the most common time and, in fact, is known colloquially in Japan as "Ghost Month."

19. Soko Morinaga Roshi, *Novice to Master: An Ongoing Lesson in the Extent of My Own Stupidity*, trans. Belenda Attaway Yamakawa (Boston: Wisdom Publications, 2002), 63.

20. Quoted in Malcolm David Eckel, *Buddhism* (Oxford and New York: Oxford University Press, 2002), 94.

21. Ibid., 95.

22. Ronald Y. Nakasone, *Ethics of Enlightenment: Essays and Sermons in Search of a Buddhist Ethic* (Fremont, CA: Dharma Cloud Publishers, 1990), 87.

23. Also called "The Parable of the Mustard Seed," this story appears in many traditional sources. This version comes from E. A. Burtt, ed., *The Teachings of the Compassionate Buddha* (London: Penguin Books, 1955), 43–46.

24. Ibid., 45.

SELECTED BIBLIOGRAPHY

Sutra of the Past Vows of Earth Store Bodhisattva. Translated by the Buddhist Text Translation Society. Talmage, CA: Dharma Realm Buddhist University, 1982. (Full English translation from the Chinese of a major Mahayana *sutra* detailing the origins and actions of Ksitigarbha ["Earth Store"], the *"bodhisattva* of the Hell beings." An important source for understanding Mahayana [especially East Asian] views of death and the afterlife.)

Coleman, Graham, and Thutpen Jinpa, eds. *The Tibetan Book of the Dead: First Complete Edition*. Penguin Classics Deluxe Edition. New York: Viking, 2006. (The most recent translation of the classic work attributed to the great Tibetan *siddha* Padmasambhava. A must read for understanding popular Buddhist views.)

Kapleau, Philip. *The Zen of Living and Dying*. Boston: Shambhala Publications, 1989. (Excellent discussion of death and how it can be approached from a Zen perspective.)

Keown, Damien, ed. *Buddhism and Abortion*. Honolulu: University of Hawai'i Press, 1999. (An important collection of essays compiled by a leading expert on Buddhist ethics. Includes contributions from various scholars on the diverse teachings of Buddhism concerning abortion, fetal life, etc. Very helpful in portraying how traditional Buddhist teachings on life and death come to bear on a complex and highly controversial subject in the contemporary world.)

———, ed. *Buddhism and Bioethics*. New York: Palgrave, 2001. (Another important and very topical volume examining a host of ethical issues from various Buddhist perspectives. As with the immediately preceding collection, so this work provides valuable information on the many different conceptions of life [and death] within Buddhism.)

Nakasone, Ronald Y. *Ethics of Enlightenment: Essays and Sermons in Search of a Buddhist Ethic*. Fremont, CA: Dharma Cloud Publishers, 1991. (A collection of pastoral essays and sermons from an ordained Pure Land priest addressing a host of issues. Of particular note are the sermons for funerals and memorial services.)

Rinpoche, Sogyal. *The Tibetan Book of Living and Dying*. New York: Harper-One, 1994. (A very readable contemporary overview of ancient Buddhists' teachings concerning the *bardo*.)

Thompson, John M. *Buddhism*, vol. 3. In: *Introduction to the World's Major Religions*. Lee W. Bailey, General Editor. Westport, CT: Greenwood Press, 2006. (A clear, straightforward overview of Buddhist history, teachings, and practices. Includes information on various Buddhist doctrines and practices concerning death.)

Ward, Tim. *What the Buddha Never Taught*. Toronto: Somerville House Publishing, 1998. (Entertaining account of the author's stay in a strict Theravadin forest monastery in Thailand. Eye-opening for what it reveals about actual Buddhist practice, the themes of death and dying run throughout Ward's narrative.)

Wilson, Liz. *Charming Cadavers: Horrific Figurations of the Feminine in Indian Buddhist Hagiographic Literature*. Chicago: The University of Chicago Press, 1996. (An insightful, highly provocative analysis of Buddhist "corpse meditation.")

5

Hindu Models of Enlightened Death

Peter Medley

King Yudhisthira, wisest of the five virtuous Pandava brothers in India's colossal religious epic, the *Mahabharata*, was once asked, "What is the most amazing thing in this world?"

"The strangest phenomenon," he replied, "is that every day, on all sides, the Grim Reaper cuts down or casts his imposing shadow over all living beings, yet we wishful mortals hallucinate that death will not visit us—at least not any time soon." As they say in Tex-Mex, it will always come *mañana*, tomorrow; not today. Freud concurred. "No one believes in his own death ... in the unconscious every one of us is convinced of his own immortality."[1]

In *The Hour of Our Death*, Philippe Aries suggested that the Western tendency to deny, ignore, or relegate death to the background is at least as pervasive as the Eastern—if not more so. "Society no longer observes a pause; the disappearance of an individual no longer affects its continuity. Everything in town goes on as if nobody died anymore."[2] Although humanity downplays physical mortality and medical science desperately fights to arrest it, the last time we checked, the death rate is still 100%.

Aries's point is that a kind of cover-up or denial of death is rampant in modern society, and the *Mahabharata* suggests this is not at all a new or localized phenomenon. While it is true that since the 1970s taboos concerning the discussion of death have been partially lifted (at least amongst society's intellectuals), it would be a stretch for anyone to claim that death's dread has been truly surmounted by the mass of people.

When I was a teenager growing up in a beach town in southern California, the most striking thing about the sudden drowning of a surfing peer was how quickly my friends and I put his death out of our conscious minds. According to Hindu tradition, our surfing friend's demise was probably not a favored subject for us because it was an unpleasant reminder of our own mortality. Taken seriously, it would jeopardize our ability to enjoy an alluring California slice of this temporary material world, which *Bhagavad-gita* 8.15 characterizes as *ashashvatam* ("impermanent") and *duhkhalayam* ("full of suffering").

DEATH IN EARLY VEDIC WRITINGS

Death has never been a particularly popular fellow among mortals, whether we speak of Gilgamesh, modern surfers, or the Vedic sages of ancient India. In the most ancient of Vedic texts, *Rig Veda* 10.18, a seer scornfully addressed Mrityu, death personified:

> Go hence, O Death, pursue thy special pathway
> apart from that which gods are wont to travel.
> To thee I say it who hast eyes and hearest: Touch
> not our offspring, injure not our hero....

> Here I erect this rampart for the living; let none
> of these, none other, reach this limit.
> May they survive a hundred lengthened autumns,
> and may they bury Death beneath this mountain.[3]

Early hymns of the *Rig Veda* did not specifically mention the doctrine of reincarnation, but rather stressed the prolongation of life and postponement of death. The Vedic Aryans understood a human being, however, to be an individual, personal self, distinguishable from his physical body.[4] The ancient seer of *Atharva Veda* 10.8.44 emphatically proclaimed that knowledge of the unity of the individual soul (*atma*) with the ultimate spiritual reality of the universe (Brahman) can eliminate man's fear of death. The *Shatapatha Brahmana* described how the gods attained immortality by ritually building a fire altar exactly according to the specifications of the Prajapati. The gods (*devas*) thought it dangerous, however, if mortal humans would try to employ the same method to enjoy immortality like the *devas*, thus cheating death. Therefore the gods deigned that no living being should enjoy immortality in a material body.

First, death personified (Mrityu) was to receive his portion, and afterward "he who is to become immortal either through knowledge, or through holy works, shall become immortal after separating from the body."[5] Indeed, while the Upanishads stressed that the immortal soul (*atman*) can attain emancipation from material existence (*samsara*) through cultivation of spiritual self-knowledge, the *Manu Samhita* later advocated that an ascetic embark on a journey "in a northeasterly direction, subsisting on water and air, until his body sinks to rest." Although this was a voluntary death brought on by starvation, it was considered a permissible, even meritorious act. In fact, *Manu Samhita* 6.60 stated, "By the restraint of his senses, by the destruction of love and hatred, and by abstention from injuring creatures, one becomes fit for immortality."

In the *Mahabharata*, the sage Narada declared, "Death has been ordained by the Creator himself for all creatures," and *Bhagavad-gita* 9.21 refers to the material world as *martya-loka*, the place of death, but all is not so gloomy. Hinduism offers much practical and esoteric wisdom to help a dying person elevate his or her consciousness at the critical moment when the soul departs from the body. While the tradition views this material world as a death trap, the *Bhagavata Purana* 4.12.30 tells how Dhruva Maharaja, a great Vaishnava devotee, dramatically circumvented the normal dying process that afflicts embodied beings. When he prepared to board a celestial aircraft (*vimana*) for the kingdom of God (Vaikuntha), suddenly death, in a personified form, menacingly approached him, but he nonchalantly used death's head as a stepping-stone, placing his feet on it to board the vehicle in his selfsame body to go to one of the heavenly realms.[6]

The *Mahabharata*'s "Book of the Forest" (*Aranyaka-parvan*) tells how the husband of a pious lady named Savitri died shortly after their wedding, but then, in response to Savitri's extraordinary prayers, austerity, and unending wifely devotion, Yamaraja, the Lord of death, revived her beloved mate. Such cases, however, are obviously rare scriptural exemptions from the general iron-clad imperative that every embodied soul in this material world—including you and me—must submit to death, and generally on its terms, not our own. Indeed, death visits everybody in the world, not just Hindus. Hence, even though it is a Sanskrit term, it can be argued that Martya-loka, "the place of death," applies to every embodied living entity on this material plane.

Death is a recurrent issue in the *Bhagavad-gita*, where Lord Krishna chided the great warrior Arjuna for hesitating to engage in a righteous battle in which he was duty-bound to oppose and to possibly even "kill" kinsmen and respected elders on the contending side. Explaining that the soul cannot be slain, Krishna regarded Arjuna as spiritually uncultured (*anarya*) because he was lamenting in ignorance of the distinction between the perishable physical body and the transcendent, imperishable soul. Arjuna didn't understand death as merely a change of bodily scenery for the soul—albeit a dramatic one. Verses 2.13 and 2.20–23 sum up

Hinduism's view of death as something fluid—a change of bodies for the deathless, imperishable *atma* (soul)—not a frozen, grim finality that should merit an intelligent person's obsessive dread:

As the embodied soul continually passes, in this body, from childhood to youth to old age, the soul similarly passes into another body at death. The self-realized soul is not bewildered by such a change.... For the soul there is neither birth nor death at any time. He has not come into being, does not come into being, and will not come into being. He is unborn, eternal, ever-existing, and primeval. He is not slain when the body is slain. O Partha [Arjuna], how can a person who knows that the soul is indestructible, eternal, unborn, and immutable kill anyone or cause anyone to kill? As a person puts on new garments, giving up old ones, the soul similarly accepts new material bodies, giving up the old and useless ones. The soul can never be cut to pieces by any weapon, nor burned by fire, nor mois-tened by water, nor withered by the wind.[7]

Jonathan Parry summarized how on many levels the Hindu conviction regarding the eternality of things mitigates death's specter:

There is at least a sense in which nothing is totally lost at death: the five elements [earth, water, fire, air, and ether] return to the common pool for re-use; the soul is immortal and is reborn [or according to Hindu theists, it may be liberated and attain the kingdom of God], the body particles a person shares with his kinsmen endure in their bodies [traced through seven generations on the father's side and five on the mother's]. The person is never entirely new when born; never entirely gone when dead. Both his body and soul extend into past and future persons....[8]

On a grand level, Indian theology tends to view time and cosmic func-tions as cyclical rather than linear. The destruction (*pralaya*) brought about by the dance of Shiva after the passage of one of Brahma's days (*kalpa*)—equivalent to 4,320,000,000 earthly years—is followed by a new creation cycle. The new creation, like the dawn of a new day, provides the sleeping souls—who are never really "dead," but rather suspended like dormant seeds—a chance to reawaken to pursue their remaining, latent material desires. Thus, the anxiety of annihilation, meaninglessness, and despair in the face of death that Paul Tillich identified in *The Courage to Be* may be assuaged for devout Hindus—depending on their faith and realization—because their scriptures provide voluminous and profound philosophical assurance of the eternality of the soul.

THE IMPORTANCE OF MODELS

Hinduism has been compared to a vast banyan tree whose branches stretch out without limit and whose root or center is difficult to locate. Besides their complexity, the sheer volume of India's sacred philosophical writings is mind-boggling; for example, the epic *Mahabharata* is considerably longer than *The Iliad* and *The Odyssey* combined. To distill some essential guidelines regarding enlightened death from this vast, difficult-to-fathom tradition, I queried a Hindu elder, but he soundly rejected pat or simplistic formulas:

I consider life transitions to be difficult and mystical, what to speak of the ultimate transition. For my taste, I would be influenced by models, rather than guidelines. I don't see death as a technique of *sadhana* [spiritual practice or technique]; rather I view it as an artful—or maybe inartful—surrender to mystical higher powers. How will Lord Krishna act at that time? I don't know. When will it come? I don't know.... I believe it will be my biggest test, but when the time comes, I am not going to listen to the rules of test-taking. I pray I will already be prepared, because I suspect that whatever is in my heart will automatically emerge. Thus, I think what you are writing is for the living, not for the dying. I would read it for inspiration in my life, not direction for death. Inspire me; don't teach me.[9]

In light of this cogent suggestion, besides considering traditional scriptural examples of death transcendence in Hinduism, this chapter will also look at inspiring contemporary models from studies of the dying in Benares, a holy city in India, as well as ones from the Chaitanya Vaishnava tradition, with which I am most familiar, and a few other sources. Vivid personal examples are vital, because religion in any culture never exists merely in a hermetically sealed vacuum of canon, theory, or the history of a faith. Although ancient in its origins, Hinduism today consists of vibrant, multifarious living traditions whose tenets impact the daily lives—and deaths—of millions of contemporary followers.

It was within a tightly knit Chaitanya Vaishnava community, not in India but in Dallas, Texas, in June, 2001, that I encountered a death that proved to be radically different from the surfing incident of my youth. In a small house near the Radha-Kalachandji temple in East Dallas, I observed how Kirtida Devi, a sixty-one-year-old Krishna devotee of South Indian heritage, approached her physical demise in a remarkably courageous, enlightened—and I dare say, elegant—manner. She and her religious community accepted and embraced her passing; in fact, it became an uplifting, memorable, once-in-a-lifetime happening for many, including several non-Hindus who witnessed different phases of the process.[10]

Kirtida was a disciple of Tamal Krishna Goswami (1946–2002), a Chaitanya Vaishnava spiritual master, author, and scholar. On the day she died, Goswami asked me to write a book on her saintly life and death.[11] In doing research for writing that work, I gained a deeper appreciation for Hinduism's ability to perceive significance and meaning in death and for the tradition to appropriately deal with that significance and meaning.

Indeed, Kenneth Kramer has argued that this is an important responsibility for all genuine religious traditions. Resisting the modern temptation to ignore or rationalize death away, their role is, rather, to bravely and squarely plumb its higher significance:

From a world religious perspective, dying is a sacred art, the final ritual, the last opportunity we have to discover life's ultimate meaning and purpose. Therefore, religious traditions ritualize the death process to remind us of the impermanence of life, and that whatever lies on the other side of death is as real, if not infinitely more so, than life itself.[12]

In *Banares: City of Light*, Diana Eck concluded that in India death can be welcomed or deemed meaningful or "good" by those who are consciously prepared for it:

For Hindus, death is not the opposite of life; it is, rather, the opposite of birth: the great transition which death occasions, is not from life to death, but from life to life.... The procession of life includes the procession of death. Here [in Benares, also traditionally known as Kashi] death is not denied. Perhaps that is why they can say that death is not feared but welcomed as a long-awaited guest. The promise of a good death takes the danger out of the transition, the crossing, death occasions.[13]

Giriraja Swami—a senior monk in the International Society for Krishna Consciousness (ISKCON) who, in 2007, established a hospice facility for dying Hindus of the Chaitanya Vaishnava order in Vrindavan, India— explained Hinduism's ultimate criterion for a "good death" to staff members of the San Diego Hospice and Palliative Care Center in 2005:

In Vedic [ancient Indian] civilization the time of death is considered the final test. In school we attend the lectures, do the assignments, take the quizzes, and write the midterm, but whether we graduate or not, it really depends on whether we pass the final examination. So in life, the time of death is considered the final examination, and passing the final examination means thinking of God. That is why the whole focus at the time of death [in Hinduism] is to help the person remember God. And the other activities that we perform during our life, besides freeing us from activities that will bring results [karma] that will oblige us to take birth again, are practice for thinking of God. And we get little tests along the way.[14]

Mahatma Gandhi's dramatic assassination was an example of someone reputed to have possessed consciousness of God in his final moments. The unexpected close-range gunshot that dramatically took his life was perhaps the ultimate in surprise spiritual "pop quizzes." Gandhi is said to have called out, "He Rama!" when attacked—Rama being a prominent name of God in his tradition—thus wonderfully passing the test.

In Hinduism, such a conscious remembrance of God at the end of one's life is considered symptomatic of an auspicious or enlightened passage from this world. Lord Krishna describes in *Bhagavad-gita* 8.5–6 that a dying person should focus on God, especially at the time of the physical body's last breath. "Whoever, at the end of his life, quits his body remembering Me alone, at once attains My nature [*bhava*]. Of this there is no doubt. Whatever state of being one remembers when he quits his present body, in his next life he will attain to that state without fail." Thus, a vital factor regarding the ultimate destination of the soul after death is its focus at the end of life—that is, the orientation of the consciousness itself, its *bhava* as it passes from this world.

THE "GOOD" DEATH

Although Gandhi's God-conscious response to his violent attack is considered praiseworthy, scriptures such as the *Garuda Purana* hold that such an unexpected, violent manner or circumstance surrounding his death was less than ideal. Parry has summed up some elements considered part of a "paradigmatically good death" in the Hindu tradition:

In the ideal case, the dying man ... foregoes all food for some days before death, and consumes only Ganga [Ganges] water and *charanamrita* (the mixture in which the image of a deity has been bathed) in order to weaken his body so that the "vital breath" might leave it more easily.... Having previously predicted his time of going and set his affairs in order ... by an effort of concentrated will—he abandons life. He is not said to die, but to relinquish his body.... He should die to the sound of the chanting of the names of God, for his thoughts at that moment may determine his subsequent fate; and he should be empty of all desire for the things of this world....[15]

Eck added that, according to Hindu teachings, death can be favorable if it initiates positive and progressive steps toward the soul's next destination. "What one thinks and sees at the time of death directs one's first steps toward the next life.[16] Those close to the dying should whisper the name of God in that person's ear. While death may be the final event in one life, it is also, in a sense, the first event in the life beyond."[17]

According to the *Garuda Purana* 9.34, fasting to hasten an already rapidly progressing natural death is acceptable in Hindu culture. However, to whimsically take one's own life while still healthy or youthful— such as in suicide—is characterized as ill-fated or sinful. In the *Bhagavata Purana*, when the great Vaishnava King Parikshit was cursed to die in seven days, he fasted and eschewed sleep until his death, listening around-the-clock to topics about Lord Krishna and His great devotees.

Such a self-willed, spiritually aware passing away, which Parry described as "an effort of concentrated will," is quite different from many deaths around the world today in which the dying—sometimes under strong medication—find themselves insensible or unaware at the time of their soul's departure from its no longer habitable corporeal host. Although the *Bhagavad-gita* characterizes such deaths as in the "mode of ignorance" (i.e., counter-productive in regard to the soul's ultimate spiritual welfare), a growing number of dying patients around the world, including some contemporary health care professionals, favor unconscious death. Rachel Stanworth noted that at respected facilities such as St. Christopher's Hospice in London, "disregarded" exits are preferable for many dying persons:

Irene's logic is, by far, the more typical. "I want death to be quick, in one's sleep." Despite the professional "near consensus," the official "script'" on the benefits of an aware death, this study supports a documented preference for "disregarded dying," or an unanticipated demise during the hours of sleep.[18]

In terms of comfort, unconscious death obviously has the advantage of being largely pain-free. But from the Hindu perspective, as a means to help a dying person carry ultimate meaning beyond the breakdown of the bodily machine or vehicle, disregarded dying obviously has serious drawbacks. *Bhagavad-gita* 16.15 warns that perishing in ignorance (*tamas*) reduces the degree to which a person may proactively influence the transition of his or her soul to a higher, "progressive" next destination.[19]

The *Gita* cautions that people who die unconsciously, a symptom of ignorance, even risk taking their next birth in the body of an animal or lower species, although there are notable exceptions to such a scenario, which we will discuss later in this chapter. Therefore, instead of dying unconsciously, Hindus aspire to retain as full concentration and God awareness as possible. In a way, they see death as potentially being the ultimate meditation exercise or stimulus for fervent prayer and surrender to God. In this regard, Ernest Becker cited Ben Johnson regarding death's possible redeeming effect. "The prospect of death," Dr. Johnson said, "wonderfully concentrates the mind."[20]

Death is conceived as the ultimate gauge by which one's spiritual attainment—or lack of it—can be revealed.

Parry suggested that for a "good death" in Hinduism, the dying person should "relinquish his body" voluntarily. This requires tremendous detachment, faith, and surrender to divine will. Though coming from outside the Hindu tradition, Cyprian of Carthage eloquently upheld the benefit of such respectful obedience to death's beckoning:

How preposterous and absurd it is that while we ask that the will of God should be done, yet when God calls and summons us from this world, we should not at once obey the command of his will! We struggle and resist, and like obstinate servants we are dragged into the presence of the Lord's sadness and grief, departing from this world only under the bondage of necessity and not with the obedience of a free will.[21]

Mahatma Gandhi concurred. "There is salvation in death when dying willingly, when dying gladly."[22] Although the aspiration for obedience to the divine will is common to all faiths, to freely surrender to the divine call at death may be—arguably—more culturally supported in India than the West. At least in the critical area of medical theory, opposing cultural attitudes seem to square off. Western allopathic medicine often casts death in a negative light, which Karlis Osis observed to be part of "a cultural pattern which not only sees all pain as pointless, but which looks upon death as the 'last great enemy,' to be outwitted and subdued at all costs."[23] On the other hand, India's holistic Ayurveda, a traditional preventative medical system, teaches, "Timely death cannot be avoided, as it is a natural phenomenon. Not even the best physician can save a patient whose life span is approaching the end."[24]

Christopher Justice, who, like Parry, studied death and dying in Benares, listed a few further details regarding a good or "bad" death in Hinduism:

The good death is one that occurs in ... a religious environment, concentrating on God and sipping Ganga [Ganges] water with *tulsi* leaves.[25] The good death is one in which there is no trauma or other indication that a store of bad karma is enacting its punishment. And the good death occurs at as old an age as possible, free from disease, with an empty stomach, awake, and that is expected.... It is good to die [between] about 3:30 A.M. to 5:30 A.M. Eleven at night to about 3 A.M. is a bad time to die, as it is a time of evil beings. It's also bad to die drunk, eating meat, during sex, or child delivery. There are, I was told, vast lists of good and bad ways of dying mentioned in "technical" texts such as the *Preta Manjeri*. These texts are essentially instructions for priests and are not generally known....[26]

Regarding Parry's point that a dying person has ideally "previously predicted his time of going," R. S. Khare collected and analyzed a series of narratives from Brahmins in western Bihar in which the prediction of death was an important theme, concluding that "Hindus attach considerable importance to the prediction of death."[27] Justice found that about 10 percent of the dying pilgrims who traveled to Benares accurately foretold the timing of their deaths.[28] Of course, an auspicious death cannot entirely be reduced to rigid formulas; most Hindus believe it ultimately rests less in externals than in internal surrender to God, coupled with detachment from the world. Prediction of the timing of one's death *is* valued, however, especially because it helps one be spiritually ready for one's passing.

Justice shared a fascinating story about a dying lady who arrived at one of the special facilities in Benares that are dedicated to helping people attain God-conscious deaths. Her husband had died at that same facility, and she had her heart set on expiring there too. However, when the lady arrived, all the rooms—and even most of the verandas—were overcrowded with dying patients, and the authorities told her she would have to go somewhere else to die. Utterly ignoring them, however, she had her son carry her to the exact spot where her husband had died, lay down on the floor there, and gave up her life within minutes. Such an ability to have a degree of control over the time, place, or circumstances of one's passing is considered auspicious in Hinduism.

In witnessing Kirtida Devi's last weeks in Dallas, I was amazed when she suddenly declared that she wanted to die during "*brahma-muhurta*," a peaceful early morning period between about 3:30 A.M. and 5:30 A.M.[29] Ultimately, it came to pass that she did die or "leave her body" during this auspicious general period, as she had predicted.[30] A number of saints in the Gaudiya Vaishnava tradition have been described as having been able to foresee the time of their deaths, such as Pisi Ma Goswamini of Vrindavan, India, who passed away at the age of 106 at the exact time and day she had predicted.

Regarding Parry's proviso that a dying person "foregoes all food for some days before death," he and Justice reported that most of the people in Benares' Kashi Muktibhavan care facility—an ashram-like spiritual hospice establishment—were able to fast during their last days, weeks, or months. Justice asked an attendant at the care facility in Benares about the value of having an empty stomach at the time of death. The caregiver explained, "If you have power in the body [supplied by food] then the *prana* [vital breath] does not go quickly from the body: you struggle. But if you are very weak, the *prana* [and along with it, the soul] will go very easily."[31]

Justice and Parry reported that fasting was a tool used by the majority of Hindus who came to die in Benares to ease their death process. In fact, after just one week of their arrival at the Muktibhavan, an astounding 84 percent of the people had already died. This suggests that religious fasting—and a strong desire to die in a holy place—can hasten a soul's release from its body. Witnesses of Mother Kirtida's departure in Dallas observed that, incredibly, she fasted from all solid foods for nine weeks, until her spiritual master's arrival from England. Then, satisfied to see her beloved guru one last time, and ready to die, Kirtida voluntarily hastened her death by ceasing to drink any liquids, even water, for the last six days of her life.

From the Hindu perspective, a good death takes place in a spiritually conducive environment (which we will discuss in greater depth later in this chapter, under *tirthas*) that allows the dying person to hear the names of God recited up until their last breath, and even beyond it. In Kirtida Devi's case, Tamal Krishna Goswami specifically arranged that various members of the Radha-Kalachandji temple community sign up to chant for her benefit during specific time slots over the twenty-four hour period, such as midnight to 2 A.M., 2 A.M. to 4 A.M., 4 A.M. to 6 A.M, and so on. This continual around-the-clock chanting was performed for the last few weeks of Kirtida's life. At the moment she died in the early morning on the 20th of June, 2001, several devotees were chanting the Hare Krishna mantra close by, and it was observed that she was fully alert, yet peaceful, listening with rapt attention to the divine names. Another sign of a "good death."

From the 1930s to the 1950s in the West, the site of death generally changed from the home, with family, to alone in a hospital. Feeling that a hospital would be a difficult place to remember God at the time of his death, A. C. Bhaktivedanta Swami Prabhupada (1896–1977), the founder and spiritual preceptor of the Hare Krishna movement, instructed his disciples that if at all possible they should not let him die in a medical facility. Initially, Kirtida found herself in a hospital in Dallas receiving chemotherapy for her throat cancer, but when her medical condition became hopeless, she chose to welcome death—but not in the hospital. Her fervent desire to relinquish her physical body in a *tirtha*-like loving, spiritual environment was realized when she moved to her devotee-friends' home near the Radha-Kalachandji temple. Justice cited several researchers, corroborating that the hospital environment is generally not considered conducive for a good death, even in the West:

Kaistenbaum and Aisenburg suggested that when people die in hospitals, those outside the hospital are protected from the sights of death [which Kübler-Ross suggests is unhealthy]. From the point of view of the dying individual, it has been pointed out repeatedly that the hospital is not a good place to die.... Sudnow demonstrated that among hospital staff efficiency is more highly valued than human dignity.... Caregivers are often not comfortable dealing with death, and as a result handle dying patients quite poorly.[32]

H. O. Mauksch has argued that hospitals are committed to the recovery process, not to dying, and Sudnow demonstrated that among hospital staff, efficiency is more highly valued than human dignity. According to Moller, in a materialistic technocratic society, life itself is experienced as a possession, something that is stolen by death. It is the loss of this most prized of possessions that is the source of the tremendous fear of dying.

In the Hindu tradition, other, less vital details may contribute to an auspicious death:

When death is near, the patient should ideally be placed on ground which has been scattered with mustard and sesame seed, freshly plastered with cow-dung, on which the name of Lord Rama [or another sacred name of God, such as Krishna, Hari, etc.] has been written, and on which a *kusha*-grass mat has been spread. Death should occur in the open air, because a roof would impede the soul's passage upwards.... One who is about to expire should be oriented with feet pointing south—a position which people are careful to avoid sleeping, for south is the direction of Yamaraja's kingdom [the demigod of death].[33]

Besides its technical advantages, death in the "open air" suggests a natural simplicity and serenity that is hard to imagine in the bustling, high-tech mega business operations that modern hospitals have become today.

One of the items Parry mentioned as another aspect of a "good death" is that the dying person has nicely set his or her affairs in order. As much as possible, modern hospice caregivers attempt to help the dying reach a state of closure in regard to worldly affairs so they can finally "let go" and accept a more peaceful, purposeful death. In an earlier work, instead of saying "tying up one's affairs" Parry phrased it "having fulfilled his duties on this earth."[34] "Duties" implies fulfilling vital or binding social, familial, legal, or religious obligations. In the Hindu context I believe it is a more appropriate word to use than "affairs," which suggests items to do that might be merely arbitrary and not obligatory.

For instance, in Hindu society parents consider it to be one of their important sacred duties or dharmas to see to the marriage of their children, especially a daughter. If a man who is close to death has not arranged for any of his children's marriages, this would normally weigh upon his mind, and a truly "good" or peaceful death would be compromised.

Yet, as stated in the *Bhagavata Purana* 11.5.41, the *bhakti* or devotional traditions hold that through *bhakti*, a pure devotee is ultimately exonerated from all material obligations:

Anyone who has taken shelter of the lotus feet of Mukunda, [a name of God meaning] "the giver of liberation," giving up all kinds of obligation, and has taken to the path in all seriousness, owes neither duties nor obligations to the demigods, sages, general living entities, family members, humankind or forefathers. Such obligations are automatically fulfilled by performance of devotional service to the Supreme Personality of Godhead.

Earlier, *Bhagavata Purana* 4.31.14 explained that rendering *bhakti* or service to God is like watering the root of a tree; by feeding the root all the branches, twigs, leaves, and fruits are simultaneously nourished. These limbs of the tree of life can be compared to duties and obligations a dying person may have to ancestors, relatives, society, employer, etc. The devotee is reassured that by fully surrendering to God, he or she is freed from the normal duties and obligations that would be binding upon a pious and devout Hindu.

In the *Mahabharata*, the wise elder statesman and warrior Bhishma, blessed with the ability to die at a time he himself chose, imparted final instructions to the soldiers on the battlefield, who observed a ceasefire as he was dying. In a similar vein, Justice spoke about an old man who was preparing to leave his village to die in Benares:

Before leaving the village many people came to see him off. They said, "Now you are going to Kashi, and nobody knows if you will come back to be with us."

They asked him to forgive any mistakes they had made and to give them his blessing. They all touched his feet [a sign of respect]. Singh told his visitors to live a long life and to be healthy. He and his family then caught a bus to Kashi.[35]

Although my friend Kirtida was a quiet person, her death in Dallas became a profoundly public event. During her final days, she was able to give spiritual advice and counsel to many devotees, old friends, and relatives, and to express her love and devotion to her spiritual master and many devotees, friends, and relatives, bringing a satisfying sense of completion and closure. By fulfilling these desires and duties in her final days, she gained a palpable sense of purposefulness and meaning in her life and death. She also left a large amount of money, which would be used to commission ornate new clothing outfits to be made annually for the Dallas temple deities—extending for many years into the future.

A "bump in the road" did arise, however, when several of Kirtida's visiting family members expressed their surprise regarding her initial plan to leave nearly all of her wealth to spiritual projects. This caused some anxiety, but she quickly addressed their concerns and decided to change her will. After this adjustment, she and her relatives were more at ease. Thus, it appears that any action or communication that helps to put a person in a more satisfied, peaceful, or fulfilled state of being at the end of life contributes toward a better or more auspicious passing, whether in Hinduism or any other tradition.

FEARLESS DYING

> It's not that I'm afraid to die. I just don't want to be there when it happens.
>
> —Woody Allen (1935–)

Sherwin Nuland insists, "No matter the degree to which a man thinks he had convinced himself that the process of dying is not to be dreaded, he will yet approach his final illness with dread."[36] While this is certainly generally true, a priest at the Muktibhavan in Benares explained how the pilgrims who come there to die are usually remarkably free from fear, and fearlessness can be part of a good death:

According to Pandey's understanding, the people who have come to die stop feeling fear once they have reached Kashi. He said, "They are not afraid of death. They take God's name and keep chanting the name of Rama. I think they are not afraid. Rather, they are happy to be dying here." The guardians of the dying people seem to agree; all of them say that the dying person is happy to have reached Kashi and almost all say that the dying person has no fear of dying.[37]

Larry Shinn explained how a theist or devotee is relieved of fear in Hinduism:

Neither Death (i.e., Yama) nor his abode (hell) is feared by the devotee. On the contrary, it is the heaven-like abode from which no man is born again that a devotee anticipates after death. Vishnu's heavenly abode is called Vaikuntha and Shiva's sphere is called Kailasa. Therefore, whichever sectarian Purana one reads, the outcome is the same: Yama's messengers are defeated by the soldiers of the supreme deity, and the naked soul of the devotee is carried off to that deity's heavenly abode.[38]

By way of an analogy, in Prabhupada's commentary on the *Mukunda-mala-stotra*, Mantra 3, he pointed out how the same phenomenon, death, can be viewed either fearlessly, or fearfully, by individuals in varying states of consciousness:

We may use a crude example to illustrate the difference between a devotee's death and an ordinary man's death. In her mouth, the cat captures both her offspring and her prey, the rat. Such capturings may appear the same, but there is a vast difference between them. While the rat is being carried in the cat's mouth, his sensation is poles apart from that of the cat's offspring. For the rat, the capture is a painful death-strike, while for the offspring, it is a pleasurable caress.

Bhagavata Purana 2.1.15 explains that key to attaining fearlessness at the time of death is to relinquish one's grip on the material: "At the last stage of life, a person must be bold enough to not fear death. One must cut off all attachment to the material body and everything pertaining to it, as well as to all desires thereof." Hospice workers often report that dying persons with positive faith in the afterlife are more forward-looking at the time of death; they can more readily detach themselves from the impermanent. Hinduism is able to interpret death as a powerful destroyer of the soul's fetters or material attachments, thus shedding its fearsome profile. "Shiva is a destroyer and loves the burning ground. But what does he destroy? Not merely the heavens and earth at the close of a world-cycle, but the fetters that bind each separate soul."[39] As Heinrich Zimmer put it, even "… destruction—Shiva—is only the negative aspect of unending life."

Maharishi Mahesh Yogi once told the story of an Indian *sadhu* or holy man who was adept at seeing something positive in any situation, an attitude that fosters fearlessness. When the man came upon a dead dog sprawled grotesquely on a roadside, he declared, "Oh my, his teeth are shining so beautifully!" In *Leaves of Grass*, Walt Whitman, one of the "American transcendentalists" influenced by the *Bhagavad-gita*, could remark with similar buoyancy, "The smallest blade of grass shows there really is no death." The residents living in the atmosphere of perpetual death and cremation in Kashi do not stereotypically display fear or moroseness; rather, they routinely exhibit "jocularity," "devil-may-care assertiveness," "amusement at the divine comedy of the world," or "carefree eccentricity."[40] Patricia Justice had the same revelation:

We leaned over the railing on a tiny Shiva temple, feeling bursts of heat from the pyres fifteen feet below and breathing air tinged with the distinctive, acrid smell of burning bodies. There seemed nothing somber or ceremonial about the scene around the pyres: the parties of mourners lounged around, occasionally poking the fires with long sticks, to ensure a thorough cremation; children laughed and played, splashing in and out of the water a few feet away from the pyres; dogs and cows wandered around, grazing on whatever they could find.[41]

Comparing death to an immersion in a holy river, the Hindu holy man Ramakrishna was able to view it as a spiritual consummation, not a fearful end:

People may perceive it [physical death] as illness, but it is really the process of spiritual completion. You are encountering the sacred river of Karmanasha, destroyer of the sense of duty. It is blissful to plunge into this swift current. All sense of being able to initiate actions—from spiritual teaching and social reform to even the simplest personal responsibility—now comes to an end.[42]

Bhakti Tirtha Swami, a distinguished Chaitanya Vaishnava guru and author of African American ancestry, passed away at the Gita Nagari farm community in Port Royal, Pennsylvania, in the summer of 2005. Blessed with the supportive companionship of loving friends and disciples during his last days, the *swami* embraced his own physical demise with remarkable fearlessness, as his dear friend Radhanath Swami recalled:

He was in immense pain and asked me to speak about Lord Krishna, which, according to him, was the "only real medicine." I started chanting the Hare Krishna mantra and his eyes became big—he had the expression of an innocent, simple little cowherd boy.[43] He was gazing at me and chanting. And he did something that no one has ever done to me before: he took my hand and kissed it. And looking with his child-like eyes he said, "Maharaja, isn't this wonderful?" He was shaking his head in ecstasy and had a beautiful, blossomed smile. He said, "Maharaja, it doesn't get any better than this! I wouldn't exchange my place with anyone; and what's amazing is that it gets better every day!"[44]

Tamal Krishna Goswami described a similar composure in Kirtida Devi during her final days in Dallas. "She told people, 'I feel so blissful: I've never been happier in my life. I have no fear of death whatsoever.'"[45]

DEATH AS *SEVA* ("SERVICE TO GOD")

Graham Schweig has stated that for Vaishnavas, Hinduism's devotional majority, activities such as fasting to death, nicely tying up one's final affairs, dying at an auspicious hour or holy place, or even attaining liberation or salvation—while all desirable as part of the traditional "good death" in Hinduism—are actually of secondary importance when it comes to "fulfilling what is pleasing to God"[46] or passing from the body in a state of willful surrender and consciousness of God. Doing what is pleasing to God is known in Sanskrit as *seva*, which in English can be translated as "service." By defining the word *bhakti* as "devotional service" rather than simply as "devotion," Prabhupada emphasized this principle of *seva* for the *bhakta* (devotee). E. H. Rick Jarow elucidated this overarching principle for Vaishnavas in general:

Seva moves beyond the ideal of non-attachment and into devoted service to the truth, which exists through, above, and beyond death. From the ideal devotional perspective, *seva* is participating in life in its fullest sense. So important, so absolute, is one's *seva* that life, death, or any conditions in between do not come in the way of it.... If one is "living well," that is, living in *seva*, then it does not matter if one's death is ritually auspicious or not.[47]

Kenneth Kramer corroborated the fact that in Hinduism, the divine love that is churned by the ladle of *seva* ultimately renders ritualistic formalities or methodical techniques at the time of death as insignificant:

At that point forms and rituals vanish, sacred texts are superceded, temples are transcended. Nothing remains to bind a person in this life. Whether through the recitation of mantras (sacred sounds) or through selfless acts of mercy, the *bhakta* welcomes everything that happens, [even death] as a gift from the beloved.[48]

Surrendered souls in Hinduism's Vaishnava traditions hold *seva* to be the guiding principle of their lives. As their body expires, they are not so concerned with the scriptural techniques or fine points of dying as they are with their *bhava*, or the state of surrendered consciousness, at the end. Commenting on *Bhagavad-gita* 8.23–24, which describes auspicious and inauspicious times to die, Prabhupada concluded:

The unalloyed devotees of the Supreme Lord, who are totally surrendered souls, do not care when they leave their bodies or by what method. They leave everything in Krishna's hands and so easily and happily return to Godhead.... for the pure devotee in Krishna consciousness, there is no fear of returning [to this world], whether he leaves the body at an auspicious or inauspicious moment, by accident or arrangement.[49]

The Medieval mystical text *Bhakti-rasamrita-sindhu* 1.2.187 tells us that "Anyone who, by his actions, mind, and words, lives only for the transcendental loving service of the Lord, is certainly a liberated soul, even though he may appear to be in a condition of material existence." This verse indicates that in Hinduism an advanced, pure devotee is recognized to have already attained salvation or liberation, even prior to relinquishing the material body at death. Bhakti Tirtha Swami, for example, in both his life and his dying, fervently utilized his actions, mind, and words in *seva*. In 2004 his Vyasa-puja essay (a written glorification of his deceased guru, on the latter's birthday) referred to a Medieval devotee, Vasudeva Datta—now a Chaitanya Vaishnava saint—who had offered to accept the sins and karma of all the fallen souls in the entire universe on his own head. "In the mood of Vasudeva Datta," said Bhakti Tirtha Swami, "I would like to ask you, 'Can you arrange that their sufferings come to me, so that many can be freed from their anguish and thus joyfully serve you and return to Krishna with fewer encumbrances?'"[50]

The swami's wish to assume the karmic debts of others was a contemporary instance of Christ-like compassion in the Chaitanya Vaishnava tradition, similar not only to Vasudeva Datta but to the Bodhisattva in Buddhism. As far as the Hindu tradition goes, this self-sacrificing disposition of *seva* was magnanimously demonstrated by Lord Shiva in the *Bhagavata Purana* when he decided to drink poison so that others would not be harmed by it, taking the suffering or inconvenience upon himself. Another example of this selfless mood was exhibited by King Rantideva, an elevated Vaishnava who risked starvation to share food with others. In *Bhagavata Purana* 9.21.12 Rantideva declared, "I do not pray to the Supreme Personality of Godhead for the eight perfections of mystic yoga, nor for salvation from repeated birth and death. I want only to stay among all the living entities and suffer all distresses on their behalf, so that they may be freed from suffering."

According to Hinduism's Vaishnava traditions, the value of acting in *seva*—unselfish service to God and his parts and parcels, in life or death—is that such unmotivated *seva* generates no karma, positive or negative. Further, it burns up preexisting karma. In Christian terms, it may be comparable to being "in the world, but not of it." According to the *Bhagavata Purana* 8.7.44, self-sacrificing, magnanimous *seva* is *parama-aradhana*—"the topmost worship of God." Parry noted that in Hinduism even one's final cremation is considered *seva*, an act of surrender to the Supreme. It is viewed as not merely an ending, but as a type of rebirth:

Cremation is known as *dah samskar*, the "sacrament of fire" or, more revealingly perhaps, as *antyeshti*, the "last sacrifice." The typical Brahmanic sacrifice is a fire sacrifice (*homa*) and the sacrificer's "last oblation" (*antyahuti*) to the fire is his own body…. Elaborate rules for the pyre, the position of the deceased (ideally the feet are facing south) and auspicious wood for the pyre, such as fragments of sandalwood, mango and wood-apple, are considered *pavitra* or pure…. According to one well-known text which deals with sacrifice, the *Satapatha Brahmana*, there are three kinds of birth: that which is had from one's parents, from sacrifice, and from cremation….[51]

TIRTHAS, IN BOTH TRADITIONAL AND UNLIKELY PLACES

A *tirtha*, a holy place, often but not exclusively where devout Hindus go to die, is considered in Hinduism to be a "transitional zone" because—

according to scripture—it acts as a mystical crossing point through which
a departing soul can readily pass to a better destination after death:

[The *tirtha* or holy place]... puts the worshipper in direct contact with the transcendental world. Transmission conditions between the sacred and profane worlds
are—as it were—optimal; and the place itself is a kind of transitional zone between
the two. The term *tirath* [or more commonly, *tirtha*] derives from the Sanskrit root
signifying the idea of crossing over, and refers not only to a "place of pilgrimage"
but also to a "ford" or "crossing point."[52]

Such sacred places or *tirthas* have sometimes been compared in Hinduism
to an embassy of the kingdom of God on earth. The *tirtha* is located in
the world, but it is believed not exactly a part of it: it is understood as a
manifestation of a higher realm on earth, as well as a transition point or
passageway that facilitates the soul's journey out of this world to a higher
spiritual situation. Parry noted, "This belief that salvation is guaranteed
to those who die at the pilgrimage center is, of course, familiar from
other world religions. Those who die at Mecca, Jerusalem or Compostella
go straight to heaven."[53]

One of the practical reasons people in India favor conscious death in a
tirtha is that in such a sacred locale, chanting and religious activities are
enacted continuously. In fact, they have been performed for hundreds or
thousands of years in such special places. This creates a powerful cumulative purifying atmosphere or vibration for the souls who die there. One
of the care providers at the Kashi Labh Muktibhavan outlined the spiritual activities performed there for the benefit of the dying:

Here, twenty-four hours per day, there is religious singing (*hari-kirtana*) and from
time-to-time the adoration of God (*bhagavan ki arti*) is performed near the sick
person, who is given Tulsi [the leaf of a plant from the Basil family that is
esteemed as holy in Hinduism] and water from the Ganga. There is the benefit of
hearing *Gita* and *Ramayana* and in this type of religious atmosphere the sick person will get the benefit of Kashi (*Kashi labh*) and, according to the scriptures
(*shastra*), their soul (*atman*) will get absolute peace and salvation (*sadgati*), of this
there is no doubt.[54]

Eck describes how in Kashi (which is traditionally viewed as an important *tirtha*, especially for Shaivites, worshippers of Shiva) Lord Shiva is
said to personally protect the souls of those who die there. "The very sick
or the distressed may lose consciousness as death approaches and be
unable to place their thoughts upon the name of God, but Shiva himself
will be there, they say, to whisper wisdom into the ear of the dying."[55]

Although my friend Kirtida passed away in materialistic Dallas, which
is known more as the site of John F. Kennedy's assassination than a holy
place, the Vaishnavas there provided spiritual services similar to those
that would be available in a *tirtha* such as Vrindavan or Kashi. For the

most part, these included the constant chanting of the holy names and the transformation of Kirtida's room into a meditative sacred space decorated with religious art, wall-photos of holy places in India, deities, Ganges water, and other spiritual relics. Her lifetime of devoted preparation and the *tirtha*-like atmosphere in the Radha-Kalachandji community helped maintain her fearless condition in her last days.

SADHU-SANGA: ASSOCIATION OF THE SAINTLY

Hinduism holds that when we die we are responsible to control our own state of consciousness, to "fly our own plane," so to speak. Certainly, no one else can die for us. However, I have argued that the beneficial effect of *sadhu-sanga*, the association of like-minded, spiritually inclined well-wishers, is vital for a dying person.[56]

In the *Bhagavata Purana*, although King Parikshit fasted and was in perfect God consciousness at the time of his death, he also benefited from the saintly *sanga* (fellowship) of Shukadeva Goswami and other *sadhus* who were present. Gian Giuseppe Filippi describes how various advantageous environmental elements can help to make a person's death spiritually auspicious. "The priest chooses sacred and efficacious verses from the *Bhagavad-gita* and the *Ramayana*. So it is in this atmosphere, consecrated by vibrations of sacred texts, by the perfumed air of flowers and incense ... sprinkled with Ganges water, and lying on the naked and fertile earth ... that man concludes his earthly existence."[57]

Part of that environment is the association of like-minded and spiritually advanced souls.

THE ROLE OF THE GURU

Susan Pattinson, a Vaishnava hospice care nurse and the author of *The Final Journey: Complete Hospice Care for Departing Vaishnavas*, described the death of a senior female disciple of Swami Prabhupada, Mula Prakriti Devi, who died in Vrindavan peacefully, without medication, calling upon her spiritual master's mercy and feeling his personal spiritual protection, right up until her final moment.[58] In a manner similar to how a Christian would approach God the Father through Jesus Christ, Mula Prakriti's intense meditative and prayerful connection with her spiritual master at the end of her life was an inseparable part of her relationship with her beloved Lord Krishna.

In the various branches of Vaishnavism, a guru traditionally assumes an essential role in helping a disciple to best ascertain how to perform pure *seva* and to attain such a "totally surrendered" state. Kirtida Devi was another example of someone who dedicated her life and her death for the pleasure of her guru, in the mood of Chaitanya Vaishnava teachers such as Vishvanath Chakravarti Thakur, who wrote: "If one pleases and thus attains the mercy of the spiritual master, then Bhagavan (God) will bestow His mercy." Although Kirtida originally wanted to die in Vrindavan, by following the instruction of her guru to die in Dallas, her death became *seva* or devotional service. It was her complete faith in her guru as God's representative that allowed her to experience ecstasy and fearlessness in the face of death.

Susan S. Trout, Ph.D., though not formally a guru, related how she assisted a dying lady named Jenny in the latter's last months:

She felt no peace and the terror of dying increased. Then, only two weeks before she died, it came to me in contemplation that maybe a Sanskrit mantra might help her, as it would carry no bias of her negative feelings about organized religion. One Saturday afternoon, I brought my selection of mantra tapes, and she selected the Robie Gass version of *om namah shivaya* because it reminded her of the Polynesian music of the South Pacific Island where she had lived and worked.... From that day on we played the tape continuously, day and night, in her hospital room. Her husband would join the chant; the nurses would join the chant. The chant wafted throughout the hospital hallway. The chant was the only thing that brought Jenny peace. I said to Jenny that she would have safe passage if she went out [of her body] on the mantra. I said that as she was dying I would walk with her and we would follow the mantra. But I could only go so far. She was to remember to "take the road of the mantra" and there would be helpers to greet her and help her across.[59]

SUKAL MRITYU: A WELL-TIMED DEATH

Parry describes how a timely death is termed *sukal mrityu* in Sanskrit. Of course, the characterization of a person's death as "well-timed" or not is subjective, but there are general scriptural criteria in Hinduism by which to make such a determination. First, an auspicious death should follow a well-lived life. A well-lived life traditionally includes a preparatory stage to ready one for a good or enlightened death. After a person reaches maturity, yet before the full debilitation that advanced old age occasions, he or she is advised to cease normal occupational duties and to begin a period of undistracted spiritual activities or *sadhana*. This stage of life is known in Hindu scripture as the Vanaprastha-ashram. Traditionally in Indian culture, when a pious couple's children had grown up and married, husband and wife would retire—either together or separately—and spend time in spiritual cultivation as *vanaprasthas*. Gian Giuseppe Filippi describes how this stage is advantageous to prepare for death:

The unpleasant discovery of the first grey hair at his temples puts him, for the first time, under the specter of death. From this moment on he begins to prepare himself to affront his remaining life in a different manner. The ideal of Hindu life requires passing into the state of *vanaprasthin*. As already mentioned, there are few who abandon their homes to retire into the forest alone or with their wives, in order to interiorize the *grhasthya* [householder] rites. The current usage is to enter into some *sampradaya* [spiritual lineage], going around dressed as *sadhus* or *sants* to holy cities ... living off alms near temples and ashrams.[60]

Gauri Devi Dasi, a senior female Vaishnava who had for years self-lessly served her spiritual master's mission by pushing herself to distribute spiritual books to the general public, did not have the classic allotment of time described above for a *vanaprasthin* to prepare for death, because in 1985 she was diagnosed with a terminal disease and retired to Vrindavan, India, expecting to die quickly. However, Gauri was known as a highly advanced devotee who was completely dedicated to her spiritual master and Lord Krishna. In this sense, she was already prepared to accept any-thing—including death—as a divine arrangement. In a letter to friends in 1986, she described how she had a sense that the timing of her departure was perfect, because the Lord was personally arranging it:

Lord Krishna is being very kind to me by giving me a little more time here in Vrin-davan in which to work on my relationship with the holy name.... I am finding more and more it is becoming my only desire—to be able to chant Radha-Krishna uninterruptedly, in ecstatic love. There is nothing left for me to desire in this world. My body is completely finished.... But I am actually finding all of this because Krishna is doing everything in such a gentle way to give me plenty of time to adjust to the idea of giving up this useless body once and for all. *I feel that He is just waiting for me to become completely ready, and then He will finish the whole thing off* [added italics]. I have absolutely no hankering or lamentation left in my heart—at least that I am conscious of. I feel very happy and peaceful, however totally unprepared I still am for the final showdown. So, whatever time Krishna gives me, I feel I can use every bit of it to try to pray more sincerely.[61]

Filippi ruminated on how saintly persons in India who died early in life, like the celebrated woman saint Mirabai (or in the West, Therese of Lisieux, who died at the age of twenty-four) are puzzling exceptions to Hin-duism's normal expectations for a full life before death at a ripe old age:

The "good" death, according to the norm, should arrive in a "normal" way, with old age as the cause. Why then, these deaths during youth? The difficulty repre-sented by this eventuality is overcome upon consideration that bodily life, what-ever its length, has the aim of furnishing a support to the real self for the actualization of an eschatological design. Premature death, in some rare cases, may even be interpreted as a positive sign of a complete realization. Positive pre-mature deaths are rare and exceptional, as [for example those of]... Sankara-charya, Chaitanya, Mirabai, etc. [Indian spiritual luminaries who all died young]... extraordinary instances, due to the special sanctity of these figures.[62]

There are other instances of positive premature death in contemporary times. Tamal Krishna Goswami, for example, passed away "untimely" in his mid-fifties in a car accident at a holy place near Mayapur, West Bengal in early 2002. His friends and disciples have tried to fathom his apparently "premature" passing from this world. Filippi's realization suggests the possibility that Krishna had already achieved through Goswami the completion of his primary God-given mission or purpose on earth, and it was a divinely orchestrated time for him to move on.

The *Padma Purana* 6.229.58 states, "Vaishnavas do not take birth according to the normal law of karma." If the births of great souls transcend normal karmic influences, their deaths may also be considered free from the binding nature of customary material laws of action and reaction. Indeed, their lives and deaths are fully in the hands of their Lord. Regarding timing, in *Bhagavad-gita* 11:32 Krishna declares "*kalo 'smi*," literally meaning, "Time I am." Vaishnavas with deep faith in the divine have a sense that God's timing, especially in regard to the passing of surrendered devotees, must somehow be perfect, although it is often incomprehensible to imperfect human reason—because He is time: it is mystically non-different from Him.

AKAL MRITYU: TIME OUT OF JOINT

The opposite of *sukal mrityu*, a well-timed death, is *akal mrityu*, an ill-timed passing of the soul from the body. The attendants at the Kashi Labh Muktibhavan accept only those people who appear to be three or four days away from a natural death, because the priests there consider a premature or *akal mrityu* to be a death that takes place less by the natural process of aging than by a disease that overwhelms one when he or she is still considered "young." The custodians of Muktibhavan also require that people must be over sixty years of age before they are accepted to die there, because they consider sixty the beginning of old age, and only old age is *sukal*, a natural or "good" time to die.

While we have been exploring Hindu understandings of a timely death, in their book *Time for Dying*, B. G. Glaser and A. L. Strauss described how many people in the West in the not-so-distant past tended to follow pious, natural, or religious lifestyles, and they were spontaneously more intuitively sensitive to the timing of their own deaths. However, the *Bhagavata Purana* 1.1.10 predicts that as the current materialistic age known as Kali-yuga continues to progress, people will be *alpa* (meager) in their *ayusha* (duration of life),[63] and they will be *manda-bhagya*—"generally unlucky or unfortunate." Glaser and Strauss opined that people's deaths now appear to be significantly less fortunate or controlled than they were even sixty or seventy years ago. From the Hindu perspective, this observation seems to confirm the rapid degradation and deterioration characteristic of the age of Kali.

Truth be told, however, India's devotional *bhakti* traditions assert that too much focus on the timing, techniques, or rituals surrounding one's death actually misses the point. The only true requirement for the practicing devotee is to live and die in *bhakti*, loving devotion to God. All other customs and rituals are subservient to this one overarching principle. This factor is ultimately more important than the exact timing of the soul's departure from its mortal coil. For Vaishnavas, if one is able to think of God at the moment of death—whether it happens at *brahma-muhurta* [the auspicious early-morning hours], noon, midnight, or any time or place—the particular timing, locale, and other circumstances will be far less relevant than the God-conscious demeanor of the dying devotee, and God's grace, which cannot be limited by time or place.

"GOOD PORTALS" FOR THE SOUL'S DEPARTURE

Hindus believe that when the soul leaves the body at the time of death, it passes through one of the natural bodily openings, some of which are considered "good" or propitious for leaving at the time of death, whereas others are not. The *Garuda Purana* 1:26–32 and 9:36–37 elaborates:

The soul will leave sinners from the lower regions [such as the anus]. For the virtuous, their souls will be released from somewhere in their heads, like their eyes....

For the person who at the last moment performs these activities [hearing or chanting the holy names of God, taking Ganges water, sacred *tulsi* leaf, etc.], the soul of these religious persons comes out through a hole in the top of the head [known as the *brahma-randhra*]. The mouth, nose, eyes, and ears: the life's breath (*prana-vayu*) of religious people comes out through these seven doors.

Filippi explains that the soul of a just and pious person will emerge with the "vital breath" through the suture at the top of the skull, or through one of the other portals considered favorable, such as the mouth,[64] eyes, nostrils, or ears. However, the soul of a sinful or materialistic person passes through the anus along with excrement, and this is considered a "bad" death. Such inauspicious departures are sometimes experienced by family members of dying patients or hospital attendants. It is therefore not surprising that in India it is considered practical to die with no food in the digestive tract.

CLEANLINESS AT DEATH

According to Vaishnava-Hindu philosophy, the greatest impurity or "uncleanliness" that can adversely affect a dying person is the subtle stain of materialistic desire that remains tightly impacted in the heart, even up to the time of death. In the *Bhagavata Purana* this impurity is compared to a knot of ignorance or contamination in the heart, known as the *hriday granthi*, which can only be cut or cleansed away by self-realization and devotional service.

However, in Hinduism, the term "cleanliness is next to godliness" applies not only to a person's internal cleanliness in the heart, but also to the external cleanliness of the body. A worker at the Kashi Labh Muktib-havan explained how *shaucham*, external cleanliness—which is mentioned as a spiritual quality in *Bhagavad-gita* 13.8—is also considered important for a "good" religious death in India:

We instruct the guardians. We tell them to bathe the sick person every day, and to serve him, to make him sit in the sun in the winter, to air their beds. We insist they keep them clean. If not, how can we perform our religious ceremonies? How can we read the *Gita* and the *Ramayana* [to the dying patients] if they are not kept clean?[65]

Because in Hindu culture one should read holy scriptures like the *Bhagavad-gita* or *Ramayana* only in a clean and sanctified place, the attendant's point is that the environment in the dying persons' rooms must also be kept hygienic and unpolluted. Traditionally, Hindus prefer to die on the ground to protect themselves from undesirable situations:

The old man should not expire suspended between heaven and earth, as he would on his bed; between heaven and earth there is the atmospheric environment (*antariksha*), populated by subtle beings [different malevolent entities]... ready to invade the body. The dying man, lying on the ground, can better grip onto an objective reality, remain in the waking state, and die lucidly while concentrated on the phenomenon he is experiencing.[66]

The people in my Chaitanya Vaishnava community whose deaths we have already mentioned, including Kirtida Devi, Bhakti Tirtha Swami, Mula Prakriti Devi, and others, have died—as far as I am aware—in a normal bed instead of on the ground. However, there are no reports of any of them having problems with malevolent subtle beings as their deaths approached. The faithful in their tradition would credit these individuals' freedom from such influences to their serious adherence to spiritual *sadhana* [practice]—many years of chanting and prayer—as well as their avoidance of intoxication, gambling, meat-eating, illicit sex, and other materialistic habits. Hinduism's general understanding is that unfriendly beings can only harass someone who has a bad habit or weakness that allows such beings entrance. In modern life, drunken persons are often seen wandering the street muttering strange things, as if ghostly-haunted. The Hindu understanding is that an alcoholic has so weakened his body by his habit that in such a compromised condition subtle beings like ghosts can more readily enter his body and disturb him. It appears that at some point in Hindu culture, sages observed that because subtle beings move in space (or ether, *akash*), it is safer when materialistic dying persons are not suspended in the air.

THE COMPLEXITY OF DEATH

Phyllis Palgi and A. Abramovitch[67] suggested that the restored and decorated corpse in Western funerals portrays a "fiction" that gives the misleading impression that the deceased's soul is idyllically sleeping. Researchers such as Elisabeth Kübler-Ross have asserted optimistically that all people are alike at birth and at death, and in her books she reported that a vast majority of dying people have positive experiences such as illumination, apparitions of angelic beings or already-deceased relatives, and the like.[68] According to Hindu scripture, however, this understanding presents an oversimplified picture that is at odds with descriptions of the afterlife in the *Shiva Purana, Garuda Purana,* and other Indian scriptures, which describe how karma profoundly influences a person's birth, life, and death—positively or negatively.

In fact, it may be argued that Kübler-Ross's scenario is also at odds with clinical reality: nurses and hospice workers routinely report "good" deaths and "bad" ones. Some dying people exhibit what is called "terminal restlessness," in which they become frightened and resistant against the dramatic change that is taking place. Sometimes such restless persons are even found to tumble from their beds as their death approaches. Other dying persons—observed to be more at peace with themselves and their understanding of the divine—are found to pass away serenely.

In the real world, while they indeed follow similar general patterns, birth and death are nonetheless highly individual. One baby may be born into health, wealth, and comfort, while another emerges from the womb of an alcoholic, mentally deranged mother who is afflicted with life-threatening diseases and mental turmoil. One person dies peacefully with satisfying closure and faith, while another dies in fear and agitation, passing stool and urine in his bed. How "alike" are all births and deaths, in truth? The *Bhagavad-gita* teaches that the ramifications of karma are unfathomably complex, inevitably impacting on how we are born and how we die.

In the religious traditions of India, dying is viewed as a process of radical, uprooting transition, and major life transitions are almost always challenging and disorienting—at least, let it be said, they are viewed as rarely serene. From the Hindu perspective, "Death is dangerous because it is a time of transition. It is a liminal or marginal space, a bridge between life and life."

In this transitional period, the soul is called a *preta,* literally one who has "gone forth" from the body but has not yet arrived at its new destination."[69] The *Shiva Purana* vividly describes how the *preta* finds itself in an uncomfortable, hungry and thirsty, body-less, ghost-like condition; in fact, during its volatile transitive state it may prove disruptive to its close survivors. This view is consistent with many cultures' folklore regarding the existence and behavior of disembodied souls after their deaths.

As soon as the soul "leaves" the body, messengers known as *yamadutas* take it to the court of Yamaraja, the king of death, for judgment. Via this judgment the *preta* gets a preliminary inkling of the punishment (or perhaps less stressed in the scriptures, rewards) it will likely receive as a consequence of the actions it has performed, but the retributions are apparently not always exacted immediately.

The common Hindu understanding is that, in most cases, for about ten days the characteristically restless *preta* finds itself in a state of limbo in which it restively attempts to get some relief or control over its destiny. During this transition period the deceased often aspires to re-enter the body it has just vacated, but is prevented from doing so by its *yamaduta* attendants. The *preta* may also vainly attempt to communicate with loved ones or sometimes to disturb rivals. The purgatory-like state in which a disembodied *preta* hovers is viewed in Hindu canon as a discomfiting, though temporary exile from corporeally advantaged life.[70]

The tradition views the itinerant soul that finds itself in this materialistic quagmire as patently homeless, because in this world even a vagrant bum who owns nothing else at least possesses a physical body as a corporeal "home" for his soul; yet a *preta* no longer has that consolation. When Eck speaks of the fragile, "liminal" uncertainty of the *preta*-stage, an analogy comes to mind: Boarding a 747 jet on an international flight. Even if a passenger is headed for a rewarding and favorable destination—for example, he or she is Hollywood-bound to receive an Academy Award—there still remains an at least subconscious trepidation in transit, in mid-air, until one has actually touched down and arrived safely at his or her destination. Because the *preta* has not yet arrived at its next bodily station, it remains in a precarious situation. As a modern aircraft flying high above the clouds can experience technical difficulties or be hijacked by terrorists or downed by missiles or explosives smuggled on board, the *preta*'s disembodied limbo renders it vulnerable to unfavorable subtle entities.

As an addendum, perhaps, there are various means by which Hinduism seeks to relieve the plight of the *preta*, not least being the famous *shraddha* ceremony. In this well-worn ritual, Hindus traditionally offer rice-balls (*pinda*) for the benefit of the departed soul each day up until the tenth day after death. On the twelfth day, a rite known as *sapindikaran* (also known as *shraddha*) is enacted, intended to consolidate the *preta*'s attainment of a body suitable for reunion with his already deceased ancestors (*pitris*). Here he or she enjoys with them an afterlife realm described in the ancient *Rig*

Veda 9.113.7–11 as replete with pleasures such as "… the drinking of *soma*, milk and honey and experiencing love."[71]

In Hinduism, the end of bodily life also has a literally bright side. "Death is not only a time of danger, for it is also held to be a time of great illumination. At death, they say, the light is very intense, and what separates this shore from the far shore is almost transparent. The time of death, therefore, is a time of clear seeing, of vision, of insight."[72] Other researchers from the West such as Elisabeth Kübler-Ross also report that many people who survive near-death experiences report them as times of great illumination.[73]

However, such data—which reported a wide preponderance of cases of peaceful serenity and illumination in the dying—was gained largely by interviewing people who had survived death, or who were just about to die, and these findings may not address the dilemma of a disembodied soul that has been suspended in a limbo. From the perspective of Hindu scriptures, which designate that different individuals have widely varying karma and extremely divergent states of consciousness at the time of death, to assume that nearly everyone who dies uniformly encounters the same sort of positive phenomena, i.e., illumination, angelic beings, or apparitions of affectionate deceased relatives who lovingly and gently lead the newly deceased through the transition—would seem an oversimplification.

GRACE FOR THE DYING

When I was passing through the New Delhi train station during the writing of this chapter, a friendly Christian evangelist from America on a preaching mission to India asked a few questions about Lord Krishna. Although he listened politely to my answers, it became obvious that he was filtering what he heard through an imposing network of deeply rooted assumptions. Having already concluded that Christianity was the only religious tradition capable of offering divine grace or mercy, he was not open to the possibility that these most sublime spiritual gifts—grace and mercy—have been an integral part of India's living religious and scriptural traditions for thousands of years, and they continue to play an important role in Hindus' approach to death today.

Historians may not agree that this has always been the case. Thomas Hopkins explained that in the early Vedic period, entrance into the celestial abode of one's ancestors did not depend on divine grace; rather, more stress was given to the proper execution of ritual performances, both by the deceased prior to their death and by surviving family members afterward. Later, however, Upanishadic metaphysical expositions explained that even residence in the abode of "the forefathers" was temporary—remaining under the ambit of *samsara*, the cycle of material existence—and it would necessarily lead, eventually, to rebirth and its concomitant suffering.

While the goal of the Upanishadic path of knowledge (*jnana marg*) was escape from the ceaseless cycle of *samsara* through realization of the transcendent nature of self, it was not destined to be the "only way" in Hinduism. During the period in which the Puranas were being written, release from rebirth became possible not just via transcendental knowledge alone, but also through the "divine gift to faithful devotees."[74] That "divine gift" was grace, pure and simple.

The translation, in 1901, of a Brahmi script engraving from the famous "Heliodorus column" discovered in central India in 1877, revealed that a Greek ambassador in India converted to Vaishnava *bhakti* more than a century before the appearance of Christ. This substantiated that the grace clearly elucidated in the *Bhagavad-gita* and *Bhagavata Purana* was not borrowed or "imported" from Christianity. On the contrary, *The Cambridge History of India* states that Krishna worship—which includes the doctrine of divine grace—predates Christianity by many centuries.

The fallacious speculation that grace does not, or cannot, exist in Hinduism, and that the only recourse the devout or devoted in Indian tradition have is to Sisyphus-like drudgery via the folly of vain "works" or well-meaning but God-less karma,[75] does not hold water in the face of Lord Krishna's unambiguous declaration in *Bhagavad-gita* 18.56: "By My grace, though engaged in all kinds of activities, under My protection My pure devotee reaches the eternal and Imperishable Abode." The word Krishna uses for grace or mercy here is *prasad*. Other important Sanskrit terms that appear frequently in ancient Hindu texts are *kripa* or mercy, *karunya* or divine kindness, and *daya*, divine compassion. In the ancient Vaishnava text *Brahma-samhita*, 5.54, Brahma declared that Lord Krishna, by His grace, minimizes or nullifies the reactionary karmic influences of a devotee's past karmic deeds, both pious and sinful.[76]

Perhaps no example of a devotee's dependence on divine grace or mercy is as moving in Hinduism as the story of Draupadi in the *Mahabharata*. When that noble lady was being stripped naked in an open assembly without any human being willing to step forward and protect her honor, she realized that it would be impossible to save herself by her own strength or karma. Thus, she utterly depended on God, throwing her hands up in the air and helplessly chanting Lord Krishna's divine name, like a helpless child in danger, desperately calling upon its mother. Miraculously, Krishna expanded Draupadi's *sari* dress material, so that the vile men who were trying to disrobe her found themselves pulling up piles and piles of cloth. But the cloth was being mystically expanded while their arms simply grew tired and they finally gave up. Through God's grace, the great devotee Draupadi was thus saved in her darkest hour. Like Draupadi in her crisis, at the time of death everyone is helpless and utterly dependent on the mercy of the Lord.

In his *Shikshastaka* prayers, verse five, Sri Chaitanya Mahaprabhu humbly begged for the Lord's mercy or *kripa*: "My dear Lord, I am your eternal servant, but somehow or other I have fallen into the ocean of this material world. By Your mercy, kindly pick me up and fix me as a speck of dust at Your lotus feet."

These are not isolated examples—grace and mercy abound in Hinduism. Lord Shiva—who some Hindus (Shaivites) consider to be God, whereas others see him as the greatest devotee of God (because he is always chanting Lord Vishnu's, Rama's, or Krishna's divine names)—is particularly renowned for bestowing his magnanimous grace on the dying in Kashi (Benares):

Whatever "liberation" is, there is almost complete unanimity that all who die in Kashi get it. Shiva's grace is indiscriminately extended to all, whether they be Brahman or *chandal* (untouchable), *raja* [king] or beggar, dog, insect, Muslim, or *mleccha* (foreigner). Not only is caste made irrelevant to one's prospects of salvation, but so too is karma. Here in Kashi, Shiva bestows his blessing on sinners, "just as a mother takes a dirty child onto her lap."[77]

In the Shaiva tradition, a scriptural story highlights Shiva's ability to bestow grace on the dying:

A childless couple prayed to Lord Shiva to grant them a son. He asked them to choose between a virtuous son who would live for a mere sixteen years, and a dunce with a long life. The parents opted for the former, and Markandeya was born. As the hour of death approached, Markandeya prayed to Lord Shiva to deliver him from death. When the Lord of Death came to ensnare the soul of the youngster, Lord Shiva intervened and granted immortality to the boy. The site of this miracle in Tirukkadavur (Tamil Nadu, India) has a temple that is visited by people praying for a long life on their 60th and 80th birthdays. Markandeya grew to become a great sage, and one of the eighteen major Puranas is named after him.[78]

Even those Hindus who consider Shiva to be merely a great devotee or demigod (rather than the supreme Godhead) have no problem accepting that he can bestow grace or mercy, because in Indian tradition it is understood that the predominant means by which God bestows grace to human beings is through an intermediary—a guru or special representative of the Supreme. The role of such an intermediary was stressed by Lord Krishna in *Bhagavad-gita* 4.34: "Just try to learn the truth by approaching a spiritual master. Inquire from him submissively and render service unto him. The self-realized souls can impart knowledge unto you because they have seen the truth." Near the end of the *Gita*, Lord Krishna declared, "Just surrender to me. I shall deliver you from all sinful reactions. Do not fear."

But earlier, Krishna explained that surrendering to Him means to follow a spiritual master, an intermediary servant-devotee.

My friend Kirtida had faith that she would go to Lord Krishna's divine abode after her death due to the mercy of her spiritual master, and by his intercession, she would receive the grace of Lord Krishna. Although she was very pious and devout, her faith was not based on any particular karma, rituals, or spiritual activities that she had performed. When she chanted the names of God, she did not do so to accrue "good karma" or piety to get an advantageous birth in her next life. When she chanted, she was calling on the mercy of her Lord, like a child calling to its mother, or like Draupadi calling out Krishna's name—"He Govinda"—while she was being stripped naked.

Although it may appear that techniques of conscious dying are absolutely necessary in Hinduism, a beautiful story from the Sri Vaishnava tradition suggests that ultimately God's grace is the most important factor in a good or enlightened death. This was related by modern-day Vaishnava evangelist Indradyumna Swami in his *Diary of a Traveling Preacher*:

It is important how one actually leaves this world. In one sense, a devotee's whole life is in preparation for that one moment.... The consciousness at death determines one's next destination. There is a Bengali proverb: *bhajan kara sadhana kara, murte janle hoy*: "Whatever *bhajan* [worship] or *sadhana* [spiritual practices] one has performed throughout his life will be tested at the moment of death!"

But what happens if a devotee cannot fix his or her mind on Krishna at that crucial moment? A doctor recently told me that eighty percent of people are actually unconscious at the moment of death! The body "naturally" goes into a state of shock before the traumatic moment when the soul leaves the body.... Once Ramanujacharya [an eleventh-century philosopher and spiritual master in South India's Shri Sampradaya], after the disappearance of Yamunacharya [his guru], was pensive with some questions. He requested Kanchipuma, the servant of Lord Varadaraja (Krishna), to ask the Lord some questions on his behalf. One of the questions was this: What happens if a devotee dies suddenly and is unable to think of you at the time of his death? Lord Varadaraja replied, "Then, I will think of My devotee."[79]

Divine grace for the dying is so prominent in Hinduism, in fact, that it is not restricted to human beings. Many Puranic accounts reveal that grace or mercy can even be bestowed upon animals as they face the threat of death. This should not be entirely surprising, because a Hindu tenet holds that all creatures, including animals, possess souls or are souls, just as human beings do; in fact, several prominent avatars—divine descents or incarnations of the Lord on earth—appeared on earth in the form of animals.[80]

Bhagavata Purana 8.4.6 describes how an elephant named Gajendra [who was *not* an avatar] was attacked by a ferocious crocodile, and he recited prayers recollected from a previous human birth, finally attaining *bhuri-karunaya,* "the unlimited mercy or grace of God" in the form of *sarupya-mukti,* "spiritual salvation" in Vaikuntha, the kingdom of God. The *Mahabharata* recounts how King Yudhisthira once refused to go to heaven unless his dog could accompany him to that celestial realm. The *Chaitanya Charitamrita* 2.1.140, a Medieval Bengali holy text, describes how a dog that had been befriended by a great Vaishnava, Shivananda Sen, attained salvation in the spiritual world after receiving spiritual food that had been offered to God (*prasad*) and the audience of Chaitanya Mahaprabhu.

Hinduism offers another special avenue by which the dying, either human or beast, can benefit from divine grace or mercy. There are many Puranic accounts describing inimical or demonic human beings or beasts that were personally killed by God or one of his divine incarnations. The ungodly living entities were purified by the personal touch of the Lord, and they attained salvation. The demons Kamsa, Putana, and Shishupal are examples of demons who all attainted liberation by dying at the hands of Lord Krishna.

DYING AS A LEARNING AND TEACHING EXPERIENCE

Hindu scriptures recount many examples of dying persons who imparted wisdom from their deathbeds, as we have seen in the case of Bhishmadeva in the *Bhagavata Purana.* Compared to the West, Hindu households are more commonly comprised of extended families. Indeed, married couples traditionally feel it is their *dharma* or duty to care for elderly parents, who often live with their married children, though with the passage of time this custom seems to be not as common as in the past. At any rate, it happens quite frequently that the death of an elder will become a family event in Hinduism.

In the West, however, elderly persons more frequently die away from their intimate family members, in old age homes. In Hinduism, it is therefore much more likely that the surviving members will get the firsthand opportunity to participate in the death experience and to thus gain a broader perspective of the whole panorama of life and death.

Elisabeth Kübler-Ross has stated that death can be an edifying learning experience—not only for the dying person, but for the entire family or extended community that participates in or witnesses the event. She recommends that a dying individual should depart in the company of loved ones and that children should be part of the death-process: they should not be excluded.

When Tamal Krishna Goswami decided it was best that Kirtida pass away in Dallas rather than sacred Vrindavan, one of the factors behind his decision was the conviction that it would be a profound learning experience for the Vaishnavas in the Dallas community, including the children, to witness the self-willed death of a saintly Vaisnavi. Kübler-Ross explained the importance of including children in this process:

We routinely shelter children from death and dying, thinking we are protecting them from harm. But it is clear that we do them a disservice by depriving them of this experience. By making death and dying a taboo subject and keeping children away from people who are dying or have died, we create fear that need not be there. The fact that children are allowed to stay at home where a fatality has stricken and are included in the talk, discussions, and fears gives them a feeling that they are not alone in the grief and gives them the comfort of shared responsibility and shared mourning. It prepares them gradually and helps them view death as part of life, an experience that may help them grow and mature.[81]

In Kirtida Devi's unusually public death, many children in the Dallas community visited her daily, either with their parents, with other children, or even on their own. Often the kids would sit on her bed, speak with her lovingly, hold her hand, massage her feet, or chant during the *kirtans* in her room. Seeing such an accessible, God-conscious, and fearless role model, the children's ability to face their own future deaths increased immeasurably.

CONCLUSION: DYING AS A BLISSFUL EXPERIENCE

Most spiritual traditions understand that there comes a time for a departing soul to let go of life in the dying, decaying body it has inhabited. The dying person at that point should be allowed and encouraged to direct his or her attention as wholeheartedly as possible to God or the transcendent, beyond the temporal. If he or she truly "lets go," death can be experienced as a release from the miserable bodily strictures and a positive source of joy. In this connection, Rabindranath Tagore declared, "Because I love this life, I know I shall love death as well."[82] Overall, Tagore advocated a brave, impassioned acquiescence to death's inevitable call:

> Death, thy servant, is at my door.
> He has crossed the unknown sea and
> brought thy call to my home.
> The night is dark and my heart is
> Fearful – yet I will take up the lamp,
> open my gates and bow to him my
> welcome. It is thy messenger who
> stands at my door.
> I will worship him with folded hands
> and with tears. I will worship him
> placing at his feet the treasure of my
> heart.

He will go back with his errand done,
leaving a dark shadow on my morning;
and in my desolate home only my
forlorn self will remain at my last
offering.[83]

The following segment from *Servant of Love: The Saintly Life of Kirtida Devi* suggests something far beyond noble acquiescence; rather it gives us a glimpse of the ineffable beatitude of spiritual bliss. It begins with descriptions by two senior Vaishnava ladies regarding the uncommonly blissful mood that permeated the group chanting sessions held for Kirtida a matter of days before her death:

One evening some days after the Vyasa-puja program, and only a matter of days before Kirtida would "leave her body," her condition took a drastic change for the worse and a long and heartfelt *kirtan* [congregational chanting] ensued, as Chandravali Devi recalls:

It was earlier in the night and Kirtida was really, really sick. We were chanting nicely, and when the chanting reached a crescendo she raised up, raised her hands in ecstasy and everybody jumped up and started dancing. It was like celebrating victory over death. You almost felt ashamed, you know, that you were enjoying someone getting ready to pass on. But that's how it felt: it felt like a joyous occasion. She had no fear of death, and she was so happy to be there in Dallas with her spiritual master and her devotee friends, the deities, her old medical friends, and her sister and brother.

Twenty or thirty devotees who were packed into that tiny room started dancing with reckless abandon, and the bliss was so thick it was unbelievable. Not a single person seemed capable of escaping the ecstasy—it was like a spiritual tsunami or tidal wave. Indranila-mani Devi described the blissful dancing:

Mother Kirtida began clapping and swaying her arms from side to side, and all of a sudden everyone got up and started blissfully dancing. Mirabai was doing Bharata Natyam dance steps, Chandravali was doing [African American] "soul" steps, Padad-huli and two other ladies formed a *mandala* or circle, and they were dancing blissfully around and around. More devotees started coming in and joining the transcendental *kirtan*. Everyone was smiling, singing and dancing. At that time I stood on a chair and started taking pictures of Mother Kirtida, who was so beautiful with her *maha*-flower garland[84] and was so happy, enjoying *kirtan* and seeing the devotees dancing. Then all the devotees, while dancing, started going around and took turns having their pictures taken with Kirtida, who was so bright and effulgent. That night everyone was in ecstasy. By her association, we were all inspired with the holy name.

During these wonderful chanting sessions, Kirtida and the devotees were totally unconcerned with her upcoming physical demise. As she raised her hands in ecstasy and swayed to-and-fro, the devotees danced into the night, like innocent children. It was clear that this was a special event, a celebration of divine love's triumph over death; it was anything but a grim ending. Indeed, it felt to the participants as if a spiritual airplane was taking off, as if that little room in East Dallas had temporarily become the center of the universe. If there were any angels or demigods lucky enough to be in the vicinity, they must have similarly danced, showered celestial flowers, played their own divine instruments, and joined in the uproarious *kirtan*, which seemed to rock the entire universe.[85]

Although for many the topic of death may be grim, in the *Mahabharata* the sage Sanatsujata told King Dhritarashtra that ultimately death is merely "a tiger made of straw"; therefore it is not to be feared by one who has transcendental knowledge.[86] Hinduism sees death as part of life, and the *bhakti* traditions view it as an aspect or stage of *seva* or divine surrender and service—which are unlimitedly blissful, not morbid. Yes, we should make no bones about it: physical death can be, and almost always is, a terribly difficult test for anyone. But according to Hinduism as well as other faith traditions, a life of *seva* can profoundly affect the dramatic transition that is death. Saint John of the Cross declared:

The death of such persons is very gentle and very sweet—sweeter and more gentle than was their whole spiritual life on earth. For they die with the most sublime impulses and delightful encounters of love, resembling the swan, whose song is much sweeter at the moment of death.[87]

When I read this moving passage, it immediately reminded me of my friend Kirtida's enlightened passing. For a Hindu, a saintly death can also be "very gentle and very sweet," as sweet as Krishna's flute-playing, as colorful as the peacock feathers He wears on His head, as exciting as the battles He wages with demons like King Kamsa and Trinavarta, and as captivating as His joking and dancing pastimes with the *gopi* milk-maidens of Vrindavan.

NOTES

1. Sigmund Freud, "Thoughts for the Times on War and Death" (1915) in *Collected Papers*, vol. 4, trans. by Joan Riviere (London and New York: Basic Books, 1959), 304–5.

2. Philippe Aries, *The Hour of Our Death* (Oxford: Oxford University Press, 1981), 560.

3. R. Griffith, *The Hymns of the Rg Veda* (Benares: 1896–97), vol. II (Delhi, India: Moltilal Banarsidass, 1993), 406.

4. Frederick H. Holck, ed., *Death and Eastern Thought: Understanding Death in Eastern Religions and Philosophies* (New York: Abington Press, 1974), 29.

5. Ibid., 39, citing *Shatapatha Brahmana* 10.4.3.9.

6. The *Bhagavata Purana* describes how Dhruva's mother also joined her son and ascended to heavenly realms in her selfsame body.

7. A. C. Bhaktivedanta Swami Prabhupada, *The Bhagavad-gita As It Is* (Los Angeles, Bhaktivedanta Book Trust, 1983) 91, 101–6.

8. Jonathan P. Parry, *Death in Banaras* (Cambridge: Cambridge University Press, 1994), 172.

9. E-mail in 2001 to author from Dayananda Dasa of New York.

10. See Christopher Justice, *Dying the Good Death: The Pilgrimage to India's Holy City* (Albany: State University of New York Press, 1997). Justice suggests that Hinduism views death as a process rather than an event.

11. Peter Medley/Sarvabhauma Dasa, *Servant of Love: The Saintly Life of Kirtida Devi* (Badger, CA: Torchlight Publishers, 2007).

12. Kenneth Kramer, *The Sacred Art of Dying: How World Religions Understand Death* (New York: Paulist Press, 1988), 1.

13. Diana K. Eck, *Banares: City of Light* (Princeton: Princeton University Press, 1982), 343.

14. Transcript of a recording made at the San Diego Hospice and Palliative Care Center on May 19, 2005, San Diego, California.

15. Parry, op. cit. 82, 158.

16. In Hinduism "next life" does not mean that everyone who dies must necessarily reincarnate in the material world. The goal of Vaishnavas, the religious majority in India, is that their soul be conveyed to Vaikuntha, i.e., the Kingdom of God, after death. Millions of Shaivites, worshippers of Lord Shiva, aspire to attain the divine abode of Shiva known as Kailash.

17. Eck, op. cit, 343.

18. Rachel Stanworth, *Recognizing Spiritual Needs* (Oxford: Oxford University Press, 2004), 103.

19. In the Hindu traditions, dying in ignorance is viewed as akin to anything else done in low consciousness—it brings uncertainty and misery. It is like whimsically dropping out of college, quitting a job, or leaving one's spouse without a reasonable, thought-out plan or alternative. If we "disregard" anything vital in life, such as our children, spouse, health, or career, it has disastrous or negative results. Hinduism teaches that death should similarly not be disregarded.

20. Ernest Becker, *The Denial of Death* (New York: The Free Press, 1973), intro., ix. While India's emphasis on heightened awareness at the time of death may be arguably more upfront than some other theological traditions, it is certainly not unique. According to Aries, after the fifteenth century in the West, Christians understood that the events of one's life would flash through the consciousness of a dying person and therefore heightened awareness—rather than smothering unconsciousness—was considered indispensable at that momentous time, to provide life "its final meaning, its conclusion." In this connection, Saint Catherine of Siena's last moment before death was depicted by her biographers as the "supreme moment of her life, which she had so much desired."

21. Paul Thigpen, *Dictionary of Quotes from the Saints* (Ann Arbor: Servant Publications, 2001), 55.

22. M. K. Gandhi, *The Complete Works of Mahatma Gandhi* (New Delhi: Government of India Publication, 1958), 271.

23. Philip Kapleau, *The Wheel of Death: A Collection of Writings from Zen Buddhist and Other Sources* (New York: Harper & Row, 1971), intro., xvi, citing Karlis Osis from "Deathbed Observations by Physicians and Nurses," *Journal of the American Society for Psychical Research* (October, 1963).

24. S. N. Bhavaskar and Gertrud Kiem, "Spirituality and Health (Ayurveda)" in *Hindu Spirituality: Vedas Through Vedanta,* ed. Krishna Sivaraman (New York: Crossroad, 1989), 356. The necessity of feeding and hydrating gerontological and terminally ill patients has developed into a controversial ethical and legal issue in North America, in which the home environment often sees pressure from family members for an elderly person to continue to be sustained by eating and drinking, even—sometimes—when the desire to eat diminishes dramatically, as a normal, natural physiological stage in the dying process.

25. The *Garuda Purana* (8:25–26) states, "The person who chants the names of Vishnu, the destroyer of sins, or chants the *Gita* or hears it from others ... [and who takes] Ganges water, *tulsi* leaves, water from the feet of Vishnu (*charanamrita*), these things give *mukti* [liberation] at the time of death."

26. Justice, op. cit., 228.

27. R. S. Khare, "Prediction of Death among the Kanyo-Kubja Brahmins," *Contributions to Indian Sociology* 2(1) (1967): 167.

28. Justice, op. cit., 199.

29. See Claudia Welch, "The Secret Potential of Brahma-muhurta," in *Namarupa: Categories of Indian Thought,* eds. Robert Moses and Eddie Stern (New York: *Namarupa*, 2003).

30. Medley/Dasa, *Servant of Love,* op. cit., 235.

31. Justice, op. cit., 230.

32. Ibid., 3.

33. Parry, op. cit., 172–73.

34. Maurice Bloch and Jonathan Parry, eds., *Death and the Regeneration of Life* (Cambridge, UK: Cambridge University Press, 1982), 16.

35. Justice, op. cit., 211.

36. Sherwin Nuland, *How to Die: Reflections of Life's Final Chapter* (New York: Vintage Books, 1993), 143.

37. Justice, op. cit., 90.

38. Holck, op. cit., 90, citing Shinn.

39. Joseph Henderson and Maude Oaks, eds., *The Wisdom of the Serpent: Myths of Death, Rebirth and Resurrection,* 2nd ed. (Princeton NJ: Princeton University Press, 1990), 81.

40. Parry, op. cit., 21.

41. Justice, op. cit., xvi.

42. Lex Hixon, *Great Swan: Meeting with Ramakrishna* (Burdett, New York: Larson Publications, 1996), 130.

43. Lord Krishna himself was a cowherd boy or *gopa*.

44. This segment was extracted from a Web site organized by disciples of Bhakti Tirtha Swami (www.btswami.com).

45. Medley/Dasa, *Servant of Love,* op. cit., appendix A.

46. Graham M. Schweig, "Dying the Good Death," *Journal of Vaishnava Studies*, Vol. 11, No. 2 (Nyack, N.Y.: A Deepak Publishing, 2003), 107 n. 8.

47. E. H. Rick Jarow, "The Good Death," *Journal of Vaishnava Studies* 11(2, Spring) (2003): 74.

48. Kramer, op. cit., 35.

49. Prabhupada, *Bhagavad-gita As It Is*, op. cit., 440–41.

50. Steven Rosen, *Black Lotus: The Spiritual Journey of an Urban Mystic* (Washington, DC: Hari Nama Press, 2007), 330.

51. Parry, op. cit., 176–79. While cremation is common for the deceased in Hinduism, saints' bodies are considered pure and are generally not cremated; rather they are buried in a shrine or Samadhi (tomb). Deceased infants are also considered pure and are generally not cremated; Parry reported that sometimes infant's bodies are immersed in a holy river, such as the Ganges.

52. Ibid., 19.

53. Ibid., 30. The *Garuda Purana* (16:112–14) identifies the following holy places as *tirthas*: "Those persons who, wanting to die, leave their homes to live in Prayag [Allahabad] or some other *tirtha* ... will definitely get *moksha* [liberation]. Ayodhya, Mathura [which includes Vrindavan], Haridwar, Kashi [Benares], Kanchi, Ujjain and Dwaraka: these are seven *moksha*-bestowing places."

54. Justice, op. cit., 81.

55. Eck, op. cit., 344.

56. Peter Medley/Sarvabhauma Dasa, "Where to Die? Is Vrindavan the only choice for devotees of Lord Krishna?" *Back to Godhead*, 36(1) (2002): Alachua, FL: Bhaktivedanta Book Trust. In commenting on a verse in *Srimad Bhagavatam* 1.19.15 Prabhupada explained that the association of devotees significantly helped King Parikshit go back to Godhead. Even though he "flew his own plane," he also had assistance: "The atmosphere *created by the presence of great devotees of the Lord* [italics my emphasis] on the bank of the Ganges and Maharaja Parikshit's complete acceptance of the Lord's lotus feet were sufficient guarantee to the king for going back to Godhead." The presence of devotees—*sadhu-sanga*—helped King Parikshit go back to the spiritual world.

57. Gian Giuseppe Filippi, *Mrtyu: Concept of Death in Indian Traditions* (New Delhi: D.K. Printworld, 1996 [English trans. from the Italian]), 117.

58. Phone conversation with the author of this chapter.

59. Stephen Knapp, *Facing Death: Welcoming the Afterlife* (Detroit: World Relief Network, 1999), 58.

60. Filippi, op. cit., 105–6.

61. Personal letter from Gauri Dasi to Virabahu Dasa and Karta Dasi, 1985.

62. Filippi, op. cit, page undetermined.

63. Hridayananda Dasa Goswami has demonstrated in his translation and commentary on *Bhagavata Purana* 12.2.2 (see bibliography under Goswami, Hridayananda dasa) that if the abbreviated life duration of aborted fetuses is factored into the data for determining the statistical lifespan of people today, the actual average lifespan for people in contemporary society significantly diminishes.

64. At the moment my friend Kirtida passed away, she conspicuously opened her mouth, a favorable portal for the soul's departure.

65. Justice, op. cit., 103.

66. Ibid., 116.

67. Phyllis Palgi and A. Abramovitch, "The Anthropology of Death," *Annual Review of Anthropology* 13 (1984): 410.

68. This seems to be a general assumption of Kübler-Ross, but I do not profess to be an expert on her research and conclusions.

69. Eck, op. cit., 342–43.

70. Neil Gilman, *The Death of Death: Resurrection and Immortality in Jewish Thought* (Woodstock, VT: Jewish Lights Publishing, 1997), 23. Although drawn from a Judaic rather than Hindu perspective, Gilman's portrayal of destitute, homeless exile in *The Death of Death* seems to mirror the *preta*'s forlorn desperation. "To be in exile is to be condemned to a life of wandering, to have no 'place,' no 'home.' It is also, as Cain understood, to be vulnerable. To grasp that sense of vulnerability, all we need do is contemplate the fate of the many homeless people on our cities' streets." The *preta*'s homelessness is even more forlorn.

71. Holck, op. cit., x.

72. Eck, op. cit., 342–43.

73. Elisabeth Kübler-Ross, *The Tunnel and the Light: Essential Insights on Living and Dying* (New York: Marlowe and Co., 1999), 93–94.

74. Thomas Hopkins, "Hindu Views of Death" in *Death and Afterlife*, ed. Hiroshi Obayishi (Westport, CT: Greenwood Press, 1992), 152.

75. *Bhagavata Purana* 1.5.12 decries any karma or pious action that is not devoted whole-heartedly in God's service: "What is the use of karmic activities, which are naturally painful from the very beginning and transient by nature, if they are not utilized for loving, devotional service of the Lord?"

76. Sarasvati Thakura, Bhaktisiddhanta, *Sri Brahma-samhita* (Mumbai: Bhaktivedanta Book Trust, 2001, orig. published 1972), 98.

77. Parry, op. cit., 27.

78. Agarwal, op. cit., 1–2.

79. Indradyumna Swami, *Diary of a Traveling Preacher,* vol. 3 (Badger, CA.: Torchlight, 2003), chap. 30.

80. These include the incarnation of Matsya-avatar (God who assumed the form of a giant fish), Narasimha-avatar (God as half-man, half-lion), and Varaha-avatar (the Lord in the form of a giant boar).

81. Elisabeth Kübler-Ross, *Death: The Final Stage of Growth* (Upper Saddle River, NJ: Prentice-Hall, 1975), 5–6.

82. Holck, op. cit., 170, citing Rao.

83. R. Tagore, *Gitanjali* (London: Macmillan & Co., 1913), 79.

84. In Hinduism a "*maha*-flower garland" is a garland or lei of flowers that has been offered to the carved icons or "deities," and then is given to a devotee, who sees it as the blessed remnant or *prasad* of the Lord.

85. Medley/Dasa, *Servant of Love*, op. cit., 250–51.

86. Holck, op. cit., 73.

87. Carol Lee Flinders, *Enduring Grace: Living Portraits of Seven Women Mystics* (New York: HarperSanFrancisco, 1993), 108.

SELECTED BIBLIOGRAPHY

Agarwal, Vishal. "Spiritual Role of Children and Adolescents in Hindu Traditions," a paper read at the WAVES Conference (World Association of Vedic Studies) at the University of Houston, summer, 2006.

Antony, C. M. *Saint Catherine of Siena: Her Life and Times.* London: Burns and Oates, 1915.

Aries, Philippe. *The Hour of Our Death.* Oxford: Oxford University Press, 1981.

Becker, Ernest. *The Denial of Death.* New York: The Free Press, 1973.

Bhavaskar, S. N., and Gertrud Kiem, "Spirituality and Health (Ayurveda)." In *Hindu Spirituality: Vedas Through Vedanta,* edited by Krishna Sivaraman. New York: Crossroad, 1989.

Bloch, Maurice, and Jonathan Parry, eds., *Death and the Regeneration of Life.* Cambridge, UK: Cambridge University Press, 1982.

Eck, Diana K. *Banares: City of Light.* Princeton: Princeton University Press, 1982.

Filippi, Gian Giuseppe. *Mrtyu: Concept of Death in Indian Traditions.* Translated by Antonio Rigopoulos. New Delhi: D. K. Printworld, 1996.

Flinders, Carol Lee. *Enduring Grace: Living Portraits of Seven Women Mystics.* New York: HarperSanFrancisco, 1993.

Freud, Sigmund. "Thoughts for the Times on War and Death" (1915). In *Collected Papers,* vol. 4. Translated by Joan Riviere. London and New York: Basic Books, 1959.

Gandhi, M. K. *The Complete Works of Mahatma Gandhi.* New Delhi: Government of India Publication, 1958.

Gilman, Neil. *The Death of Death: Resurrection and Immortality in Jewish Thought.* Woodstock, VT: Jewish Lights Publishing, 1997.

Goswami, Hridayananda dasa. *Srimad Bhagavatam.* Los Angeles: Bhaktivedanta Book Trust, 1988.

Griffith, R. *The Hymns of the Rg Veda* (Benares: 1896–97), Vols. I and II. Delhi, India: Moltilal Banarsidass, 1993.

Henderson, Joseph, and Maude Oaks, eds. *The Wisdom of the Serpent: Myths of Death, Rebirth and Resurrection,* 2nd ed. Princeton, NJ: Princeton University Press, 1990.

Hixon, Lex. *Great Swan: Meeting with Ramakrishna.* Burdett, NY: Larson Publications, 1996.

Holck, Frederick H., ed. *Death and Eastern Thought: Understanding Death in Eastern Religions and Philosophies.* New York: Abington Press, 1974.

Hopkins, Thomas. "Hindu Views of Death." In: *Death and Afterlife,* edited by Hiroshi Obayishi. Westport, CT: Greenwood Press, 1992.

Jarow, E. H. Rick. "The Good Death," *Journal of Vaishnava Studies* 11(2, Spring) (2003).

Justice, Christopher. *Dying the Good Death: The Pilgrimage to India's Holy City.* Albany: State University of New York Press, 1997.

Kapleau, Philip. *The Wheel of Death: A Collection of Writings from Zen Buddhist and Other Sources.* New York: Harper & Row, 1971.

Kapoor, O. B. L. *Experiences in Bhakti: The Science Celestial.* Caracas, Venezuela: Sarasvati Jayasri Classics, 1994.

Khare, R. S. "Prediction of Death among the Kanyo-Kubja Brahmins." *Contributions to Indian Sociology* 2(1) (1967):1–25.

Knapp, Stephen, *Facing Death: Welcoming the Afterlife.* Detroit: World Relief Network, 1999.

Kramer, Kenneth *The Sacred Art of Dying: How World Religions Understand Death.* New York: Paulist Press, 1988.

Kübler-Ross, Elisabeth. *Death: The Final Stage of Growth.* Upper Saddle River, NJ: Prentice-Hall, 1975.

————. *The Tunnel and the Light: Essential Insights on Living and Dying*. New York: Marlowe and Co., 1999.

Medley, Peter/Sarvabhauma Dasa. *Servant of Love: The Saintly Life of Kirtida Devi*. Badger, CA: Torchlight Publishers, 2007.

————. "Where to Die? Is Vrindavan the only choice for devotees of Lord Krishna?" *Back to Godhead* 36(1) (2002): Alachua, FL: Bhaktivedanta Book Trust.

Nuland, Sherwin. *How to Die: Reflections of Life's Final Chapter*. New York: Vintage Books, 1993.

Osis, Karlis, and Erlendur Haraldsson. *At the Hour of Death*. New York: The Hearst Corporation, 1977.

Palgi, Phyllis, and A. Abramovitch. "The Anthropology of Death." *Annual Review of Anthropology* 13 (1984): 385-417.

Parry, Jonathan P. *Death in Banaras*. Cambridge: Cambridge University Press, 1994.

Pattinson, Susan (Sangita Dasi). *The Final Journey: Complete Hospice Care for Departing Vaishnavas*. Badger, CA: Torchlight Publishing, 2002.

Prabhupada, A. C. Bhaktivedanta Swami. *The Bhagavad-gita As It Is*. Los Angeles: Bhaktivedanta Book Trust, 1983.

————. *Srimad Bhagavatam*. Cantos 1-12. Los Angeles: Bhaktivedanta Book Trust, 1987.

Rosen, Steven. *Black Lotus: The Spiritual Journey of an Urban Mystic*. Washington, DC: Hari Nama Press, 2007.

Sarasvati Thakura, Bhaktisiddhanta. *Sri Brahma-samhita*. Mumbai: Bhaktivedanta Book Trust, 2001 (originally published 1972).

Schweig, Graham M. "Dying the Good Death." *Journal of Vaishnava Studies* 11(2, Spring) 2003.

Stanworth, Rachel. *Recognizing Spiritual Needs*. Oxford: Oxford University Press, 2004.

Swami, Indradyumna. *Diary of a Traveling Preacher*. Badger, CA: Torchlight, 2003.

Tagore, R. *Gitanjali*. London: Macmillan & Co., 1913.

Thigpen, Paul. *Dictionary of Quotes from the Saints*. Ann Arbor: Servant Publications, 2001.

Tillich, Paul. *The Courage to Be*. 2nd. ed. New Haven, CT: Yale University Press, 1952.

Welch, Claudia. "The Secret Potential of Brahma-muhurta." In: *Namarupa: Categories of Indian Thought*, edited by Robert Moses and Eddie Stern. New York: *Namarupa*, 2003.

Conclusion: A Shepherd in the Trenches—One Chaplain's Work with the Dying

David Carter

INTRODUCTION

I am a hospice chaplain. Each day I work with the actively dying and the loved ones who attend them as they negotiate the dying process. A few glide through gracefully. Most struggle.

The in-patient unit I serve accommodates fifteen patients. Some come for symptom management, and some to resolve a caregiver crisis. Most, though, come for end-of-life care. The unit is a comfortable and pleasant environment congenial to the intimate exchanges necessary for a "good death." For example, each patient has a private room able to accommodate many family members and friends who may and often do stay overnight with the patient, sometimes for days on end—until the end. Each day, round-the-clock care is provided by a highly trained and obliging team of professionals without whom the patient would, in most cases, suffer terribly. Medication for pain relief, breathing treatments, wound dressing, periodic repositioning, daily bathing, oral care, personal grooming, and therapeutic music—all of these and other interventions are provided for patients.

Still, in the end, without the chaplain's spiritual interventions, can there really be "a good death"? After all, doesn't a "good death" mean effectively addressing the spiritual concerns that are common to all, but that are all too often left unresolved even up to the point of death?

People of all backgrounds tend to be extraordinarily receptive to spiritual truths when death is imminent. Hospice chaplaincy thus affords a rare opportunity to arouse or to heighten love of Godhead in any of those going through or witnessing the dying process. Clergy, especially if they are nonsectarian, can be uniquely helpful to the dying due to their background, training, and, most importantly, their own personal experiences in devotional service to God.

As a hospice chaplain, I am in an uncommon position to appreciate just how active the "angel of death" is. Many times at the hospice, I have witnessed "the bus coming through." All at once, for no apparent reason, a large number of the patients, say five or seven of the fifteen, will die, sometimes within minutes of one another. Those who "get on board" when the bus comes through neither know nor have contact with the others, for each has lain dying in a private room. They differ widely in age, cultural background, spiritual understanding, and the types of diseases suffered. Some die alone. Others die surrounded by loved ones. Some have faith in God and the afterlife, while others believe that God is merely a creation of man's wishful thinking. Yet all die within moments of each other.

Is it just coincidence, or is there an angel of death who comes for the soul at its appointed hour? Could it be that some other similarly mysterious phenomenon occurs—perhaps an entourage of spiritual beings passes by unseen plucking from this world those souls ripe for the next "stop" or for their ultimate destination? Whatever the truth, one thing is certain—the bus stops when it will, and when it rumbles off, it leaves in its wake many a weeping person abandoned to cope with, as best as he or she can, the mystery we call death. But what marvels might we see if our mortal eyes, now dim with the things of this world, could peer beyond the sensory realm to the world on the other side?

In my ministry, I provide spiritual support and guidance when death comes to fetch a soul. Having been present at many deaths, I have many stories to tell. Black or white, educated or ignorant, believer or nonbeliever, joyous or fearful, young or old, rich or poor—the soul cannot postpone death when the "bus" comes through. I try to enrich each dying person with direct experience of God's unexceptionable love, or at least instill hope that such love exists and is within reach. Although some of the dying manifest serenity, fearlessness, or great joy at the time of death, others lose all composure. As singular as the stories of each person's life and death are, still, in another sense, all my stories are finally one story, the story of the burden of our humanness, our mortality.

HOW I CAME TO HOSPICE WORK

But let me begin with my story, the story of my own mortality and how I came to work with the dying.

Night had fallen and cross-eyed with fatigue I was about to do the same. My fellow monks had already crashed out inside our frugally outfitted RV. Alone I lingered outside savoring the quiet, bathing in the balmy breezes, and gazing up under a full moon as it plied through white clouds overhead. Our days that summer—as we crisscrossed America—had been a frenzy of distributing spiritual books and collecting donations for our mission.

Occasionally we would conscript a newcomer to our way of life as well. Like us, he would submit himself to the demands of self-willed vagrancy—hard work, little play, and no pay; yet each of us, poor as birds, felt better remunerated than any of the six-digit executives we would sometimes meet out on the road. Still, no matter how spiritually rewarding, our days were physically exhausting, so at the end of each, in sleeping bags sprawled out on the polyurethane-coated hardwood deck of our "traveling temple," we would sink into well-deserved sleep.

Just as I had begun to drag my tired bones into the moonless dark of the RV, the black womb of night—benign a moment before—bore down on me, constricting and suffocating my chest. What was happening? The air was squeezed from my lungs and my heart, like a redheaded woodpecker drilling a hollow stump, hammered wildly. In the dark there was no sound, no sight, and no smell that should make me afraid. But I was afraid, more afraid than I had ever been. What was happening? Why was I suddenly afraid? Why couldn't I catch my breath? And then I knew. I felt it and I knew. I felt it as clear as the summer sun. Death had come for me.

I froze there under the silent stars. What should I do? I could shake one of my colleagues, Travis, from his sleep. But what would I say? "Listen Travis, get up, I'm scared. Oh God, I'm scared! I'm going to die, Trav! Tonight, Trav, tonight. I'm going to die. And I'm not ready, I'm not ready. Help me. You have to help me, Travis. Help me."

That would be crazy. Travis or any of the others would think I was mad. And they would be right. What I was feeling was mad. After all, there was nothing at all threatening me—no fever, no twitch, no pain, no cough, no worrisome diagnosis, nothing at all. Somehow though, my chemistry had been altered radically, and my body quaked with icy dread.

I tried to think. Decades before, in my late teens and early twenties, I had endured a few panic attacks. Now, resembling these attacks was this current tsunami of nameless, nonlocalized terror rising up from out of nowhere. Only this attack was worse, more intense. Still, I thought, "I am older now, in my mid forties. I must be more spiritually equipped to deal with this than I had been as a young adult." No, waking a friend from much needed sleep to irritate, frighten, or bewilder him with the news that I was succumbing to some peril nowhere to be seen or sensed—it was out of the question.

Despite my terror, the midwestern night was mild and pleasant. High trees canopied one area of the rest stop, while manicured paths snaked through a thinly forested park in another area. Besides the stars, a few small man-made lights punctuated the dark—those of the rest stop's welcome board and public bathroom. Also, parked nearby our own RV were three or four additional RVs or "traveling temples" with low lamps burning. Our traveling party had kept a rendezvous with more than a dozen other monks from our spiritual order according to a plan worked out beforehand, but my contemporaries were all asleep, and so were the dozens of other weary travelers in their respective cars or vans. Alone under a stand of oak trees in the dappled moonlight, I decided to pray. Fingering my prayer beads, I began pacing through the sentinel trees, murmuring my prayers. My mind still reeled, but I was determined not to disturb my companions.

I felt death pacing with me. Surely, this was to be my last night on earth. In the years since, I have tried to convey my impression of that moment by recounting it as a visitation by the "angel of death." But I skip ahead of myself.

I paced and prayed. According to the sacred vows I had taken in my faith tradition—which is Gaudiya Vaishnavism, often considered a part of the Hindu tradition but which partakes of the nonsectarian, universal philosophy found in Vedantic texts—obligatory daily prayer takes about two hours to complete. Even though I had hours earlier finished my required daily prayer, I still paced and prayed. After several more hours of pacing under the oak trees, I had certainly exceeded my quota of daily prayer. But I wasn't pacing to fulfill a vow of obligatory prayer. I was praying for dear life.

As the night wore on, one part of my mind busied itself calculating the cost: "You will need to sleep sometime soon, you know. You can't run on empty, you know. You had better watch the time." Another part, still haunted by stark fear and hoping against hope to somehow forbid death its due, was busy cheering on the prayer: "That's it, that's it. Just focus on the holy name of the Lord. Just hear the name, God's holy name, whatever else may come, even death. Just bind your attention to the mercy of God's holy name and all will be well by dint of its distinct virtue. All will be well." I paced and prayed, gradually becoming oblivious to my mind's internal tug of war.

I prayed as my spiritual master had bidden me pray. I asked for nothing, only that the Lord engage me in loving service—to become the servant of the servant of the servants of the Lord, whoever they may be, wherever they are. I neither asked that death be forestalled, nor did I ask for more time.

I simply recited God's holy names as they had been taught to me with all the attentiveness at my command. With each utterance, I begged only to be granted unmotivated, uninterrupted, loving devotional service to God.

Hours passed in unceasing prayer. As I paced I forgot everything—the fatigue, the lack of rest, the threat of death—everything but my fervent prayer. Little by little, the prayer restored my gravity and peace stole over me. My chemistry changed too as my terror-stiffened physiognomy relaxed into calm. My frightened consciousness was gradually soothed by an inner light more cooling than the moonlight that brightened the path on which I paced. Even as peace settled in my heart and mind, I continued to pace and to pray. Not a soul stirred around me. Only the breeze-blown clouds, the gypsy moon, and my penitent feet glided through the midnight hours.

And then dawn roused the day with a twittering of birds, the tug of sleepers from their beds, and the resumption of the ordinary sights, smells, and sounds of the world shaking off its slumbers. I was pacing still and deep in prayer. Not only was I utterly calm, but I was suffused with joy, energized more than if I had slept the whole night through. After all, I had been reborn into a higher life of prayer. It was exactly as if I *had* in fact died and had been miraculously reincarnated into that happier, infinitely more robust existence all seekers after enlightenment crave. I knew it was the prayer, the constant, unbroken, fervent prayer. It had worked an unexpected miracle, and just as I had earlier intuited the unworthiness of waking a godbrother to burden him with my mortal dread, I was now enriched with another intuition. Life, I sensed, had just whispered into my eager ear, qualified by desperation, one of its sweetest and most profound secrets: Heartfelt prayer is the source of life.

As we monks traveled around the country, it was not uncommon for one of us to rise earlier than the others and complete his obligatory devotions. This I would let my friends think I had done that night, for I had no words to convey the depths to which I'd been plunged, no language sufficient to conjure the uncanny terror and despair I'd undergone, nor any to depict the heights to which I'd been mysteriously lifted. In fact, years would pass before I spoke to anyone about that odd night and its extraordinary gift.

Whatever had been my belief about prayer before, as a monk and spiritual aspirant, my encounter that night with "the angel of death" transformed that belief into a finer asset—realized knowledge that far surpassed the theoretical understanding I had lived by previously. Most important, I had received a tool for helping others gripped by fear of death. If prayer could rescue me from the depths, could it not rescue anyone else who took to it earnestly?

That night, prayer had become a fruitful dialogue, a blissful rendezvous between friends. Constant prayer, I learned, results in a locking of hearts. It is the transcendental ecstasy of spiritual lovers inseparably bonded—sitting, standing, walking, running, resting, or sleeping together—heart bound to heart, everywhere and always, together heart-to-heart. Just as with care and attention we make plans to be with a lover or friend, so it is with heartfelt, constant prayer that we make plans to be with our one true Beloved, the Lord.

Love dawns. Death dies. Then, clinging to the memory of that love, we constantly dream about the next time of meeting. We telephone ahead to secure tentative plans; we take special pains to protect the appointed time on the calendar; we journey long and far; and we even lose sleep over or miss meals to be sure of the meeting, never caring whether we must face dangers or dig down into our savings to facilitate the assignation. Prayer is just such an affair of the heart. Conducted by love, impelled by love, flavored by love, watered by love, dictated and narrated by love—the lover and beloved meet, the two rushing together all smiles, parting in tears, and then yearning, endlessly yearning, as only lovers can.

We may identify death as an enemy, but for me that night it was death, life's twin, who by his perceived visit had bestowed on me the wisdom that I still to this day own. So is death an enemy? The spiritually awakened speak otherwise. How often have we heard spiritual authorities speak of death as "love's nightingale" or "life's harbinger?" For example, we may recall Sri Krishna's teaching in the *Bhagavad-gita* that the soul never dies and His admonition that those who develop love of God are blessed even in this world and at death enter God's kingdom; or Socrates' disquisitions in *Phaedo* wherein he derides the fear of death and insists that for one who has lived as a devotee of the absolute, death is a blessing; or Christ's exhortations in the Bible to prepare for the world to come by developing love of God through cultivating a nondifferential outlook toward so-called friends and foes. In all of the world's great spiritual traditions, we receive the testament of saints and sages averring confidence, not only in the soul's spiritual survival of death, but also in the bliss that awaits those rightly situated at the time of bodily demise.

Since my own vivid encounter with the "angel of death" at that midwest rest area, I see death as just another of God's infinitude of purposeful disguises. This has been borne out for me in my years as a hospice chaplain as I have witnessed that those patients intimate with God through prayer can peer through his disguise, however beguiling. Even as death comes to claim the body, the spiritually prepared soul recognizes death to be his or her beloved God standing there, eager to translate love's dealings to a higher level. Such a soul does not fear death.

REWRITING THE DEATH NARRATIVE

Not everyone is so intimately connected with God through prayer that they recognize death as a friend. Most people see death as the enemy and struggle with fear. One goal I set for myself in working with the dying and their families is to evaluate the "death narrative" they subscribe to. That death narrative determines their experience, reflecting as it does their sense of what death means or what it portends as it draws near. If its effect is pernicious, I seek to reshape it. Instead of a narrative that equates death with defeat, I offer an alternative narrative equating death with victory.

My role is to strengthen the patient's ability to see death as the ultimate friend, despite coming in a disguise so consummate as to bewilder all but the most perspicacious. I draw on two separate sources—the patient's own death narrative and the extensive spiritual training I received from my spiritual mentors. To be effective, I must be a good listener to discern the nature of the inherited death narrative. At the same time, I must also live constantly in the spiritual presence of my own mentors so that I may be a conduit through whom their wisdom and knowledge may flow. It is their wisdom that guides me in reshaping the narrative.

I first grasped the importance of evaluating death narratives in my early weeks of hospice work after an eye-opening encounter with a patient who subscribed to a negative death narrative. Here's how it went down: Knocking at the door of D7, I waited. "Mr. Jack Cooke," the chart read. "Liver cancer." When after a few seconds there was no response, I slowly pushed open the wooden door and slipped into the private room. I was unprepared for what I encountered inside. Stark naked on the carpeted floor, his legs sprawled out, his skin from head to toe as yellow as a lemon, was Jack, the patient I had come to visit. Tall, thin, hairless and bald, he was slouched back, elbows propped against the room's single hospital bed, half lying in a pool of foamy fecal matter colored as yellow as his skin. The stench was unbearable. His scrotum, grossly distended, lay alongside one skinny thigh almost down to the knee. Unblinking eyes, wide with horror and disgust, stared into the empty space in front of him. He made no effort to raise himself up, spoke no word, made no sound. Alone and helpless, he had given up all struggle.

It was my first or second week at the hospice inpatient unit, and I had been worrying about what I would say and how I should dress. I had not yet seen a person die. Now, in a moment, all those anxieties were quelled as I began to fathom what my real challenges would look like. Circumspection over my choice of necktie that day or deliberations over how colloquial or formal my salutations should be instantly faded in the face of the malodorous yellow puddle before my astonished eyes.

Acting quickly, I scanned the room for the call button and summoned the patient's nurse. Though Jack was still breathing and very much alive (he would live a few more weeks) and though I did not know it at the time, this was the first time I witnessed the "death-as-enemy" mindset seize a struggling soul and, like an invisible boa constrictor, strangle the quaking life away. In the few short moments before the nurse arrived, I had time to apprehend the stony, wretched look on Jack's face. Never before had it crossed his mind that he could be laid so low, rendered so bereft of power, so vulnerable, so defeated.

I can't remember just what, if anything, his nurse said when she first gazed on the fiasco before us. But I can still picture her. Plucking bright green latex gloves from a sanitary box on the wall, she stretched them up over her forearms. "I am going to need help," she muttered to herself and went to work.

I moved toward her. "I can help."

"No, no. You're the chaplain. I'll get another nurse. It's all right. Don't worry. I'll get someone to help." She unfolded a towel and began wiping the fecal matter from the man's body.

I would not have it. I followed her example, plucking a pair of latex gloves from the box and pulling them up over my forearms. There was no way I would agree to spare myself the messiness of helping this patient. If I were to recoil from this messy opportunity to serve, I would be cultivating disgust in that space meant for cultivating compassion. I would be teaching my heart to shut down rather than open up and serve another in distress.

The nurse saw that my mind was made up because she offered no further protest. On the count of three, we lifted the patient from the excrement puddled on the floor and swung him back onto his bed. When we had settled him safely there, I carefully pulled off the soiled gloves and discarded them. Then, feeling out of my league, I excused myself to go "do the things chaplains do."

Jack, in his prime, had been a university professor. Well respected in academe by colleagues and students alike, he had been celebrated as a brilliant, cultured, and successful scholar. But now this cruel reversal wrought its worst on his fortunes. Later, I learned that he had been a stranger to spiritual culture and practice, having failed to discover in his many years of scientific inquiry and learning any compelling reason for having or seeking to acquire confidence in the claims of religion. My subsequent attempts to visit were all declined. Except for the episode above, I never had contact with him again.

Encounters like the one I had with Jack taught me early on in my work that in order to comfort the dying or their family members, often enough the chaplain can do more harm than good relying on chapter and verse alone. Rather, what is crucial is a reinvention of the narrative that instructs us how to make sense of our experience. How does one comfort family members witnessing a loved one in the throes of the death struggle? Death may come slowly, extending the miseries of dying. Hours or days pass, but still the dying drags on. Family members watch as their loved one labors hard to breathe, speak, and hold on to consciousness. Toward what end is it that they are laboring hard, struggling?

Every theology proffers the hope that one may experience death as the portal to eternal life, but unless we mere mortals are aided by a skilled spiritualist when confronted with the stark reality of death, we often find these proffered hopes small recompense. Here is where the art of spiritual teaching is vital for effective chaplaincy. Just as a poet endows the most ordinary occurrence with strange beauty, so the effective chaplain must help the dying to envisage the great beauty inherent in death.

Indeed there can be great beauty in death as in each and every phase of our life's journey. But often, the art of uncovering that beauty lies in deconstructing and then reinventing the common cultural narratives and values that blind us to the beauty. Narratives such as death as loss, death as defeat, death as the enemy: these must be reworked. As most theologies aver, even in dying there lies a hidden treasure, but that treasure belongs only to those spiritually fortunate enough to jettison the inherited negatives associated with death. These fortunate souls more accurately understand the process as a spiritual event pregnant with beatific meaning. They see death as renewal, as victory, as consummation.

Scriptural and religious tradition is replete with positive portrayals of death, or counter-narratives to the conventional idea of death as defeat. For instance, the Sufi master Jalaluddin Rumi in his writing insisted that death should not be understood as the beginning of nonexistence. Rather, it should be understood to be, simultaneously, departure from one plane of existence, and arrival upon another. He cites the sun's setting on one horizon and its rising on another as the divine's playful way of disclosing the secret of death's mystery to us mortals. Like a bucket disappears into the depths of a well, only to be drawn up again bearing a wealth of life-giving waters or as a seed disappears into the ground only to reappear as living vegetation, so the individual disappears for a time from our mortal vision, that it may reappear to express its increased and enriched being in another, richer realm.[1]

Similarly, Thich Nhat Hanh, a now-famous Vietnamese Buddhist monk, compares the body's disappearance at death to the disappearance of a wave when it sinks back into the ocean from which it has risen. Death for the wave ends with the realization that, in fact, its identity as a wave is temporary, but its identity as water is perpetual. Hanh's proposition is that just as the wave is naught but water temporarily transformed, the body is naught but a temporary transformation of that enduring reality that outlasts all transformations. The wave, through all phases of its trajectory, never loses its integrity as water. Similarly, when human illusion is transcended, there is the realization that death does not diminish the dignity of our being one with "the Buddha nature." Water is the wave's essence, "suchness" that of the human.[2]

Counter-narratives such as these furnish springboards for the conscious mind to plunge deep into the mysterious death struggle, gradually comprehending in a new light the long, hard labor of dying. How striking is the silence that obtains when the death struggle finally ceases! How penetrating is its opposite—the loud and inconsolable wailing of the bereaved!

As a father, I have been present at the birth of each of my three children. In each case, I shared in the birth labor, toiling to support, coach, comfort, and encourage my beloved until the sacred moment when her long and hard confinement finally bore its fruit. Each time, after the long exertion, we were drowned in a sea of thanksgiving and great joy. Now, as a chaplain, I have also been present at the death of many of life's sons and daughters. One glorious day, the multiple impressions of those birth moments and of those many death scenes finally crystallized in me, cementing the realization that death's labor is akin to the labor of childbirth. On that day I saw clearly that death's labor also bears new life as its fruit. However, to see this truth, one must have love-awakened eyes or eyes anointed by faith, divine knowledge, or mature mystical aptitude. Anyone fortunate enough to view new life as the natural fruit of the dying process would be elated not devastated.

I don't remember the first time that I either encouraged a family member to read the death struggle as a birthing process or dubbed an assisting family member a midwife. But whenever I do, I am able to supplant the negative identity of "mourner"—with its connotations of loss and diminution—and to conjure instead the life-affirming identity of "day bringer," "harbinger of dawn," or "liberator."

However, only when I was able to perceive the death vigil as spiritual midwifery could I effectively instill in family members a sense of joyous celebration in the hospice room. This celebration gave way to hope rather than despair, to envisaging death as an angel of God restoring the soul to glory rather than a grim reaper plundering the heart of its treasure. In my years of chaplaincy, as the truth that death is unreal has become more fixed in me, it has become easier for me to show this vision to others. With the eyes of faith or spiritual knowledge, one can see the spiritual birth of the soul into its new life. Only when one sees this way can he or she become a joyful assistant, a midwife of the divine.

Of course, this is easier said than done. Have you ever witnessed a midwife or *doula* at her work? For hours on end, or days even, she will labor right along with the birthing mother. She will forego sleep to coach, massage, encourage, joke with, sing songs to, or otherwise edify the mother as her contractions bring on waves of intense pain and/or fear. A chaplain's work is similarly demanding. Bringing a family member around to the realization of death as the dawn of a new life can be a long and challenging one. Take for instance the case of young Isabella.

Isabella's grandfather had just passed away. Picture a withered man, well past his three score and seven, lying dead on a clean and neat hospital bed. An uncanny stillness clasps his thin figure. The winter sun pours through Venetian blinds and into the room. His death was not unexpected. Its circumstances were ideal insofar as all that modern medical science could have done to alleviate bodily pain had been done. Close family members and friends had visited or had remained present with him until the very last to assure him of their undying love. Finally, he had slipped away after hearing the heartfelt expressions of love and spiritual faith each of his family members had had to offer.

Two grey-haired daughters stand by the bed tearful but composed. In silence, the man's son sits beside them, hands folded in his lap, his tears of mourning spent. A scant distance from the silent corpse, but facing away, a granddaughter, Isabella, sits in rage. Her unblinking eyes are red-rimmed and weeping. Copious tears glide down her stunned face. She sits with a box of Kleenex in her lap, tearing out one tissue after the other. First, I console the several older family members and then quietly move across the room to sit down on a chair beside her. We remain silent for several minutes.

"Why did he have to die?" she turns to me and suddenly sobs.

I extend my hand and rest it gently on her shoulder. "It's so hard to lose one we love. The burden of our human mortality is immense." I feel her anguish. Her question is clearly spiritual. After all, she knows perfectly well the host of material reasons that brought about her grandfather's death. "You weep as every mortal weeps," I continue, "to bear the wound of separation from one you love dearly."

Her grandfather had been ill for years with prostate cancer. She had in recent months, as had every other member of the family, witnessed her grandfather's condition become increasingly fragile due to advancing age and disease progression.

"But he was doing so well here at the hospice. He was getting better. What happened?" She wads up her Kleenex and, in a flash of anger, pitches it five feet into the trash can.

Though considerably younger than her parents, aunts, and uncles, she is nevertheless intellectually mature, being in her twenties and educated. She knows that medical science had had no cure for him. He was in his eighties, withered and worn, and for weeks she had witnessed his increasing dysfunction. She has had ample opportunity too to witness how joyless existence had become for him.

I offer more words to Isabella. "What happened is that his soul finally flew free of the confinement that his debilitated body enforced on him. Now he is no longer a hostage to incapacity, to the indignity of being restricted by illness and age from each and every one of the pleasures that life affords us in the world. His suffering is over."

Death, she knows, has liberated her grandfather from the miseries of utter confinement in a hospital bed, but she cannot welcome death as a liberating friend. Rather, she feels death's presence as a cruel enemy. No, she is not questioning the physical event. Instead, her question is a plea for a solution to the ancient metaphysical perplexity of life and death. As I venture to console her further with these or similar words, I find myself listening too.

"Really," I say to her, "you weep because you feel you cannot know when, where, how, or even if you will ever meet with your grandfather again. And that misgiving hints at the underlying existential anxiety that troubles us all—which one of our cherished joys can endure forever? But please consider this: Haven't you sensed this vexing apprehension, this threatening shadow lurking offstage, hidden in the wings somewhere, for as long as you can remember?"

"Why, what do you mean?" Isabella asks, pulling another tissue from the box.

"I mean, isn't the burden of our mortality ever present? Every one of us must die—isn't it true? Who is exempt from death? When a child is born, that child must advance through the years to its final days. What choice does any one of us have? What I am asking is only this: Why now? Why do you weep now?"

"Because I am sad ... because he had to die."

"Yes, and it is sad. But it has always been sad. So why do you cry now?"

All this time, she had been crying. My probing, though, triggers a calming reflex, and her tears abruptly abate. She sets the box of Kleenex on the floor.

"I don't know," she says.

"I'll tell you why. You weep because your heart tells you that love is eternal. As such, its subject, in this case you, and its object, in this case your grandfather, must also be eternal. You intuitively know this to be true. But death is a problem. It gainsays your heart's wisdom with its refutation of love's eternality. But this challenge goads everyone, always. Therefore, I ask again, why do we not weep always to feel this terrible anguish? We must lose everyone we love by death's cruel hand. Is it not true that the cruelty of our existential position has become overwhelming at this particular moment only because of the sting of death? Death has suddenly thrust before your unwilling mind what you have always known—that the wound of separation is inevitable."

"Yes, I see that."

"And most assuredly every mortal who stops to think about it feels and inwardly mourns at all times the inevitable wound of separation, its imperiousness and cruel efficacy. But credit the swoop of death with rendering visible the wound we otherwise mask. When death unmasks the existential anguish of our mortality, then we can no longer stave off the weeping. To be mortal then is to walk and weep. We hide the tears so well, but we humans are walking weeping, walking weeping." Here I find myself misgiving the words I speak. To my listening ear, they sound depressing. "Where am I going with this?" I ask myself.

Isabella begins to weep again. I bend forward to lift the box of Kleenex from the floor and set it in her lap. "But, Isabella," I continue, "here is the important thing: At every moment we also have in our grasp the key to immortality! If love is, as we intuit, eternal, then its subject and its object must, in fact, also be eternal. Otherwise we wouldn't suffer this constant longing for love and its fulfillment. Otherwise, we wouldn't weep at all."

She was again listening with keen interest, and by her growing composure indicating a growing acceptance of what I was stating.

"You and your grandfather are not subject to death. None of us is. You are, and all else that lives is, eternal. And that is because we are each an eternal, inseparable part and parcel of the divine reality, of God's infinite, eternal being. As such, deep within, we own a cause for the highest rejoicing, because at all times we carry within, however dimly or vividly it may be portrayed to our conscious mind, an awareness of God, who never dies. Covet this awareness, Isabella, because it imparts delights. It summons spring to waken winter from its deep dreaming, from its blistery winds, its frost, and its hoar. Always we carry and are carried by God, our source and our destination."

Isabella's face relaxed and she nodded in agreement. "So you're saying I shouldn't be spiritually lazy?"

"Yes," I smiled. "Whatever you do, don't be spiritually lazy."

Later I would reflect on my meeting with Isabella. She was right. Death certainly does occasion our weeping. But what occasions laughter? It is the divine presence hidden within our consciousness. It is that presence that tells us with certainty that death is a lie. But we must convene with the spiritually minded to come to a perfect understanding of this fundamental truth that every child intuitively knows, that love never dies.

For the truth is that neither the lover nor the beloved ever die. Only by grasping that spiritual truth will we waken the laughter that cannot be quenched; only by that consciousness will we ring in the gladness that cannot be overthrown; only by that realization will we make palpable to the heart the divine ecstasy it already owns, the treasure from which it can never be separated. It is experience of the intimate and unbreakable love that exists between us and the Godhead that will alone awaken our freedom and establish our triumph over death. If it is death that unmasks our deep and abiding existential anguish, then it is spiritual work and the realizations that ensue that are needed to counteract death's sting and reveal our intrinsic ecstasy.

But spiritual work is an elective. Whereas age, disease, decline, and death are unavoidable, spiritual work is not. Truth be told, spiritual work is scrupulously avoided by most humans. How sad. We won't meditate regularly; we won't offer prayers; we won't inquire about the afterlife, and we won't fast or make pilgrimage.

Nevertheless, the longing for God remains despite our willful negligence. It is this longing for God that is the essence of our spirituality. And God has a longing also, that we be delivered from suffering. As a result, whenever we elect to go against the norm and engage in spiritual work, we begin to experience a diminution of fear and an increase of hope. Thus, our commitment to spiritual practice will elicit a response from the divinity. We will have inaugurated a search for and ultimately a celebration of God's existence, and then and only then can we invoke bliss.

The celebration can be the simple act of privately acknowledging the mystery of our origins and naming that mystery "God." Or the celebration can be silent meditation on being. Or it can be the recitation of the holy name in speech or in song. The celebration of God's existence can be realized in the midst of congregational worship at a church, synagogue, mosque, or temple. But it is always an elective. Spiritual beatitude has nothing to do with bodily life or bodily death. It is aroused by seeking out and relishing encounters with the divine, whether those take place in solitude or in the company of many. But it never comes to the spiritually lazy.

Isabella's grandfather had escaped. She wouldn't want him to be forever confined to a bed, unable to enjoy the pleasures he once knew. Neither would he want her to linger on in misery because of his escape. Rather, he would be glad to see his granddaughter embrace the means of her own escape from suffering into freedom.

When we seek spiritual truth, we escape from suffering and find our eternal happiness. That is how Isabella finally came to understand the answer to her question, "Why did he have to die?" He did not die. He is holding the mirror for us all. Look into the glass. In it is your own reflection, and the light that enables you to see is the light of consciousness. Trace that light to its roots. Beyond the consciousness of death's cruelty is the consciousness of God and of God's love. God awaits our turning to Him to lift us beyond the fetters of bodily mortality.

While Isabella had to be coaxed into revising her narrative and Jack Cooke never changed his, there are those people who are so genuinely committed to and sincerely practicing spiritual life that they have no fear of death whatsoever.

Jonathon was one such person. Just weeks before his death, I met Jonathon. By that time, he had endured three brain surgeries, the third of which greatly diminished his functionality and rendered him incapable of speech. Whenever I visited his room, he would rock back and forth excitedly and smile, indicating his pleasure to have a visit from the chaplain. This smiling and rocking was almost all that remained of his ability to communicate. Although I liked him readily, I might never have gotten to know him were it not for his wife, Grace, who was there whenever I visited.

Grace shared with me the details of her husband's life. She recounted how after the second surgery, as the sleep of anesthesia lifted, Jonathon woke in great excitement. "God spoke with me," he exclaimed, "I was talking with God!" Jonathon's eyes were sparkling as he spoke, and his face was aglow with the radiant ecstasy of the holy encounter he was describing. He then shared God's message with his wife and family: "Our grandbaby will be born on September 4th [a birth date that contradicted the doctor's expected birth date by fully a month] and the child will be a boy [there had been no attempt to ascertain the expected child's gender]. Oh, and God said that his name is to be Gabriel for he is to be the messenger of God [no one had even thought of a name yet]!" Grace didn't know what to think. Had Jonathon, while unconscious on the operating table, actually somehow communed with the Supreme Lord? Or was he mistaking a dream or some hallucination for a holy experience?

Whatever doubts Grace entertained were dispelled when their grandchild was born—a beautiful baby boy who appeared on the very day that Jonathon had foretold months before! Of course, no one doubted what to name this child. After all, he had come bearing God's message of imperishable love—"Lo! I am with you always. Be of good cheer!"

Jonathon first came to hospice for symptom management. After a few days at the in-patient unit when his pain was brought under control, he returned home. During his short stay, he had shown his appreciation through smiling for my prayers and spiritual talks. But Jonathon especially liked my singing of hymns, for whenever I sang for him, he would reach for a guitar (that wasn't there!) and, although he could no longer sing or even speak, he would attempt to sing along with me. He would play "air guitar" and his eyes would shine with delight while his whole body rocked and rolled with the rhythm of the song.

As a result of his stay in the in-patient unit, Jonathon's symptoms had been effectively managed, and he returned home to spend his last days there, with homeside hospice staff still looking in on his care.

A short while later, I learned from Grace the remarkable details of his death. I was as affected as I would be had a friend or family member died. Grace and their five children had been keeping vigil. Jonathon's vital signs had become increasingly feeble as he lay unconscious in bed. Suddenly he sat upright in bed. Eyes shining brightly and looking upward, he began smiling broadly, seeming to greet an unseen presence. He opened his arms and raised his hands high over his head. His eyes were dancing excitedly, drinking in details of a vision privy to him alone. Moments passed with Jonathon remaining oblivious of his terrestrial surroundings. Then, still looking up in rapture, he sank back onto his bed and breathed his last. Jonathon had died as he had lived. Steeped in love of God, certain of God's love for him, confident of his destination, he left this world glowing with love and joy.

After his death, the family asked me to be one of the speakers at his service. Several hundred mourners gathered at the Baptist church for Jonathon's memorial. Not only did I sing a medley of spiritual songs, but I also related the anecdote of Jonathon's conference with God regarding his grandson Gabriel. Then I shared another amazing story Grace had shared with me.

One day, Jonathon was high up on a shaky ladder, nailing new gutters to the house when disaster struck. The ladder slipped and suddenly he was falling! Worse yet, his small daughter was below, deep in play. If he were to fall on her, she'd be killed! But that could be prevented only if he could manage somehow to fall on the wrought iron picket fence below, thus impaling himself! Praying with all his heart, he begged God: "Let me die, but spare my child!" Then as he fell, he struggled to redirect his fall away from his child and onto the wrought iron spears below. But it was useless. Try as he might, he was plunging straight toward his daughter.

Meanwhile, Jonathon's next-door neighbor had seen the impending tragedy and dashed across the yard with the aim of snatching the little girl from harm's way. Although he could not reach the child in time, he bade his legs pump as he ran with all his might. Before his eyes, just before Jonathon crashed to earth, the most extraordinary thing happened. Jonathon's little girl was suddenly snatched from the spot where she was playing and mysteriously transported several feet away. Then Jonathon hit the ground and lay without moving.

Jonathon was rushed to the hospital and treated. After it was clear that he would recover from his injuries, his daughter's story and that of the neighbor's became prominent in everyone's mind. The small child kept asking everyone if they had they seen the beautiful man all dressed in white come down from the sky and snatch her up in his arms before gently setting her down again. She repeated over and over that he was the most beautiful person she'd ever seen. And she wanted to know if they had seen him too. Of course, they had not.

Whatever one makes of such stories, they speak to the concerns and the faith of the people who believe them, and, arguably, such concerns and beliefs enrich their lives. Without doubt, I was a comfort to Jonathon and his family. But by ministering to their needs, I discovered anew how powerfully devotion affects our life experience and our understanding of the reality in which we live. Despite all that Jonathon had been through physically, he was unafraid of death. His death narrative brought him through effortlessly to the other side.

USING PARAPSYCHOLOGICAL INSIGHTS IN HOSPICE WORK

Sometimes I encounter persons who are resistant or even hostile to religion. Usually, when I meet a dying person or that person's loved one, I introduce myself. "I'm the chaplain."

Most people who are opposed to religion make their inclinations known: "Yeah, well, I'm an atheist." What is left unsaid is understood: "There's the door, buddy, and don't let it hit you as you leave, okay?"

"Not a problem," I reply, "I'm a theist too." Using deliberate inflection to emphasize the double *entendre* usually evokes laughter. Ice melts and a door opens. "We share a lot in common." I continue, "And I mean that. You see, what I hear you telling me is that you exalt truth above all things. You're unwilling to endorse as true something you're not persuaded of as being true."

"Well, yeah, you could say that," the "atheist" replies. Most often by this point, my would-be adversary is disarmed—"this chaplain is different"—or at the very least interested or amused enough to welcome productive conversation.

I seize the opportunity. "Well, I deeply respect your critical tough mindedness. You see, I'm the same."

"Really? How's that? Don't you believe in God?"

"Let's have an understanding here. What I'm getting at is that you're identifying yourself as an idealist; truth is your ideal. Well, I'm also an idealist. And truth is my ideal. So we have this in common, right?"

"Not so fast," my challenger replies. "There's still a problem, you know. A small problem called God."

"But we're alike in that respect also, my friend. I have serious problems with many people's conceptions of God. And I would wager that if we were to reason together for even a little bit, you would discover that I don't believe in the same God that you don't believe in. I'm also certain that we agree rather than disagree about many more things than you might guess."

The man nods and relaxes back into the pillows. "Go on," he says, now willing to indulge me.

I take this as my cue to sit down on the edge of the bed. "You have no use for the claims of religion as they have been presented to you. Again, I salute that as integrity, a virtue indispensable for any idealist. So tell me, which of religion's many claims seems most absurd or patently wrong to you?"

With that we're usually off to a good start. And as the proverbial wisdom goes, "Well begun is half done." In these cases, though, I'll scrupulously avoid invoking scriptural reference or theological argument for support. Instead, I will use an approach more suited to the requirements of the skeptic. After all, here is a soul who wants fact, not faith. I turn to the field of parapsychology.

In this twenty-first century, an age of unprecedented scientific achievement, some researchers have produced peer-reviewed studies of parapsychological phenomena, concluding that a significant number of reported near death experiences (NDEs) or out-of-body experience (OBEs) can be rationally explained only by accepting that personal consciousness, the soul, can and does continue to operate after the death of the body has been clinically verified. (NDE and OBE phenomena are so popularly known of these days that recently I saw a billboard advertising some product or other encouraging the consumer to "have an 'out-of-office' experience.") In my hospice work, oftentimes I find that persons who were moments before reluctant to talk about something as fraught with contention as religious beliefs, are now elaborating the details of an OBE or NDE that either they or one of their intimates has experienced.

A striking case comes to mind. Lucinda, a middle-aged woman, is a rigorously intelligent and highly educated medical professional who came to hospice when her father was dying. A decidedly spiritual woman, she nevertheless expressed a rooted dislike for religion that stretched back to her youth when she had witnessed abuse and hypocrisy within her church. The few times we met, whether at the hospice or at the chapel where her father's service was held, she always comported herself with intelligence, sensitivity, and aplomb—her demeanor and appearance were never offbeat or strange.

But what she related to me was decidedly strange. Because she is a credible source, I have shared her story on numerous occasions for what it suggests about the spiritual potency of the soul. She and I had been talking about how the soul is never diminished or impaired, not even when bodily illness severely restricts its functioning in the realm of the senses. We were considering the internal spiritual realms as they have been delineated in various spiritual, scientific, and parapsychological literatures. I had just related to her how, as a student at NYU, I had learned that parapsychologists claim that talking to a person in a comatose state is meaningful because the soul is able to comprehend and process communication despite the bodily decline or impairment. So personally affected was Lucinda by what I had been saying that after a moment's hesitation she recounted the following story:

"One night," she began, "I was wakened from sleep by a disturbing dream. A very close friend appeared to me. It was so vivid. She needed my help, she told me. She had been murdered! She urged me to contact the police and tell them that they would find her corpse in the trunk of her car and that it was her boyfriend who had murdered her. She wanted him apprehended and tried for killing her! It was so uncanny. I really didn't know what to think or do. But it seemed so real. At the risk of appearing to be a madwoman, or worse, a criminal or murderer, the next day I did what she asked. I went to the police. You know what? They found her dead body in the trunk of her car, just as she said. Then, after a trial, her boyfriend was convicted of the murder. So I agree with you that the soul is never impaired or disabled, not even by death itself."

While perhaps hard to swallow, we must ask whether Lucinda's story is inconsistent with other narrations of the inexplicable. In literature, for example, there are famous instances of the parapsychological, such as the ghost of Hamlet's father in Shakespearean tragedy or the descent of the angelic host who intercedes on behalf of the heroine in the denouement of Yeats' *The Countess Cathleen*. Then there are reports of precognition of events where people tell of being visited by a relative or friend who discloses to them details of some far distant or imminent event, details impossible to know, details which are later substantiated. Then, of course, there is the report of the world's scriptures, replete with instances of extrasensory or trans-empiric phenomena: apparitions, transfigurations, astral realms, prophetic dreams, and the like.

Certainly, a good many of these reports might be fraudulent. But what of those that are not? Too many people, in too many diverse conditions of life, attest to their veracity. As do reliable saints and sages of the past.

How sad when the liminal condition of being nonresponsive or comatose brought on by illness is equated with spiritual absence or with death. As a consequence, family members or loved ones conclude that there is nothing they can do or say to comfort or assist their loved one. This mistaken conclusion leads to one or another unfortunate situation. In some cases, people remain in the room but just ignore the dying person altogether and instead divert themselves, watching their favorite soap opera, playing computer or card games, or engaging in other frivolous activities. The dying person is abandoned to negotiate the dying process bereft of their help. In other cases, those who remain in the dying person's presence will refrain from such conduct, but ignorant of the soul's ability to interact despite bodily incapacity, they too will ignore the person lying there. Thus the torrent of loving expressions remains bound up within their mournful hearts, and though perhaps more considerate and respectful than their television-viewing counterparts, still again the dying person is effectively abandoned to face death alone and unaided.

By contrast, how powerfully liberating, how profoundly healing is the knowledge that can be accessed through a study of the parapsychological. Many times, on the strength of my understanding of the soul's transcendental nature, I have interacted with a person whose bodily decline prevents not only speaking or gesturing, but prevents even the lifting of closed eyelids to peer out at and see me. How then can I know that the person is cognizant of my presence?

Once in my hospice service, I was prompted by an intuition to visit an actively dying patient. As I entered the room, sound was conspicuous by its absence. A slip of a white-haired woman, aged and wasted by cancer, lay motionless with eyes closed in a tidy white hospital bed, unable even to lift her head from the big white pillow. She was breathing audibly but was nonresponsive. I sat close by the bedside and identified myself by name and occupation. I proposed reading to her from scripture for a while, and then in a soft, clear, and audible voice, I read into her ear. Selecting biblical verses glorifying the Supreme as the nearest and dearest friend, I read as follows:

Give thanks to the Lord, for He is good, for His faithful love endures forever. Give thanks to the God of gods, for His faithful love endures forever. Give thanks to the Lord of lords, for His faithful love endures forever. He alone works wonders, for His faithful love endures forever.

Despite profound fatigue and debilitation, her spirit was invigorated. As she turned her aged face towards my voice, I could see her eagerness and attentiveness. Eyebrows that had been motionless now quivered and arched in the direction of my intonation. Her still closed eyes fluttered and darted behind the lids, indicating rapt attention to the messages of Godhead. I read further:

Even darkness to You is not dark, and night is as clear as the day. You created my inmost self, knit me together in my mother's womb. For so many marvels I thank You; a wonder am I, and all Your works are wonders.

Minutes slipped by. Abruptly, the audible breathing ceased. I looked up from my text and realized I was suddenly alone. She had gone.

I pulled the cord to summon the nurse, and in the remaining moment, while still alone with the serene looking body, I dropped a single bead of holy water on her forehead. Another moment passed before the nurse appeared. She probed for vital signs and, finding them absent, confirmed the death. Who was it who prompted my timely visit? Who was so concerned that this lonely, otherwise neglected soul be encouraged and guided by holy verse at the final moment as she stepped free from this worldly plane? Who orchestrated this magical turn of events? Can I doubt for a moment that it was the Lord acting, making me instrumental as His servant to open the way for this humble soul at the threshold of eternity? No, I cannot.

How better to understand what has just transpired than that she let go on the strength of having been so edified by focused meditation on God's love? If I were certain she couldn't hear me or understand my words, would I so patiently and purposefully have read to her words of healing and power? Hardly. And yet it is because of the mentoring I have received, borne out by experiences like the one just narrated, that I continue to treat the dying thus. And I say with confidence to the loved ones eager to assist their beloved in this most difficult task, "the soul is never diminished or impaired, it is simply the body that is declining. Your words of love and encouragement are the food and drink your loved one needs to complete the journey."

THE IMPORTANCE OF BEING NONJUDGMENTAL AND NONSECTARIAN

Nonjudgmentalism is essential in serving the dying and their families. If I am to serve effectively, first I must learn who it is I am hoping to serve. I must be together with the one I am to serve, listening and learning, so that my heart can join with his or her heart. Every adventure is uncharted, each destination brand new, every story its own, alone. Only when I truly meet the other can I be of any real use to him or to her. Otherwise, without genuine rapport, my attempts at benefiting the other may be worse than useless. The happy fortuity that permits rapport may be divine, but the desire that rapport develop is a function of our own sweet will.

Blake Sutherland was prepossessing—a lady killer, as they say. Indeed, whenever he managed to smile, the room lit up. I was amused each time I visited him because his Hollywood good looks always reminded me of a prominent American political leader whom I had met years back in the 1960s. Except for Blake's head full of silvery white locks contrasting sharply with the '60s senator's dark wavy hair, the two were dead ringers for each other. It was uncanny. Soft spoken and gentlemanly, Blake related that he had been a successful farmer. Now, advanced in years though still youthful in appearance, he was dying of cancer.

Family visited him daily. His wife was always well-dressed and solemn. She and I had no meaningful exchanges, and though I wished it were otherwise, I respected her well-defined if unexplained boundaries. I was informed by other hospice staff that on evenings after I had gone home, grown sons and daughters regularly visited Blake, but I met none of them. There was his grandson, Chad, a young college student, who would sometimes visit during my shift. Handsome as his grandfather, neat, and always polite, Chad and I too hardly exchanged anything more than cordialities. He would invariably ask me to pray for his grandfather, we three would pray together, and moments later Chad would leave. Even though contact with the Sutherland family was minimal, my talks with Blake were many and meaningful.

Blake was a Christian, well-churched his whole life and faithful. Despite his lifelong faithfulness, I was surprised to learn how anxious he was about what lay in wait for him after death. He was sure he would never see heaven. I would counter that notion, reminding him of various scriptural assurances that anyone who calls upon the Lord for mercy is surely saved from perdition. I would emphasize Christ's repeated assurances to that effect, but Blake was convinced that these assurances did not pertain to him.

"But Blake," I would remind him, "what about the thief whom Christ assured would be in heaven with him that very day? This thief was a sinner, no better than you." Blake would light up momentarily. "Do you think?"

"Yes, yes. The thief's happy destination was not due to worthiness on his part. Rather it was another powerful evidence of the Lord's mercifulness. Why should you not receive the same?" I recalled my own fear of death and how it drove dread into my limbs and cast me out under the stars that midnight to pace in prayer upon the moonlit path. But, more important, I recalled how it was absorption in the holy names of God that rescued me.

This was exactly what Blake needed—to be engaged in contemplative prayer and opened to God's healing presence. Fear of death and of hell had stolen all hope from him. The only antidote, I reasoned, was the regular experience of peace and joy that results from a conscious coming into God's presence through uninterrupted, contemplative prayer. Daily, when we'd meet, I engaged with Blake in the Prayer of the Heart: "Lord Jesus Christ, have mercy on me, a sinner." At the end of each session, I assured him that by having "called on the Lord," he had accepted the freely offered grace of God, and he would not go to hell at the time of death.

Though he'd smile and hold my hand while gazing into my eyes, he would have only brief respite from his fears. Later, I learned from other staff that Blake would ask for me, claiming I was the only chaplain who "understood" him. I suspect I was the only one he met who conveyed unflinching faith in the teaching that no one who surrenders to the Supreme Lord is ever condemned to eternal hell. For nearly a week, we met and engaged in the Prayer of the Heart together.

Then, returning to work one Monday morning after the weekend and inquiring from coworkers about Blake, I learned that he had refused to see the other chaplains who had come to call. Again his plea was that I was the only one who understood him. The nurses described how as death drew near—as evidenced by increasing lethargy, fewer periods of lucidity, mottling to the extremities, and long periods of apnea—Blake kept asking for me, insisting that no one else would do.

I hastened to his room, stood before the door for a moment in silent prayer, then knocked, and entered. There he lay, on his back with eyes closed, alone in the neat hospice room, apparently sleeping. It was midafternoon, a sunny spring day. From the large window by his bed, one could see rolling lawn and shrubs, blooming red bud trees, a small pond, park benches along a winding path, and a quaint wooden gazebo. I sat down on the bed next to him and gently spoke his name. "Blake." Slowly his eyes opened and when he recognized that I had come, he smiled.

Then, as on many previous occasions, he asked about God forgiving sinners. I stated again what I'd emphasized in past visits—that any sinner, however sunken in sinfulness, who sincerely asked God's forgiveness would receive His mercy. Although I recited numerous examples and assurances, as I had before, he was still unsatisfied. Something was deeply bothering him.

"Any sin?" he asked. "Will God forgive any sin?"

"Yes, Blake."

"But God will never forgive me," he whispered.

"Why?" I asked. "What sin or sins have you committed that God will not forgive?" We sat hand in hand, peering into each other's faces. His eyes, tear-filled, held mine. I could see he was feeling too abashed to answer my question, so I continued. "There is no sin God will not forgive, if we but sincerely ask. Your remorse is your silent plea. Blake, please know that desire is the subtle form of prayer, and the Lord's hearing is the most subtle thing of all. Listen to what I say. Moses, before he led the Israelites, committed murder; King David, in order to enjoy illicit connection with his servant's religiously wed spouse, intrigued the death of a trusting and loyal subject; and the apostle Paul, whose checkered career encompassed the cruel persecution of Jesus' first followers, was among those who martyred Saint Stephen. Do you think they dwell in fire?"

This was all it took for Blake to finally pour out his heart to me. Our eyes were still locked, woven into a knot of love and trust. He scrutinized me, and peering through me he sought sight of God the beloved, trusting that he might somehow find what he sought. I held his gaze staring straight ahead into his eyes hoping to ignite trust therein, while simultaneously I looked backward, upward, and within to my Sweet Inspiration, and pled Blake's case.

"But Moses and Paul never had sex with animals," he whispered. "I had sex with pigs." There, the secret was out now. "You know I raised pigs," he ventured. "Hundreds of 'em. I had sex with them again and again. And when they got old, I killed them and invited my friends over to cook and eat them. I had sex with them and I ate them." As he unburdened his heart of his lifelong secret, he told of his childhood on an isolated farm, his mother's early death, his father's tyranny, his suffocating loneliness in the midst of the swine, and the burgeoning of his adolescent libido.

I commanded my face to freeze right where it was, to not go where it might, whatever it felt. I had been taken by surprise. As blindsided as I was, I knew that my face was at risk of betraying how surprised and challenged I was by this revelation. If even in the least, my face registered the disgust my conditioned self felt at his confession, if by the tiniest shudder of my eyes I intimated the repugnance that was my knee-jerk reaction, he would slip back out of the newfound light he had just lately entered and in which he was barely situated, to be plunged again into fear of death. Luckily, my face must have surrendered to the command.

Judging by Blake's soft eyes, he understood my reply to his confession of sex with animals and his concern that God would not forgive him: "But that is the substance of the Prayer of the Heart. 'Jesus Christ, son of God, have mercy on me *a sinner.*' We don't feign a purity we don't own. Rather, we confess and ask pardon for our sin. We are not rescued by merit. We are rescued by divine love, by mercy. Now, pray with me as before."

In voices barely audible, we recited the familiar words together; still hand in hand, eye to eye, we prayed the Prayer of the Heart. Time begot time, and we continued to pray. The sunlight shifted by degrees across the room, and we prayed the Prayer of the Heart.

When we finished, Blake had been transformed. He had felt peace after confession, followed by absolution, and then the joy that love alone brings. And I had also been transformed, having learned to suspend to the uttermost my judgment in order to bond with another human.

Not only is nonjudgmentalism toward sinfulness essential in serving the dying and their families, but nonsectarianism is as well. How can I serve effectively if I refuse to honor and respect the religious preferences of the persons whom I serve? Again, I must listen and learn from them so that my heart can join theirs and I can be of use to them. This hasn't always been as easy as it is for me now.

As a young African American growing up in mid-twentieth century America, I often heard terms like "underprivileged" or "disadvantaged" applied to blacks. My father, desperately "underprivileged" at birth, was almost universally thought of as having escaped "disadvantage" because in time he ruled over (or was ruled by) a small fiefdom of material opulence. In fact, at the height of his prosperity, he employed dozens of skilled men and women in his successful insurance business and paid them large salaries. Each year, he sojourned in Spoleto, Italy, for a whole month to enjoy the classical music festival. One year, he spent more than the combined yearly income of both my wife and me to remodel his already elegant and fully equipped kitchen.

Despite his wealth, never for a moment did I subscribe to the narrative of his escape to privilege. Unimpressed by his monetary affluence, I continued to view my wealthy dad as "underprivileged" because for the whole of his life, he never possessed lasting peace or inner happiness. In fact, I fled from his affluence because I witnessed how thoroughly it had estranged him from the real wealth I and others of the countercultural youth of my generation so fervently sought: true self-knowledge. As a refugee from "privilege," by sheer grace, I have been led to the "advantage" of spiritual life, and, by the various disciplines of spiritual life, to the inconceivable opulence of loving service to God. I have come to associate with billionaires—"bliss billionaires," that is, connoisseurs of love's extensive repertoire of ecstasies. However, hospice work is continually broadening my horizons, and, lately, the question dawns anew: Just what does it mean to be "underprivileged"? Who are the "disadvantaged?"

For a while, I thought of as "underprivileged" anyone whose theology placed them outside the parameters of God consciousness according to the theology I regard as unexcelled. But hospice work has helped me to realize a teaching that my mentor stressed again and again: love of God and loving service to God are not sectarian phenomena. Christians, Muslims, Jews, Buddhists, Hindus, Sikhs, Unitarians, Pagans, and others—if they are genuine—are God conscious. Until I met certain of my coworkers and patients, I never directly experienced the truth of this, which meant I was underprivileged. I felt I could only be intimate with persons who shared the intricacies of my own faith tradition.

Now I discover and genuinely admire mature spiritual qualities in many of the people I meet through hospice; I am able to learn from and be spiritually enriched by them, and I perceive them to be engaged in the same process I am engaged in. They love the same Supreme I do, albeit according to a catechism and understanding different from my own.

In ways, Sama Nyugen's spiritual process was similar to mine. Each day at the same hour, five Buddhist monks came to visit her and her family. With their simple ochre robes and their shaved heads, they resembled the Vaishnava monks of my order. Being cordial, the monks would chat with family members, amuse themselves looking at magazines, or occasionally watch as images floated by on the large-screen television. Then they would get down to their real purpose, and for the better part of an hour, they would ring bells and chant elaborate Sanskrit prayers at Sama's bedside. Then they would be gone until the following day.

Like Vaishnavas, Buddhists hold that death is illusory. Like Vaishnavas, Buddhists strive to rise above illusion as the means of extinguishing suffering. Nonviolence is a central principle and practice of both traditions, and, in both, celibacy is an honorable means of accelerating one's spiritual progress. Concepts like the *sanga* (association of likeminded devotees), the *dharma* (duty, religiosity), and *nirvana* (enlightenment) are central to both. But there are fundamental differences also. Buddhists hold that the self is illusory; they neither believe in nor worship the deity (an image usually found in Vaishnava temples).

Despite these differences in our spiritual perspectives, I relished our visits because they afforded me a chance to witness Sama's preparedness for her imminent death. In her late seventies, still she was wrinkle-free and youthful looking. Gracious, calm, and friendly, she always greeted me with a smile, but remained distant and reserved during our visits, after the first couple of which, I asked her if she wanted me to read to her from the *Dhammapada*. She was surprised that I, a Westerner, knew of this masterwork of Buddhist lore. She was even more surprised to learn that I respected it enough to own a copy, which I read frequently and with pleasure.

She began to ask me the details of my spiritual life, so I shared with her salient points of Vaishnava theology. She was delighted and right then and there decided that she could share a confidence with me. "Do you know where I'm going?" she asked me.

"You mean when you die?" I replied.

"Yes, when I die."

"Please tell me, Sama, where are you going?"

"I am going to be with my father. The Buddha is my father. I am going to be with him in his place, and I will be happy. Do you believe me?"

Without hesitation, I assured her that I believed it was so. I will never forget her delighted smile. Then she happily showed me the shoes, gown, and silk shawl she had selected to wear at the time of her death.

"I will be wearing these when I go to meet my father," she said.

CHAPLAIN AS TOUR GUIDE

Despite its being hackneyed, the metaphor of life as a "journey," with death being but another twist in the road, is an apt one. Dying may be likened to entering a foreign country—language, customs, attire, climate, and terrain all change. Who would travel abroad without having first made sufficient preparations such as learning a few phrases of the language, becoming acquainted with important customs, and the like? Why should dying be different?

As it draws near, in fact, death will likely "change the terrain" radically. Who then would dream of making that mandatory journey without having made preparations to ensure a good trip? Of course, the chaplain or spiritual worker is expected to be that individual who can effectively guide those about to navigate that particularly significant "bend in the road" we call death. Here then are a few observations from my experiences in hospice that might be compiled in a chaplain's handbook entitled *Holiday in Eternity: A Travel Agent's Guide*. These are observations, incidentally, that will not only be useful for chaplains but also for anyone who finds themselves interacting with those on the ultimate journey known as death.

Learn Key Words

Chaplains have the responsibility of becoming well acquainted with key phrases in many different languages, not only because dying people come from all the various religious traditions but because a chaplain's task entails "journeying" with the dying person across various "borders" as that person prepares for death, the ultimate "border crossing."

"Language skills" thus become essential. How can you travel with someone as a helper and friend when a language barrier prevents communication? For example, what if a chaplain hears from a person who is dying, "I am a witch"? The chaplain may recoil, convinced that "we're simply on different journeys, headed for different destinations—this person is beyond help and might even be going to hell." But what if beforehand the chaplain has become conversant with the history, beliefs, and practices of Wicca, and instead of meeting the dying person's revelation with incomprehension and consequent recoil meets it with a smile and speaks one of the Wiccan cordialities, "well met," or "blessed be"? It is easy to predict. Walls will fall down. The heart will open, cautiously perhaps, but it will open to allow entry. There is nothing difficult, sinister, or corrupting about expanding our lexicon to include phrases such as *salaam alakaam, scholem ubraka, hetepu, namaste,* or *Hare Krishna*—they are keys that unlock the heart and permit entry thereto, especially when spoken with the sympathy that arises from prior study and genuine understanding. They belong in our repertoire.

Get Immunized

As there are many infectious diseases that can lay one low or even bring about death, the wise traveler gets shots to ensure a safe return home after journeying is done. When venturing down the "road" with the dying to proffer spiritual aid, best take a shot of mature faith, be inoculated with the vaccine of alert critical thought, and have surrounding you at all times the hedge of spiritual education fortified by the willingness to learn on the job.

Arrange Provisions

If travel requires suitable food and drink, what then is suitable food and drink for the journey of death? Obviously, a dying person's requirements for nutrition and hydration undergo change and will differ increasingly from those of an active person in good health. A dying body is shutting down. Often, as the disease process advances, it gradually makes a dying person's body unable to process food and drink. (Usually, by that time, the person is physically and verbally nonresponsive.) As that happens, the beverages and foodstuffs that once supported and gratified the body become detriments rather than aliments. Healing words now become the food and drink needed to comfortably complete the journey across the border that separates this world from the next. Why is this so? It is because the shutting down of the body is not synonymous with shutting down of the soul. In fact, the soul is never impaired by bodily decline, because the soul is eternally distinct from the body. The soul is not dying. Rather, the soul is preparing to journey beyond bodily life.

Ignorance of this spiritual truth can result in guilt feelings that can and often do lead well-meaning loved ones to impose regimens of nutrition and hydration on their loved one that are not only unhelpful, but painful and injurious. Therefore, advise well-wishers that all that is needed, in fact, to nourish and strengthen the soul on its journey, are words such as "I love you," "thank you," "I forgive you"—"please forgive me," and "goodbye." When a well-wisher imagines he or she is starving their loved one to death, the chaplain, spiritual worker, or other staff person may attempt to educate that well-wisher: "It is because she is dying that your wife is not eating; it is not that she is dying because she is not eating. But your words of love and thanksgiving are the nourishing food and refreshing drink she needs now to edify, comfort, and sustain her for the journey she is on...."

Learn the Culture and Customs

Oscar Wilde, speaking of Britain, once quipped, "We have really everything in common with America nowadays except, of course, language." This witticism draws its strength from how disparate the two cultures were and are. An intelligent traveler must anticipate and prepare for the cultural disparities that will be encountered, with the plan in mind to whenever possible conform to prevailing customs rather than inadvertently send a wrong message, or worse, be presumed a barbarian or lout. Likewise, to be effective, a chaplain ought to ascertain the customs and culture of the persons she or he wishes to serve. Who are these people? Are they introverted or gregarious? Do they display emotions or keep them concealed? Is touching reserved for intimates, or is bodily contact in greeting and parting considered normative?

In America, for example, the gesture with which one communicates an enthusiastic hello and goodbye is lifting the arm and vigorously waving the arm and hand from side to side, but in Britain (and in many other European countries) that particular gesture communicates an emphatic "No." Brits, by contrast, wave hello or goodbye by raising the arm up and holding it there while opening and closing the fingers of the hand. What a great many miscommunications could be avoided if, for example, U.S. citizens traveling in the United Kingdom were aware of and honored this simple but important point. There are similar principles in working with the dying.

When in Rome, Do as the Romans

If the natives look bizarre to you, consider for a moment how bizarre you look to them! The recommendation here is to abandon (temporarily) your inherited or adopted spiritual identity and try on that of the "other." For example, if relating to an atheist, try abandoning for awhile your theistic perspective and consider instead how repugnant "religious" talk may be to one who was exploited—whether sexually, financially, emotionally, or otherwise—by a spurious *representative* of God. Maybe all you can do is listen empathetically and validate the wounded person's hurt feelings, but the willingness to step outside of your identity and your expressions of understanding and caring can make all the difference in whether or not you can be a resource for that individual.

We are all fellow journeyers under the sun, and the *border crossings* are inevitable. But are we convinced of this, or are we still traveling blind? Have we not seen, for example, that time's transformations render the body alien? I see this every day in my work. How foreign to the vigor of youth is the infirmity of age? Still, while these crossings over into alien or unknown regions are inevitable, the suffering that may be occasioned by them is not. By adopting strategies from those outlined in the above-imagined *primer for tour guides*, one may avoid spiritual suffering altogether and at the same time help others to reach the final destination with confidence and with many fond memories of the journey.

EPILOGUE

There is one more piece to the story of how I came to hospice work. My story, in the end, is Kirtida's story, a story briefly recounted by Peter Medley in this book's chapter on Hinduism.

My wife and I stood outside the dilapidated house in the hot Dallas sun. As we were about to climb the stairs into the home where Kirtida lay dying, I hesitated and turned to my wife, saying, "O God! I really don't want to go in. I don't want to see her body racked by pain, disfigured by disease. It's just horrible."

The expression on my wife's face probably mirrored my own. "Yeah, I know what you mean," she said. "This is going to be a drag. I'll bet she is wasted away by the cancer." Neither of us expected anything uplifting.

Kirtida was in her sixties and for twenty years had been struggling with health problems. Gradually, in the struggle against painful ulcers, her stomach had been removed section by section. Early on, medical experts diagnosed her as having only months to live. Then, miraculously, after abandoning medical treatment in favor of a life of prayer, holy pilgrimage, and loving service to others, her health had improved. During those years, her spiritual life blossomed, and in America, Europe, and Asia she came to be regarded as a saintly and highly evolved spiritual personality. But in 2001, an untreatable esophageal tumor returned, and by June of that year, the end was near.

My spiritual mentor had asked me and others in our international spiritual community to be present as Kirtida had her death experience. Like many other of the disciples, my wife and I came from afar and stayed on for what turned out to be weeks as Kirtida left her body.

I had known Mother Kirtida for years and admired her from afar. I call her "mother" out of respect because she was an elder in my spiritual community. Slender as a wisp of air, she was graceful and jaunty in her gait. Whenever we met, her eyes danced as if she had just heard an uproarious joke and was still inwardly delighting in the fun. Surprised by the merriment her eyes and smile could never camouflage, I always wanted to be let in on the fun. Even so, there was an air of gravity about her and of extraordinary spiritual advancement. Her silvery gray hair was closely cropped in a gesture of renunciation. Two lustrous dark eyes beamed purity, joy, and strength, and each was as curvaceous and large as petals of the sacred lotus. Coffee-colored smooth skin contrasted sharply with the austere and simple white robes she wore, identifying her as a nun. Kirtida traveled frequently, spending much of her time in pilgrimage places abroad, but when she knew that death was imminent, she returned to Dallas to die.

My wife and I had heard from others in the community that she had dwindled away to almost nothing. Now we just wanted to pay our respects and get out of there as soon as possible. "What a bummer," we thought. "Death. Cancer. An old woman wasting away." Neither of us wanted to confront death, but somehow we plucked up the courage to climb the few battered stairs and step through the door. What a surprise lay in store for us on the other side!

Kirtida was sitting upright in a hospital bed, a radiant smile beaming from her face. Joyous light shone from her eyes as she welcomed us. She was wasted away, to be sure, probably down to about sixty pounds from her usual ninety-five, but that was not what we noticed. What we noticed were those huge warm eyes—the biggest part of her person—mirthful and radiating her love to us. And her smile, it was rollicking, conveying ever-fresh youth and boundless happiness. Kirtida was all eyes and all smile. Little else remained of her. But her bliss was contagious, and all of our morbid expectations were routed. Actually, we had never seen anyone more alive, more radiant, or more relaxed and at peace with herself. We were captivated.

We spent the next several weeks seeing Kirtida daily. There were frequent unscheduled visits when along with other members of our community, we would sit with Kirtida reading aloud from scriptures, telling stories, singing spiritual songs, or listening as our mutual spiritual mentor, Tamal Krishna Goswami, who visited her almost daily, spoke with her.

There were also scheduled visits. Our mentor asked that around each of the watches of the day someone always be present with Kirtida. My wife and I chose the midnight until 4 A.M. shift. During these early morning visits, we would sing standard prayers and devotional songs while softly playing musical instruments. Sometimes we would gently massage her feet. At other times, we would read to her from scripture or just talk, but in any case we were present with her.

Kirtida was an unusual person in that the whole of her life she gave to others all that she could, never calculating the cost or holding back for her own sake. She had an illustrious career as a nurse where she was celebrated for her skill as well as her determination, energy, and compassion. Later she became a disciple of my spiritual mentor. As a disciple, she gave as fully and selflessly of herself as she had as a nurse. Her devotional life, because of its sincerity and depth, was ideal. Not surprising, then, at the time of death, the fruit of her devotional practices manifested in joy, fearlessness, and freedom from regret.

Although a sprig of a woman, no bigger than a child, her mightiness and courage had been remarked upon by everyone who met her. Years earlier, she had journeyed from America to India, to holy Vrindavan, to die there because of its special sanctity to Vaishnavas, never caring that the medical facilities there were radically inferior to those she had easy access to in the West. There was no question that the medical facilities in India were ill equipped to effectively manage her intense pain and difficult symptoms. The move to Vrindavan took great courage. Once in Vrindavan, she applied herself to spiritual life, going on holy pilgrimage and performing acts of charity well beyond the ordinary. She gave generously to support a number of temples and the saintly persons who maintained them. Meanwhile, she herself lived in humble conditions despite having the means to live opulently. Moreover, even though she was sick and dying, she continued to provide crucial care to the ill and the dying as a nurse, never complaining about her own pain or fatal diagnosis.

Apparently it was her enthusiasm for serving God in Vrindavan that staved off death. She grew attached to living in the holy pilgrimage place and would never have left its precincts of her own desire. Later, though, when our guru, Tamal Krishna Goswami, became dangerously ill with advanced prostate cancer, she gave up her residence in Vrindavan and returned to America in order to serve as a member of the medical team caring for him. After successfully helping him through his life-threatening illness, her own illness returned.

When my wife and I visited, Kirtida would be surrounded by well-wishers singing devotional songs accompanied by keyboards and drums. The words of the prayers being sung were well known to her, and she would begin to dance in the bed by raising her toothpick arms above her head, the IV swaying from side to side. As a trained nurse, Kirtida knew the options she had regarding her death. If she chose to cling to her bodily life for as long as possible, she would experience death by suffocation as the growing tumor finally choked off the esophagus. She would die of acute, unrelieved air-hunger, which triggers an escalating panic reflex that cannot be checked. This is a painful and frightening way to leave the body.

There was another option. If she honored her body's inability to process food and drink any longer and instead accepted only what little hydration was needed for palliation, gradually her kidneys would shut down, and a peaceful transition would ensue. Thus, in consultation with her physician, Kirtida decided to simply fix her mind on the Supreme Lord, ceasing food and drink, and for the last several weeks of her life subsisted on ice chips alone. One time, her doctor made a homeside visit to check on her. When the doctor witnessed Kirtida's ecstasy, she remarked, "I came here to do for you, but there is nothing I can do. You are doing everything for me!"

Kirtida's dying process was a revelation, because it taught me that a person genuinely committed to and sincerely practicing spiritual life has no fear of death whatsoever. The degree of joy she displayed was amazing and enviable more so than persons with money, fame, and position. Oftentimes, when her small bedroom was crammed with twenty or twenty-five well-wishers seeing her off, I had the overwhelming sense that death's sting had been removed. Because of the grace with which she freely entered into the arms of her next life, the time we spent there did not feel like a death vigil. Rather, it felt as if we were seeing her off on a sea journey—she standing on the ship's deck waving to her friends in the harbor as the ship plied the waves.

After she departed, I knew that my conception of death had been transformed. Firsthand I had witnessed someone stepping through the door of death with the same ease as if they were stepping into the next room to greet a friend. Still, it would be several months before I came to understand that my own vocation lay in work with the dying. In March of 2002, my guru unexpectedly departed from this world after a fatal car crash on a country highway south of Calcutta, India. At the time of his death, he had been meditating on how much he missed Kirtida and was in fact writing a book about how to die a good death, a spiritual death, with grace. It was all coming together. Nine months earlier, he had instructed us that the time spent with Kirtida should be considered one of his teachings to us. As it turned out, it was his final instruction to us and the last time most of us would ever see him. This instruction I have taken to heart. This instruction has shaped my livelihood. My work as a hospice chaplain, then, in seeing souls over the threshold into the next life, is, in the end, my service to my spiritual mentor.

NOTES

1. Coleman Barks, trans. *The Soul of Rumi: A New Collection of Ecstatic Poems* (San Francisco: Harper Collins Paperback Edition, 2002), 94.

2. Thich Nhat Hanh, *Living Buddha, Living Christ* (New York: Riverhead Books, 1995), 138.

Index

About the Editor and the Contributors

The Editor

STEVEN J. ROSEN is an initiated disciple of His Divine Grace A. C. Bhaktivedanta Swami Prabhupada and editor-in-chief of the *Journal of Vaishnava Studies*, an academic quarterly esteemed by scholars around the world. He is also associate editor of *Back to Godhead*, the magazine of the Hare Krishna movement. The author of over twenty books, his recent titles include *Essential Hinduism* (Praeger, 2006), *Krishna's Song: A New Look at the Bhagavad Gita* (Praeger, 2007), and *The Yoga of Kirtan: Conversations on the Sacred Art of Chanting* (FOLK Books, 2008).

The Contributors

DAVID CARTER, a hospice chaplain for five years, is currently affiliated with Harry Hynes Memorial Hospice, Wichita, Kansas. He was ordained in the theological tradition of Gaudiya Vaishnavism in 1989, in New York City, by His Holiness Tamal Krishna Goswami. In addition to studies stateside, his absorption in the theory and praxis of Far Eastern spiritual culture has led him abroad several times, both to Europe and to India, where he was mentored by the tradition's masters. He has trained numerous meditation guides and teachers, helped dozens of aspirants to become Vaishnava ministers, and as an administrator he has been part of the management team in Vaishnava Temples in New York and Michigan.

PETER MEDLEY graduated from the University of California at Berkeley in 1971, majoring in Literature. In 1972 he completed training to become a teacher of Transcendental Meditation in Fiugi Fonte, Italy, and then, in 1981 became initiated into Hinduism's Gaudiya Vaishnava tradition by revered guru and scholar Tamal Krishna Goswami (TKG). In 1983, he was ordained as a Brahmin priest, assisting his spiritual master TKG for two-and-a-half years during his Ph.D. studies at the University of Cambridge and his work with the Oxford Centre for Hindu and Vaishnava Studies from 1998 to 2001. He was the chief compiler and editor of *TKG Memories, Volumes 1–3*, and has written articles for *Back to Godhead* magazine. Currently he is working on a historical novel on Heliodorus, a Greek who converted to Vaishnavism in India during the pre-Christian era.

Having earned his D.Phil. from the University of Stellenbosch, South Africa, in 1992, with his dissertation topic, "Esoteric Themes in the Book of Jonah," RABBI ARTHUR SELTZER holds two Masters Degrees, one from the University of Stellenbosch in Pastoral Counseling and the other from Hebrew Union College, Jewish Institute of Religion (HUC-JIR) in Hebrew Literature. Rabbi Seltzer holds degrees as Doctor of Naturopathy and Doctor of Oriental Medicine as well as a rabbinic ordination from HUC-JIR. He received the honor of Semichas Rabbonus from the Chief Rabbi of South Africa.

Emerging from the Graduate Theological Union in Berkeley with a dual focus in Buddhism and Chinese traditions, JOHN M. THOMPSON's work spans a broad range of fields including philosophy, theology, Asian Studies, history, translation and interpretation, and anthropology. He recently authored *Buddhism*, the third of the six-volume series *Introduction to the World's Religions* published by Greenwood Press. His second book, *Understanding Prajna: Sengzhao's "Wild Words" and the Search for Wisdom*, a monograph based on his dissertation on a fifth-century Buddhist monk's struggle to articulate the transformative "knowledge" of Awakening to a learned Chinese audience, is currently in production at Peter Lang Publishers. This latter book includes annotated translations of two medieval Chinese texts. He is currently Assistant Professor in the Department of Philosophy and Religious Studies at Christopher Newport University, Virginia.

HUSSAM S. TIMANI is assistant professor of Islamic and religious studies at Christopher Newport University (CNU), Virginia. He holds a Ph.D. in Islamic Studies from the University of California, Los Angeles, and has taught Islam, religion, and cultural studies at various universities in the United States and Lebanon. Dr. Timani, a native of Lebanon, is a frequent speaker on Islam, Christian-Muslim relations, and interfaith dialogue. He's also closely involved with CNU-MENA Cultural-Educational Exchange, which brings students from the Middle East and North Africa to the United States.

FATHER FRANCIS V. TISO is Associate Director of the Secretariat for Ecumenical and Inter-religious Affairs of the US Conference of Catholic Bishops (USCCB), where he serves as liaison to Muslims, Hindus, Buddhists, Sikhs, and others. Before coming to the USCCB, Father Tiso was assigned to the Archdiocese of San Francisco where he served as Parochial Vicar of St. Thomas More Church and Chaplain at San Francisco State University and the University of California Medical School. Father Tiso is a priest of the Diocese of Isernia-Venafro, Italy, where he holds a Canonry in the Cathedral.